*The* **NAIPAULS** *of* Nepaul Street

# *The* NAIPAULS *of* Nepaul Street

SAVI NAIPAUL AKAL

SPEAKING TIGER

SPEAKING TIGER BOOKS LLP
125-A, Ground Floor, Shahpur Jat
New Delhi – 110049

First published in the UK by Peepal Tree Press Ltd
This edition first published in India by Speaking Tiger Books 2024



ISBN: 978-93-5447-840-6

10 9 8 7 6 5 4 3 2 1

Printed at Chaman Enterprises, New Delhi

In loving memory of my parents

Seepersad and Droapatie Naipaul

There is a comfort in the strength of love;
'Twill make a thing endurable, which else
Would overset the brain, or break the heart.

— William Wordsworth

# CONTENTS

# Capildeo Family Tree

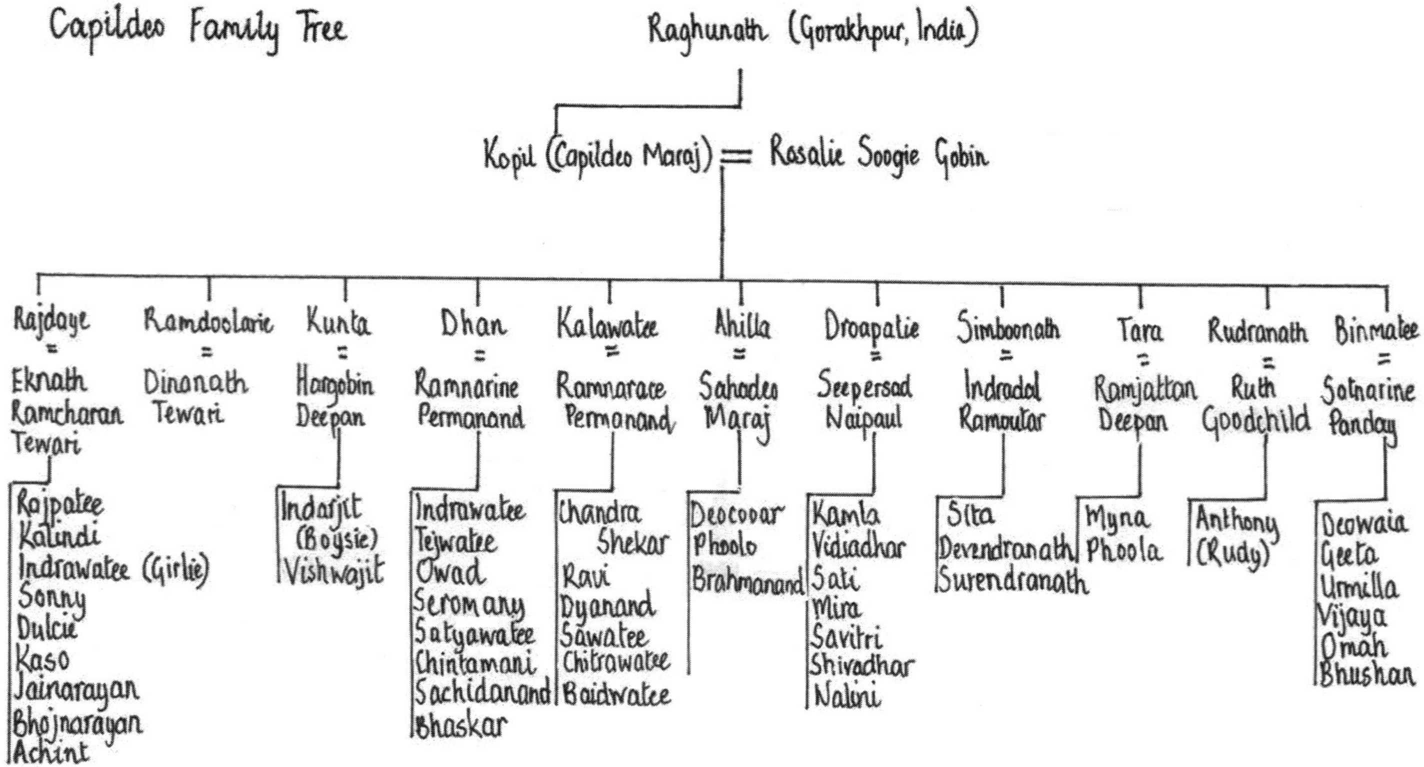

# Seepersad Naipaul's Family Tree

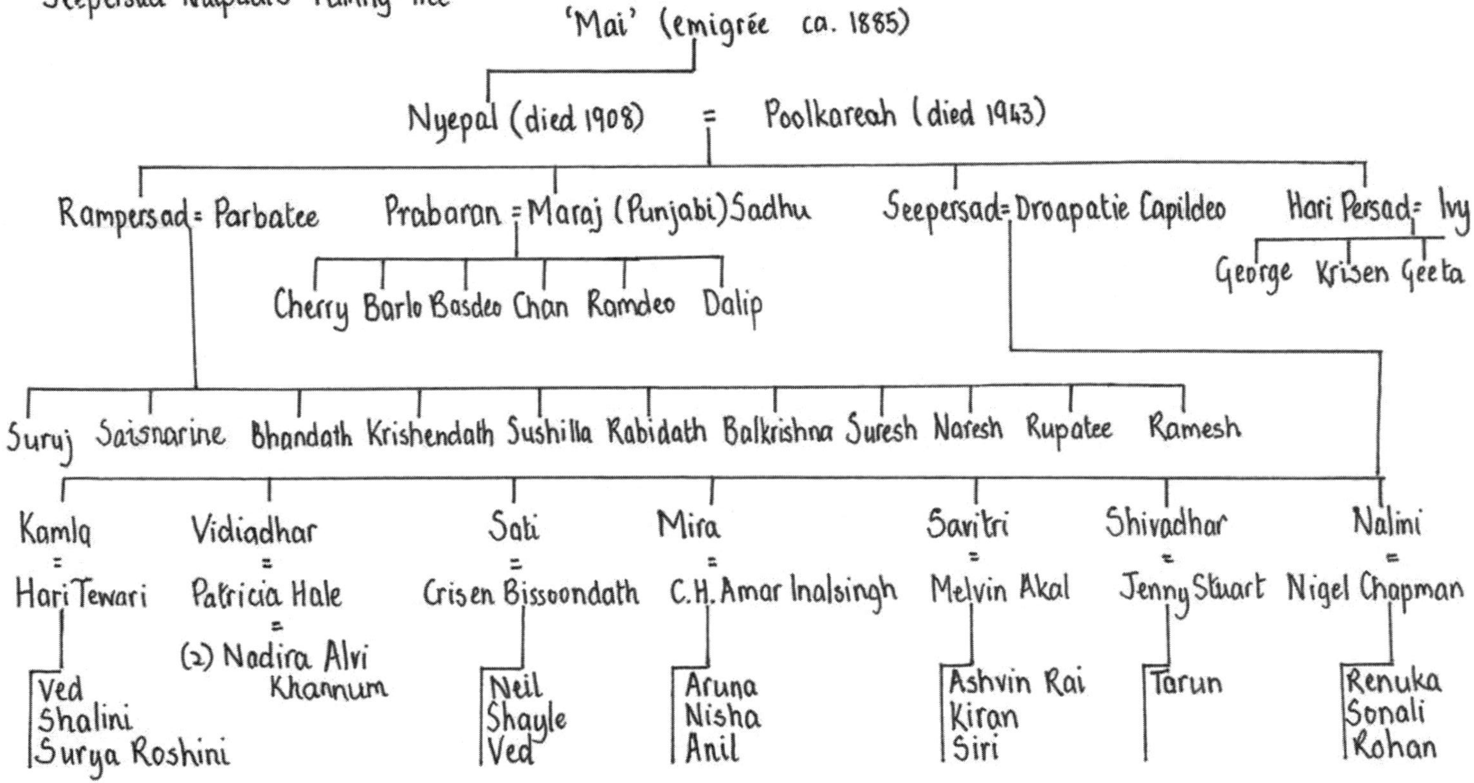

# CHAPTER ONE

## *Cunupia, Chaguanas, Chandernagore, Caroni . . .*

My father seemed destined to be surrounded by women. At first there were four aunts, a sister and four female cousins. There was a mother too, but no father he could or would recall.

Seepersad Naipaul was born on 14th April 1906 in the settlement of Cunupia in rural Trinidad. On his birth certificate, his name is 'Supersad'. The name and occupation of the 'informant' (normally the husband or father) is given as Nyepal. He is identified as a labourer. His mother's name is Poolkareah, with no occupation cited for her. Most likely she was wife as well as mother – occupations daunting enough.

Nyepal, our Pa's father, was not intended to be a labourer. An only child, he had come from India with his devoted mother, an indentured servant. In other words, she came under an agreement that would oblige her to work on the land, mainly in the sugar-cane fields. Why did she and so many others leave India in this way? Perhaps she had committed some indiscretion, or was running away from a bad marriage. After her term of indenture expired, she had the choice of going back to India or staying in Trinidad. She decided to stay, along with her son. Devoted to him, and a proud Brahmin, she sought to have him trained as a pundit. (In Hinduism, only Brahmins can perform the most sacred rites.) To that end, he travelled to Diego Martin, the large valley immediately west of our capital, Port of Spain, to sit at the feet of a venerable pundit. Being a pundit meant having knowledge and understanding of the sacred texts and rituals, and thus the ability to read and write Sanskrit and Hindi. Whether Nyepal ever practised as a pundit we never knew, but he apparently sold goods and supplies used in *pujas*, or sacred rites.

His mother also found him a wife. On the ship coming from India there were two brothers from Patna. They, too, were Brahmins. One of them had six daughters and one son. Pa's mother chose one of the girls, Poolkareah, as her son's bride. The wedding took place, and Nyepal and Poolkareah went on to have three children of their own: Prasad, Prabaran and Seepersad (or Supersad).

When Seepersad was two, his father Nyepal died. Did he drown? There is a vague story of a diver who drowned. Nyepal's mother was distraught after the death of her one and only precious son, whom she had nurtured and cared for during those challenging and difficult years. Inconsolable, she drifted into her own world and became something of a recluse and an eccentric. She appears never to have remarried or formed a new alliance with another man. Curiously, my own mother Droapatie remembered this woman well. Tiny in size and very fair of complexion, she wore nothing but white clothing after her son's death (white being the Hindu colour of mourning). She lived in or around Chaguanas, where young Droapatie would have seen her, and sometimes came into the town. Other children would sometimes jeer at her as she walked about waving a wand in front of her to protect her from unclean shadows, from people of lower caste. She spoke to no one, did her business, and then disappeared until her next visit. Droapatie would never have imagined that one day she would marry this strange woman's grandson, Seepersad. But the caste was always right.

Death was not a subject my father liked to dwell on. Several years after his father's passing, his mother died of an unspecified illness. Unlike his father's death, Seepersad was evidently old enough to feel this second loss keenly. In the early nineteen-forties he wrote a five-page letter in an old ledger book to the doctor who had not saved his mother. The doctor was late in responding to their call for help, my father wrote in anger; he had not seemed to care about Poolkareah's crisis; evidently, in his selfishness and arrogance, he was not suited to his profession. The gist of the letter was that his mother had died because she was a poor woman and therefore unimportant to the self-important Dr. Ramesar.

Perhaps the letter was never transcribed, never posted. The written word may have expiated Pa's anger and supplanted his sense of primal loss. Could my grandmother have been saved? Her five sisters, his aunts, lived on and on despite their emphysema and other medical issues. They took a long time to 'pop off', he would say.

Soon after his father's death, a half-brother was born. He was called Hari, or Hari Chacha to us children. Pa's mother, Poolkareah, a widow with three children, would have been a burden on the closest relatives. Another liaison would have been encouraged. In my own family, all these details were rather vague. For example, it took us many years to learn that Hari Chacha was Pa's half-brother.

The older Indian people were tight-lipped about the family's history. They never spoke about my paternal grandfather, Nyepal, and Hari's father never had a name. Hari's son George carried the title or surname Persad. This seemed to fit, as Pa's elder brother, Prasad, carried the surname Rampersad. Pa, however, eventually called himself Naipaul. He was the only one in his

Poolkareah, Seepersad Naipaul's mother

Droapatie Naipaul (Ma) and Seepersad's sister, Prabaran (right)

family who carried that name. Even the name Naipaul seems irregular. In its exact form, it does not appear to be previously used in India, or among Indians in Trinidad. In all of his early purchased books, he wrote his name as Naipal: Seepersad Naipal. The change to Naipaul took place, apparently, in the early forties, after he began work at the *Trinidad Guardian*, our leading newspaper. On Pa's first driver's licence, dated 22nd August 1928, his name is given as Bholah Supersad (not Seepersad), and his residence as Tunapuna. However, on its renewal on 24th January 1944, his name is Seepersad Naipaul (of Luis Street, Port of Spain).

Seepersad Naipaul and his older brother Prasad, his sister Prabaran and his half-brother Hari at first lived in the village of Cunupia. They then moved in with their aunts, in a home or homes at Back Street in Tunapuna. We know that Prasad went out to work in the cane fields as a young boy. Prabaran did not go into the fields but lived with her aunts until her marriage. Schooling seems to have been absent from the daily lives of either Prasad or Prabaran. But education, formal or otherwise, was crucial to my father's upbringing. Through him, it would have a lasting effect on generations to come.

Hari Persad (Hari Chacha), Seepersad's half-brother, and wife

Cunupia, where my father was born, was part of the ribbon settlements, almost all of them at crossroads, that extended along the Old Caroni Savannah Road. All were located in County Caroni, which extends roughly from the Caroni River at the foothills of the Northern Range to about midway on the western side of the island. This was the heartland of Indian culture in Trinidad. The Caroni is the island's major river, running westward until it empties into the Gulf of Paria between Trinidad and Venezuela. Further to the west, County Caroni includes the Caroni Swamp, the home of the dense expanse of mangrove that is the habitat of the scarlet ibis, the gorgeous bird that became our nation's main symbol. In the old days, Caroni was synonymous with agriculture of various kinds, but especially with sugar-cane. Cane ceased to be central to the island's economy and eventually ceased to be cultivated at all. The end of sugar came parallel with the expansion of our oil and natural gas production, when prices of these fuels began to soar on the world market. But in the era when it thrived, sugar sustained Trinidad and Tobago. To cultivate cane after the abolition of slavery, an influx of officially sponsored 'indentured servants' came to Trinidad from India, starting in 1845. These 'servants' (especially those who opted to stay in Trinidad) and their offspring altered forever the culture of Trinidad.

Tunapuna, the larger market town where my father found a home after Cunupia, served both the cocoa estates that flourished then in the valleys to the north and the great sugar estates of northern Caroni in the plains to the south. Despite its economic importance, it was a humble place in many respects. Even in my childhood, there was no running water or electricity outside the major settlements in Caroni and elsewhere. People collected their water in barrels. In fact, life was as gruelling in County Caroni in those days as it had been in earlier times. These harsh conditions brought out the best, but also the worst, in its inhabitants as they struggled to survive and make a viable future for themselves and their children and grandchildren. Other people, including the Creole descendants of African slaves, also faced these harsh conditions, but for Indians, far from their ancestral home, life had particular struggles. They lived in a land where no other ethnic or racial groups spoke their language, where they struggled to master English, where their religions were seen as heathen, and where the elite often saw schooling as a luxury not to be wasted on 'servants'.

In County Caroni at the start of the twentieth century, there were thirty-one estates devoted to the growing of sugar-cane. Almost all the labourers were Indian. These estates were privately owned, either by white or near-white French Creoles or by prominent, moneyed 'coloured' families. By the mid 1930s, the sugar industry was dominated by the British firm, Tate & Lyle. During the indenture period from 1845 to 1917, estate owners applied to the central colonial government for labour, according to their needs or means. Though aspects of the laws that governed indentured workers and their contracts changed over time, the core of the system remained the same. All indentured workers were legally bound to live and work on the estates to which they were assigned for a period of five years, at which point they were often pressured to sign up for a further five-year period. Workers were not free to leave their estates unless they were ill and had to be hospitalised, or if they had to go to court for some misdemeanour which could not be handled by the estate managers. Even this exemption required written and stamped approval. There were a host of punitive labour laws that employers used to discipline workers. When workers went to court, the magistrate was usually a fellow planter or manager of a neighbouring estate. The estates provided housing in the form of barracks. Everyone was treated as equal regardless of religion, caste and sub-caste – which were and are crucial distinctions in Indian culture. At best, housing accommodation was poor. Single men and women were given rooms roughly ten feet by twelve feet. Families, husbands, wives and children had slightly larger rooms. All cooking had to be done outdoors. Latrines and bathrooms were communal and outdoors.

The managers of the estates provided rations of foodstuff for a sum that was then deducted from the worker's pay at the end of the week. Only on the most enlightened estates were workers allowed to plant or grow food on uncultivated areas of the estate. Nearly all of the conditions of life and work ran counter to the traditions of the civilisation in their Indian homeland, however poor and beleaguered they might have been there. Marriages conducted solely by Hindu pundits or Muslim maulvis were not regarded as legal. With men outnumbering women almost three to one, there was often intense sexual and romantic rivalry. Personal relationships could be fragile and tenuous. Crimes of passion were common, and the weapon of choice was usually the cutlass. For many, family life was difficult and fractured during the estate days. It was a sign of the strength of Indian culture that extended family networks and traditional kinship relationships were restored when Indians settled in villages away from the estates.

At the end of a ten-year period of labour service (at least five of it indentured), the workers had certain choices. If particular workers were considered valuable by their employers, the estates tried to keep them. Some estates offered a cash bounty for these prized workers to stay. Those who insisted on being repatriated had to be accommodated on the next outgoing vessel and roughly a third of all those who came chose to go back to India. Those who wished to stay and make Trinidad their home had the choice of either a sum of money or an area of land varying in size between five and ten acres. These plots were Crown Lands, belonging to the colonial government. In those days, large areas of Trinidad remained underutilised. Often the plots were of poor quality, badly drained or heavily forested and remote, almost inaccessible. Trespassing was commonplace. The new owners often had to sell their land in order to survive. Many people found themselves homeless and destitute as they waited for repatriation. In Port of Spain, when I was a child in the early nineteen-forties, you would see roving bands of homeless Indian beggars. Some were forced into criminal acts. Most of the hangings at the Royal Gaol were of Indians.

Most Trinidadians undoubtedly saw Indians as occupying the lowest rung on the social ladder – if they were on the social ladder at all. Most people assumed, I am sure, that Indians would stay in that bottom place forever. Certainly that was the situation for Indians in Trinidad when my father was born.

It must have been before the arrival of Hari Chacha, my father's half-brother, that some members of the Back Street family in Tunapuna decided that they wanted to go back to India. Since there were children among the group, there must have been husbands or menfolk intimately involved in that decision. Though I do not know the names of any adult males in that household, I am as certain as one can be that if there were men, the decision to go back to India was probably taken by them. I am equally ignorant of how my grandmother and father became part of this Back-to-India group or what their motives were.

My knowledge of this event came personally from my father. The family, according to him, had secured their passages on a ship. Officials had approved and stamped their papers for repatriation. The group even went to tiny Nelson Island in the Gulf of Paria to board the ship for India. Like the more celebrated Ellis Island in New York, Nelson Island served as a major immigrant station. I am guessing that my father was then about five or six years old. He did not want to leave Trinidad. His story was that he doggedly hid in a latrine located on a ledge overlooking the sea. His frantic mother refused to leave without him. Two of the aunts also panicked, and the adventure came to an abrupt end for some of the women. Never again would a man be seen in their household on Back Street in Tunapuna. The men, if indeed they had been the planners and movers, left without them.

This episode of repatriation to the motherland and the act of resistance to that repatriation is, to me, of great importance. Call it fate or luck, the 'latrine intervention' by my father, Seepersad Naipaul, would change the entire history of our family.

Young as he was, he had rejected repatriation to India. Whether he knew what was involved is unlikely. The terms and times of repatriation were always fluid, as the price of sugar went up and down. The sugar barons and the colonial government made and changed the rules according to fluctuations in the prices. What happened to Indians who returned home was another fraught aspect of the story. Ships' records show that returnees tended to include both those who had saved most money and those who were most impoverished. Because they had crossed the *kala pani* (black sea) returnees were regarded as people who had lost caste. Some had changed more than they recognised in Trinidad and could no longer fit in to traditional Indian village life. Pa would eventually write a story about the plight of workers who had returned home, regretted the move, and then pined for a return to their countries of indenture. As a journalist, he also wrote about those workers who chose to stay in Trinidad, but were no longer needed or wanted on the estates and who became beggars. In our family, we became sensitive to the vagaries of migration and homelessness.

My father, seen as the main culprit in the repatriation debacle, had a stroke of luck when one of his aunts, Roopkal, having married a prosperous, generous man named Sookdeo Misir, accepted Seepersad into her household. His new home with the Sookdeos placed him in a burgeoning family.

Sookdeo Misir had fathered two daughters of about my father's age, Jassodra and Basdai. Later he would also absorb into his household his brother Ramdin's children. Ramdin was a widower with five boys and four girls. In spite of the size of his household, Sookdeo would also adopt yet another young girl, Sonmat. She was reputed to be a pundit's daughter whose wife had died in childbirth, as had his brother's wife.

So my father grew up in a household with at least eleven offspring of varying ages. Sookdeo Misir lived on an acre or more of land on El Dorado Road in Tunapuna. The plot was large enough to include an empty playing field. Sookdeo kept cows but also owned a shop and more than one estate. He would later take over the Arima Bus Company of which Ramdin, his brother, had been one of the original shareholders. In Sookdeo's household my father was always called by his family name of Bhola. Sookdeo, whom we children often called *ajah* or grandfather, while Pa called him uncle, was a small, lean, bird-faced man. His skin was taut, his eyebrows grey, and he ate frugally. Although he was always gentle to us as Bhola's children, we understood him to be a harsh disciplinarian otherwise, especially to the boys in his family. Pale in colour, he lived to a ripe old age without a wrinkle on his face.

Although Seepersad lived apart from his siblings, his older brother Prasad and his sister Prabaran, he always maintained a close connection to them. Back Street was not far from El Dorado Road. My father would describe it as 'a hop, skip and jump' away. Back Street was also parallel to the crucial Eastern Main Road. A dirt road, it was more of a trace than a street. All the houses were humble *ajoupas*, with hibiscus hedges and mango and tamarind trees abundant around them. (Freshly cut hibiscus stems, pounded and fibrous at one end and dabbed in soda powder, were used as toothbrushes in the morning.) Seepersad's sister Prabaran was his favourite among the girls, and their bond and devotion was everlasting. Prabaran's life and travails provided the basis for many of Pa's earlier short stories. Although Pa was angered by the unkindness to her of Prabaran's first husband, an uncouth Punjabi, he kept in touch with this man out of an expansive sense of loyalty to her.

After abandoning Prabaran, this Punjabi lived in squalor in a ground-floor room of a tenement building in an unsavoury section of declining George Street in Port of Spain. In my father's company, I remember visiting this old man. His room smelled sour. Not knowing exactly who he was, I hoped that the visit would soon end. But my father lingered. He had a way of thinking that practically anyone was potential subject material for a new story.

Prabaran's second husband was a man of inferior caste. He was called Sadhu. Very dark and sinewy, with a heavy moustache, Sadhu worked in the fields with Prabaran. We, as children, were never taught to give him a name, much less a title of respect as an aunt's husband. We visited quite often, but always felt that the visit was to our aunt. The romance of thinking that we would be spending the night in her quaint ajoupa usually ended at dusk, when the mosquitoes began to hum and sting and seek new blood.

Village ajoupa c. 1900. Photo from *John Morton of Trinidad,* 1916

While we maintained a fond relationship with Prabaran's first three children, our relations with her children with Sadhu were more tenuous, except for Chan, her eldest, who found a job in the Sookdeo Misir household as a cook and general helper. In his memoir *Finding the Centre*, my brother Vidia describes a chance meeting with a young man who identified himself as Sadhu's grandson. This encounter led Vidia to an urgent, unplanned visit – his first – to the frail and declining Prabaran, his aunt (whom we called Phoowah in the family). She died a few days after speaking to him.

My father's elder brother, Prasad, married a much younger woman. Prasad Chacha lived in his own property in Longdenville, a village a few miles to the east of Chaguanas. His first home may have been an ajoupa, but then he moved into a wooden house on stilts. He lived about five minutes or so from Prabaran's house. Later, as his family increased, he built a concrete house on the same spot.

Prasad Chacha never visited our family. Probably this came about because we were now living in someone else's house – one that belonged to my mother's family – or, more likely, because we were then part of the much larger and almost formidably prosperous clan of our mother, the Capildeos. Yet even after we moved to Nepaul Street in 1947, in a house of our own, I cannot recall a visit by him. Prasad Chacha's brood carried the title of Rampersad, until some of the children suddenly changed their name to Naipaul. His many children are today scattered over the world. One of his younger sons lives as a writer and carries the name Naipaul.

With my father's death in 1953, the one-sided visits ended. The children of the two brothers went their separate ways, hardly seeing and scarcely knowing each other. There was a widening of the gap in spite of the closeness of the relationship.

Seepersad's education began in Sookdeo Misir's household. While the younger members of the household spoke English, the language of the elders was Bhojpuri, a dialect of Hindi in Uttar Pradesh (formerly United Provinces). Sookdeo Misir believed that education was the surest route to success. For high school, the Ramdin girls were sent to the elite St Joseph's Convent school in Port of Spain. Some of the nuns were local, but most were from Europe. Where the boys went to school is hazy, but certainly the two youngest went to the equally prominent College of the Immaculate Conception, or St Mary's as it is also known, also in Port of Spain. A school bus came on mornings to collect the children of the household for the journey to school. Pa, however, went only to a local, non-elite elementary or primary school. He did not go on to high school, much less to one as prominent as St Mary's.

Pa seldom spoke about his schooling, but his lengthy short story 'Gurudeva' (published in 1943) and another short story he wrote both allude to an enlightened Presbyterian schoolmaster. So one presumes that Pa, like many other Indian children in Trinidad, attended a school run by Presbyterians. These schools were called CM or CMI, for Canadian Mission Indian. The CM schools were set up to help missionaries educate and convert the children of Indian indentured labourers. In the 1860s, a young white Canadian named John Morton of Nova Scotia had visited Trinidad. Touring some rural estates, he was appalled by the treatment of the Indians in general and their children in particular, who were generally denied education. It reminded him of the treatment meted out to many poor Scots immigrants in his native Canada. Morton returned as a Presbyterian missionary with a project to build schools and convert Indians willing to abandon Hinduism and Islam. Later, his son continued these efforts, with such success that a new class of mainly Christian Indians emerged in Trinidad, one better educated and much more at ease with British colonial traditions.

The only school story Pa told me personally was about a bully whom he met frequently on his way to school. At a certain dip in the road the two boys, going in opposite directions, passed each other almost every day. The bully, on approaching Pa, would look him in the eye and call him 'Chinee Butter Mouse!' (Pa had inherited the pale skin and heavy-lidded 'Chinese' eyes of his mother.) He, with his head down and eyes turned upwards under his brow, would quicken his pace uphill. On reaching the top of the hill the Chinee Butter Mouse would look back and shout: 'Is yuh mudder, man!'

To me, the encounter and his rejoinder show that my father was then fairly grown up, although still at primary school. Perhaps he was already working in Sookdeo's shop, or even (as he did later) in the adjacent rum shop, at one end of the same building. Pa obviously relished listening to the conversations, especially in the rum shop. The arguments among the patrons about which was the better or best rum always amused him, and he would sometimes attempt to provoke them. He knew that all of the rum, whether it was called Red Rooster or Seventh Heaven, came out of the same cask. Rum bottles were filled and labelled in the shop. The conversations and the arguments in the rum shops, at the *puja* religious gatherings and in the law courts always fascinated my father. As long as there was rum he knew there would be good talk.

Apart from working in Sookdeo's shop, my father developed a hand for 'lettering'. Painting signs allowed him to doodle and observe the scene about him. It also took him to the Arima Bus Company, where he was employed for a while, and which accounted for him having a driving licence as early as 1928. It is said that the practice of art often brings mental and physical healing. From early on, Pa needed mental healing. In spite of being accepted within a large household in which he apparently was, in basic ways, fairly well treated, he must have seen himself as an outsider. Sign painting would have been restorative and satisfying, an occupation that kept him apart and yet made him feel useful.

My father was always aware of the poverty in his family. Certainly he was grateful to Sookdeo Misir for permitting him to go to school, which spared him from backbreaking work in the sugar fields. Unlike Prasad and Prabaran, who were parched and wrinkled by the tropical sun, Pa as a youth remained sallow and under-exercised. He would have been flabby had he not been so thin. His flesh hung loosely on his body. He was always sensitive about the way his body looked. When we were children, he would ask my sister Mira and me to walk over him as a form of massage. We would often slip off his body, sometimes pinching his flesh. Then he might utter some mild swearwords in Hindi.

Reading would not have been a regular pastime in the El Dorado Road household. I believe that Pa often read to his 'Uncle' Sookdeo, who liked to learn the news of the day. Perhaps the reading of the daily newspapers led to the awakening of my father's interest in journalism. Later, my brother Vidia would sometimes read the papers for his 'grandfather' Sookdeo Ajah. Reading and keeping books, even buying books, must have been a quietly conducted habit for Pa. His stack of books grew over the years to require, finally, a bookcase. I still have the bookcase. Roughly made of cedar, it has weathered the years nicely. It was constructed simply, not quite six feet tall and about forty inches wide. Wooden frames encased glass doors one could peer through to look for a book. Like our dining table, it was probably made by someone with a 'feel' for woodwork, but no real training. Pa had a way of sympathising with amateurs, especially if they could make some money out of doing a job. My mother cared for the books and the bookcase. She worked to prevent attacks from silverfish and cockroaches as well as termites.

The bookcase was simply a part of the house, that moved with the family as we changed addresses. Many of the books have disappeared – probably taken by my siblings. Apart from books which we children studied at school, the bookcase held many works for those of us who wanted more general reading. Pa taught us to value books. One weekend, instead of a chicken for our Sunday meal, he bought the British writer H.E. Bates's popular novel *Fair Stood the Wind for France*, and it remained in our library. As we grew up, we came to value the diversity and worth of Pa's choices. When I discovered John Donne at university I was amazed to learn on returning to the bookcase that Pa evidently had valued him many years before. So we became familiar with names such as Flaubert, Tolstoy, H.E. Bates, Samuel Smiles (*Self-Help*), Somerset Maugham, O. Henry, Lin Yutang, Radhakrishnan, Dickens, Balzac, Bertrand Russell, Mark Twain (*Tom Sawyer* and *Huck Finn*), and Pearl Buck – I think we all read her novel *The Good Earth*.

No one can readily explain where Pa's love of the written word came from. Few of the people around him appreciated his ambition to write. In the mainly agricultural setting of his extended family he was an anomaly; in the Sookdeo Misir household he was perhaps seen as vain and overreaching. Was he also seen as an idler? Reading books, sign-painting and writing stories were not plausible or realistic occupations for a peasant boy. Perhaps some saw these interests as a ruse to avoid getting a real job. Small wonder, then, that for years the bookcase held two books that intrigued me. One was an English grammar, the other a book entitled *Popular Mechanics*. The grammar book was red, the mechanics book black. I understood the English grammar volume. But *Popular Mechanics*, for a man who could not change a fuse, must have been an attempt to please someone else.

Sign-painting at the Arima Bus Company led Pa to a job in Chaguanas. With an Amerindian name, like so many similar settlements, Chaguanas lies along what was then the most important north-south corridor, the Southern Main Road. As a town, it was several steps up from Cunupia, his place of birth, and one lengthening step up from Tunapuna. (Now Chaguanas has become the fastest-growing town in the nation.) My father was rising, if ever so slightly, at this point.

The job in Chaguanas took my father to what was already known widely as the Lion House, the stronghold of the proud Capildeo family. The Lion House was the name given to it by the awed people of Chaguanas (its real name was Anand Bhavan, or House of Bliss). All the family members also called it the Lion House, or simply Lion House. Only two minutes or so by foot from civic landmarks such as the railway station, the police station and the courthouse, it was built of bricks made, or supervised in their making, by my maternal grandfather in the back yard of the building. The Lion House was completed in 1926, the year my grandfather (Pundit Capildeo) left for India and never returned. The building was three stories high and trapezoidal in shape, with its arcade front fitting snugly into its narrower frontage on the Chaguanas Main Road. At the back, a covered bridge linked it to a wooden upstairs house. Family members called this wooden house the 'old upstairs'. The plot on which the two buildings stood stretched from the Chaguanas Main Road to Cumberbatch Street at the back, and must have been at least three-quarters of an acre in extent. The unusually thick walls (eight inches or more), the thick, sturdy decorated pillars, the two lions above the arched arcade at the front, the building painted white with tall, heavy, wooden doors – all made it more like a fortress than an ordinary home.

Why was my maternal grandfather so eager to create this illusion of grandeur? I think he wanted the house as a sign of Indian pride, at a time when the Indian community was generally despised and not recognised as part of the larger and wider society. Indians took pride in it. When the store closed on evenings, the cool verandah of the arcade provided a meeting-place for the villagers to meet and smoke their ganja *cheelum*-style, or as rolled cigarettes. Later, Syrians, who would become prominent merchants, were allowed to peddle their cloth with the permission of my grandmother, who ran the store with the help of her children after their father left for India and died there.

The Lion House, Chaguanas, showing the shopfront

What gained Pa admittance to the Lion House? A general store located on the ground floor needed a painted sign. He was hired to do this minor job. However, he was not there long when his fate was sealed and his future determined. When he tried, one day, to communicate with a young girl at work in the family store, whose beauty had impressed him, Pa's letter to her was intercepted. Someone handed it over to the young lady's mother, Soogie Capildeo, a widow but a commanding matriarch if ever there was one, and the absolute ruler of the Lion House.

Droapatie Capildeo, my mother, would have been fifteen or sixteen at that time. It was unusual for someone so slender and beautiful not to be married at such an age in the days when child marriages were still quite common. At any event, Pa must have learnt that she was unattached, and he was brave enough to take a step beyond the heavy front doors of the Lion House. Investigating him, the matriarch of the house found him acceptable as a suitor. His Brahmin caste made him more than acceptable – he was desirable, because the Capildeos were themselves Brahmin. Next, the mere mention of the name of the prosperous Sookdeo Misir as a close relative worked its magic. In 'two twos', as my father said, the marriage was arranged.

A Hindu marriage was the linking of two families and not just two

Pundit Capildeo and Soogie (Nanee)

individuals. Marriage in Hinduism is an inviolable sacrament. But in Trinidad it was not until 1945 that Hindu marriages were accepted as legal. The Hindu marriage rituals of old took the form of a premarital period, called a *tilak* or betrothal or an engagement, months before the actual wedding date. Formal rites binding the families with agreements as to dowries, especially, were decided upon. The pundits in charge of the wedding would seek an auspicious date. Two days before the wedding, purification rituals would be held in both the groom's home and the bride's home, attended by family and friends. On the third day the marriage ceremony took place at the bride's home or at a place chosen by the bride's family. The marriage knot was tied and the bride was literally handed over to the groom by her parents in a ceremony called the *Kanya Dan*. The bride's palm rested on that of her husband after the parents withdrew their own palms as the officiating pundit chanted the sacred mantras. Around the sacred fire, the two took their vows. The ceremony ended when the groom applied red powder, called *sindoor*, in the middle parting of the bride's hair. In many arranged marriages, the groom would then see his bride for the first time, when he lifted the marriage veil. Consummation of the marriage could only take place after the couple had completed rituals at the groom's home and also after the bride had returned to her home for a formal final departure to join her husband's household, to which she now belonged. Here her status and role would depend on her seniority in the family.

One of the reasons the Capildeos were so keen on the marriage was because Droapatie Capildeo had been married before, though the marriage had not been consummated. She was the seventh child and the seventh daughter of her parents. Arguably the most beautiful and most intelligent of the nine sisters, she was given the nickname Bhola by which she was known throughout her life. (Bhola means the quiet or peaceful one. It is interesting that both she and Seepersad, her husband-to-be, carried the same nickname.) Altogether there were eleven Capildeo children. A boy and a girl had not survived infancy. Had they lived, they would have completed the baker's dozen, not too startling for the times.

For a Hindu from India, seven daughters before the arrival of a son meant seven dowries. To most men, having to marry off so many girls would have been daunting and onerous. But Pundit Capildeo was well-known and well-respected in the Hindu community, and he had prospered in his own marriage. He would short-circuit the wedding situation by marrying off his daughters in pairs: two for the price of one! Droapatie had been married on the same day as her elder sister Ahila. When the time came for the brides to leave their parent's home, Ma's father decided that he had made a terrible blunder. He had discovered some flaw, something objectionable, about Droapatie's intended in-laws. He had the marriage annulled on the spot. Droapatie never left her parents' home. This would normally have caused gossip and scandal, but most people, without knowing his precise reason, would have accepted Pundit Capildeo's decision because of his lofty position in the community. The reason remained unknown, part of family

The Capildeos: Ma standing 4th from the right

lore. Ma thus enjoyed a longer period of life with her father than did most of her sisters, though when she eventually married Pa, her father had already died and her mother was in command of the family.

My father, too, had been married before. In his case, the complete marriage took place, but the bride then ran away, convinced that my father had malaria because he was so yellow! The three-day period of abstinence from any sexual activity after the marriage ceremony guaranteed that the marriage had not been consummated.

Seepersad Naipaul and Droapatie Capildeo were married at the Registrar's Office in Chaguanas on 28th March 1929. The witnesses were Ma's mother Soogie Capildeo and someone named Baden Semper, presumably a clerk in the office. There was no grand traditional wedding ceremony – perhaps because both my parents were, in a sense 'on the shelf', because of their previous abortive weddings – but marrying at the Registrar's office allowed all the Naipaul offspring to be deemed 'legitimate' on our birth certificates. Because Hindu marriages were still not legal, most of our cousins were registered as illegitimate. This was important because denominational Christian schools would not admit illegitimate children.

Like most young Hindu couples my parents were penniless. The usual expectation or custom of the day was that the young couple would go to live in the household of the bridegroom's parents. But Seepersad could not take his bride to his mother's home, because she had no house of her own, and besides, because she was a widow it would have been considered bad luck for her to perform the welcome ceremonies. So it was to Pa's adoptive home, the house of Sookdeo Misir, that my mother, now Droapatie Naipaul, went on her first day as a newly-wed.

Droapatie Capildeo had been lucky in her own mother. Soogie Capildeo was a formidable woman by almost any accounting. Following her desertion by her husband, who had repatriated himself to India, leaving her behind – but escorting another woman aboard the ship going 'home' – she had taken charge of her wealthy family's affairs. She was the best person for the job, having done far more to build up that wealth than he had. She, not her husband, was the true entrepreneur in the family, who understood the value of owning land and other property. Above all, perhaps, while his roots harked back to India, her roots were planted in Trinidad.

Born into a Roman Catholic family – hence her baptismal name Rosalie – Soogie Gobin had become, after her marriage to Pundit Capildeo Maharaj, a stern conformist to Hindu dogma. However, our Nanee, as we called her affectionately, all her life celebrated Christmas in addition to Divali and the many other Hindu calendar observances. (After Nanee's death in 1952, we would each retreat to our separate homes on Christmas Day and celebrate Christmas there. Sadly, the family dynastic traditions would lapse, without completely dying out.) Perhaps because of her Christian upbringing, she had enlightened views about certain basic matters. It was Nanee, not her husband, who insisted on education as the essential vehicle of social progress. She, not our grandfather, determined that all of her girls must go to school, at least until puberty. But Soogie was hardly reckless. Her girl children, unlike her sons, stopped school just before puberty. The idea was to reduce the chance that they would make certain terrible mistakes. One of Soogie's older sisters had strayed and married outside her race.

Soogie sought to instil pride in her family concerning exactly who they were and what they stood for as Hindus, along with the deep belief that they could match anyone in ability and performance. She possessed a powerful, persuasive will. The principal of the desirable Tranquillity School in Port of Spain, Umilta McShine, herself a famously strong leader, liked to tell the story of Mrs. Capildeo asking her quietly one day to admit some of her grandchildren into the school. Miss McShine agreed, but was dumbfounded when Nanee showed up soon after with a dozen or more children to be placed into various classes. In that way, Nanee cleared the path for virtually all members of the Capildeo clan to follow those first charges into Tranquillity.

Whenever my mother or her sisters spoke of their childhood, it was with joy and fond recollection. Their eyes lit up and they became animated with tales of Teteron Bay, moonlight games and storytelling, vats of steamed crabs and other culinary delights. Yet if I reflect, I realise that these girls must have had very few childhood years: the elder girls were married by the ages of nine and eleven. Small wonder they clung to their childhood memories and stories with so much warmth and passion.

I believe that my mother and her siblings were sent to a Presbyterian elementary school in Chaguanas. Most members of the family wrote in the easily identifiable script of the Presbyterian teachers. Ma's schooldays were few but happy. Excelling in her studies, she seemed never to forget the poems, stories, history, geography and arithmetic she learnt at school. Her younger brother, Simbhoonath, was in her class but never outperformed her. That fact, unfortunately, proved her undoing. Her mother refused to allow her to sit the bursary exam for Naparima High School out of fear, or certainty, that she would outshine her brother. It was a bitter pill for Ma to swallow. Her teachers begged for her to continue at school, but Nanee would not budge. At the age of eleven Ma's schooldays were over. Until her death she kept the handwritten goodbye page of poems and sentiments given to her by her classmates when she was taken out of school.

She would keep ledger books for her mother until she married Pa, and later she would do the same for Simbhoonath at a quarry he owned in Diego Martin. But Ma would never go back to 'real' books again. I am almost certain that she never read any of Pa's stories in his collection, *Gurudeva and Other Indian Stories*. I am also not sure that he ever read any to her. I do not know if she read any of her sons' books, all published after Pa's death. But I am sure that she read Pa's articles in the *Guardian*, as she dutifully pasted them for him in the ledger book as they appeared in the newspaper starting in the nineteen-thirties.

My mother did not always speak grammatically correct English, although she expressed herself well enough given the limits of her education. My father, also weakly schooled, taught himself to master writing in English while she was busy raising their children. If Ma had been given the opportunities at school which she would later seek for all of her children, she would doubtless have learned to express herself with boldness, skill and clarity. But her intellectual growth was stifled and stunted. Her ambition was snuffed out by a myth present in our culture that gave much more credence to the ambitions of males over females. I believe this to be essentially foreign to the deepest roots of Hinduism, which honours the feminine in all ways and forms. In Trinidad, Ma should have had the opportunity to show her true ability. Instead, she developed a compulsion to withdraw, a powerful if muted sense of reserve reflected in her family nickname, Bhola, the quiet one. Her strong speaking voice, which many of us inherited, disappeared for years into some suppressed inner chamber of her being.

The welcoming bridal ceremonies over, Seepersad and Droapatie moved into a rented apartment in a house on El Dorado Road owned by a Mrs. Harry. The young couple occupied half the house, while Mrs. Harry had the other half. Droapatie, accustomed to brewing 'good tea' for her father, made sure to maintain her reputation in her new home. Soon Pa's siblings from the Sookdeo Misir household began drifting in for her tea.

Seepersad was twenty-three years old when he married Ma. Until Mrs. Harry's house, his dwellings had been mainly the lowly ajoupa common to poor Indian life. The Sookdeo house, new and substantial, existed along with an ajoupa in the back yard. The Back Street ajoupa, which we visited during our childhood and where Pa's aunts lived, was quite large, or so it seemed. The house itself ran in a north-south direction, on the western side of the lot. The bedrooms – I believe there were three – were at the northern end, with the kitchen at the southern end. On the side of the building, beyond the bedrooms, and facing east, there was a gallery or verandah with low walls. The furniture was no more than a couple of benches.

Our *ajees*, for so we called our great-aunts (*ajee* being the Hindi/Bhojpuri word for paternal grandmother or her sisters), often squatted when chatting and smoking. This relaxed session took place usually at the end of the day. Then they all smoked, holding the hand-rolled cigarettes (*bidis*) between their thumb and forefinger while cupping the burning end with the rest of the hand. As if they were hiding the cigarette, they calmly passed it to each

The ajees, Back Street, Tunapuna

other. Thus they shared what was obviously a pleasant communal ritual. To us children, the Back Street *ajees* looked Chinese. In general they wore white skirts and tops and covered their heads with their *orhanis* or veils knotted at the back of their heads. One or two wore the heavy silver *caras* or ankle bracelets popular in Patna. We knew of only one brother, Ramjit. A driver or *sirdar*, he lived apart from his six sisters with his wife and two daughters, Khatrani and Siewbass, in a wooden house on the Eastern Main Road.

Later, when we were living in Port of Spain, where we had electricity and running water, as children we were curious and intrigued by the ajoupa when we visited our country cousins. In ajoupas, the bedrooms were always dark, some of them windowless. Kerosene lamps were used at night and bedtime came early. One awoke to the smell of coffee. The earthen fireside in the kitchen was always immaculately kept. The black soot of the wood fire would only show in the funnel and the tops of the burners. These firesides, called *choolhas*, had to be lit at least three times each day. Wood was the fuel. In the kitchen, a mixture of cow dung and mud was used as a veneer to keep the dust down. To plaster the cooking area, a rag was used to spread the mixture. Ochre in colour when wet, the plaster became a creamish wash when dried. The act of coating the fireside area was called to *leepay*, or leepaying. The pots were of cast-iron and enamel. All their utensils were of enamel or metal. Special foods, such as *kheer* or sweet rice, were cooked in clay pots that were glazed on the inside. Dried mango, limes and tamarind for making chutneys were kept in similar jars. The fare was mainly vegetarian, always simple and delicious, never oily. The religious rituals at the start and end of the day were generally not followed, as they were in our mother's family. The aroma of smoke from cooking fires and burning bush at dusk still awakens in me memories of rural Back Street in Tunapuna of the 1940s. Tunapuna is now a built-up town.

Between 1930 and 1938 my parents had five children. Kamla, their first, was born on 8th February 1930. Vidia, soon called Vido at home, came in 1932; Sati in 1934; Mira in 1936; and I, Savitri or Savi, in 1938. (Two more children would come later.)

Every name was carefully chosen by Pa and written in a particular book. Vido, being the first boy, was honoured with two names: Vidiadhar Surajprasad. The girls had one name only. Naming a child, according to Hindu custom, is a serious matter. There is always a certain mystique attached to the horoscope or *Patra* names. The names, with their syllabic starters, are based on the time, the date and the planetary alignments at the moment of birth. The *Patra* or *Rasi* name is to be held secretly by the parents until the birth rites are completed. But here, as in so many other areas, Pa could be irreverent. Pundits were supposed to advise strongly on the choice of names, but he often chose the name himself and paid no heed to the pundit. The names he chose were our 'calling names'. I doubt if breaking any of these taboos felt of grave consequence to a man like my father, who frequently questioned the intelligence and also the ability of pundits. Another form of his ingrained irreverence.

Today, his precious book of names no longer occupies a place in the family bookcase. Is it in an attic in fashionable Wiltshire, where Vidia lives? Is it in Tulsa, Oklahoma, where his papers are stored following a financial arrangement with the university there? Not so long ago Vidia told me that he had boxes and boxes of things yet to be sorted in the attic of his house. Perhaps Pa's book of names is there.

Until 1938, all Seepersad and Droapatie's children were born in the Lion House on the Chaguanas Main Road. For my mother, her confinements must have given her some badly needed respite from the constant moving and changing of locales which she and Pa underwent with their children. My mother had grown up in a stable situation in this respect. By 1938, however, she and Pa could recall Tunapuna, Cunupia, Chandernagore, Chaguanas, St. Joseph, Belmont and Petit Valley as temporary resting-places while their family grew. These areas covered a substantial swathe of Trinidad. Belmont was even then a densely populated district in Port of Spain, whereas Petit Valley was still largely virgin territory, mainly rural, with extensive private landholdings. (It has been transformed since those pre-war years.) Pa, Ma and their children – we Naipauls – had to relocate and adapt constantly. And the prime mover here was usually Nanee, our Capildeo grandmother, who owned various houses when Pa and Ma owned none, and who even owned a three-hundred-acre estate in Petit Valley.

For my father, as a man without education or money, being married to a Capildeo meant that he was continually negotiating troubled waters. The chance of him ever 'paddling his own canoe' seemed slim. In addition, he had views that were often at odds with those of the leading Capildeos and with the sons-in-law who made up the fortress that was Capildeo family culture.

Apart from my father and perhaps three others, all the sons-in-law in the Capildeo family were trained pundits and members of the first generation of immigrants from India. They would have been thoroughly schooled in Hindu customs, scriptures and rites by parents who were themselves also pundits. It was never taken for granted that they planned to make Trinidad their new home. Their parents had the choice of renewing their contracts or commuting their return passage in return for land. They trained their children in the ways of the old world. They all read the scriptures even if they did not perform the religious rites. Men such as these were straddling two different worlds. They relished their status as Brahmins, even if being a Brahmin meant little or nothing, officially, in Trinidad and Tobago under

British law. Further, by clinging to the orthodox Sanatan Dharma version of Hinduism they limited their possibility of employment (because they were debarred from entering the Presbyterian secondary schools) and their range of intellectual and cultural interests. Unlike Pa, they were not willing to accept change and choose an occupation as, say, a teacher that was in keeping with their high caste, but nevertheless secular. So they remained impervious to new ideas and new social movements.

Pa was also a follower of the progressive Arya Samaj movement, which though founded in India in 1875, had only fairly recently sent missionaries to Trinidad. The Arya Samaj valued and encouraged religious change and reform, so Pa was bound to find himself in conflict with the conservative Capildeos. The Capildeo clan was fiercely Sanatanist, although the *kala pani* (the black water) had been crossed in getting to Trinidad, and crossing the *kala pani* meant obliteration of caste, which is the lynch-pin of orthodox Hinduism. Seepersad, not steeped in or clinging to tradition, found it difficult and stifling to steer clear of trouble when pitted against eight sisters-in-law, seven husbands, two brothers-in-law and a mother-in-law who ruled with a hand of steel. In addition, the Capildeo clan was held in high esteem as the most *pukka* or high-toned of Hindus. They were also already dabbling in politics, albeit only (for the moment) at the local level. Wider ambitions were understood to be a matter of time.

Arguments in and among members of the extended family were a part of daily life, but Seepersad was always trying to be an extra step or even a leap away from his wealthy, powerful in-laws. He wanted to establish his own separate household well apart from that of the imposing communal one ruled by the Capildeos. But with Sati newly born, and Kamla and Vidia getting older and needing to start school, Pa and Ma had little choice but to off-load them on to the affluent, influential Capildeos in Chaguanas. There they joined umpteen cousins at the Lion House, all largely dependent on Soogie Capildeo. Helped by her young aunt Tara (our mother's unmarried sister), Kamla looked out for her younger brother Vidia, and did so conscientiously. A special bond formed between them.

In having to send Kamla and Vidia to the Lion House, Pa gave in to Capildeo reality but he resented this arrangement. He hated the idea of our mother having to go for help to her mother 'cap in hand', as he often said. Friction grew between him and her family, especially the menfolk led by Ma's princely bothers, Simbhoonath and Rudranath, with whom Pa now and then feuded. Then, in 1933 or early 1934, his resentment led to an incident that seriously damaged his sense of wellbeing, and indeed his sanity.

Somehow, despite his weak formal education, but driven by his literary interests, Pa had become the Chaguanas correspondent of the *Trinidad Guardian*. Largely self-taught, he had acquired competence in writing and perhaps had published a few brief pieces that are now lost. Being a correspondent for the *Guardian,* he was on virgin ground as an Indian reporter on the national scene, in particular in reporting on Indian culture as a topic of island-wide newspaper interest. Hitherto, little of Indian life had been covered and reported to the largely white or aspirational coloured and African readership of the top newspapers and magazines. Mainstream Trinidad society regarded Indian culture as beneath its notice, if not beneath contempt. A novice in journalism, but stimulated and encouraged by a new, enterprising British editor of the *Guardian*, Gault MacGowan, who was seeking to enliven its pages and especially its coverage of local affairs, Pa began to use the comings and goings of prominent Chaguanas personalities as the subject matter of newspaper stories. His sometimes cheeky coverage of local events, whether festivals or feuds, was occasionally serialised in the *Guardian*.

One day, however, Pa went too far. He reported with some levity that someone had thrown a decapitated pig's head on to the tent of a seven-day *yagna* or prayer meeting in Chaguanas. To the Capildeos and to most Hindus, this was a diabolical and unforgivable act. That a son-in-law of the Capildeo family could treat such profanity as an amusing news feature brought down shame and disgrace on the entire community. Pa faced the wrath of the Capildeos, including the cadre of pundits among its various sons-in-law. My father's position was held to be indefensible. The clan demanded an unequivocal retraction in the newspaper.

The retraction was not forthcoming. Indeed, the family feud was fair fodder to the budding journalist and his editor. So the serial continued on a daily basis. As far as Seepersad was concerned, his reports were creating a lively diversion for his readers across the island. In addition to advancing himself, he was bringing the sleepy town of Chaguanas into national focus. He deserved to be praised, not condemned. But he soon discovered that he was in deep trouble. To the Capildeo family, the daily news items were no laughing matter.

Pa received a death threat. At first, this was carried in the *Guardian* as yet another piquant episode of Indian country culture. Then Pa discovered that the threat was real. Suddenly his point of view changed. Given exactly one day to relent or die, he capitulated. He did so, apparently, without a murmur of protest. Did my mother have anything to do with his surrender? Did Pa suddenly recall that he had a wife and three children? Did he suddenly feel real fear?

A truce was called. The father of three children decided that he had to atone by making a sacrificial offering of a goat to the Goddess Kali. Who insisted on the sacrificial offering? No one knows. Seepersad Naipaul, the Arya Samajist, the defender of reform and change, the journalist who could turn local events into an entertaining serial narrative in Dickensian style for the amusement of readers across Trinidad, had won several skirmishes but lost the war. The primitivism of the sacrifice, its cruelty, the pleading doe eyes of the innocent animal, every aspect of the sacrifice overwhelmed Pa's sensitivity. A few days later, he could not look at himself in the mirror. My father had a nervous breakdown. He was twenty-six or twenty-seven years old.

My father, for all of his love of storytelling, never told this story, never wrote it down. No one in either of the extended families related this tale. This was a story that was too painful for my father to tell or write. As we, his children, grew older, the knowledge of our father's nervous breakdown was always there. We had to grow up ourselves to understand fully the term 'nervous breakdown'. To most of us – not all – our mother's unyielding reticence on the subject was as understandable as it was regrettable. It seemed the events would have been buried forever.

From 1964 to the mid-nineteen-seventies, my brother Vidia visited Trinidad from time to time. This was a period in which he felt particularly unsettled living in Britain. Together we drove through many scenic spots in and around the Montserrat Hills in central Trinidad. He was mulling over the idea of settling in Trinidad, and looking for a place to do so.

But Vidia's visits always had a professional purpose or purposes as well. During one of them he decided to research our father's career in journalism. It was Vidia, inspired and directed by the discovery made by an American writer, who had alerted him to the existence of a newspaper account of an incident in Trinidad involving Seepersad Naipaul and the ritual sacrifice of a goat, who pieced together the events which led to Pa's breakdown. Angry and aggressive as he often was, Vidia put our mother

The Inquisition: Vidia and Ma

through an inquisition. What did she know? When did she know it? Why had she kept this information from us? Intimidated, Ma bore the brunt of Vidia's blame game. The increasingly tenuous relationship between mother and son – more like son and intimidated mother – would never soften or completely heal. 'There are some things that are better to forget,' my mother would say, plaintively, with a tear or two.

Pa resigned from the newspaper. His breakdown must have seriously dented his local and professional lustre and shattered his confidence. He had broken the shackles of his family's agricultural past in Trinidad, but the future was uncertain. He knew he had no talent for business or the service industries. The only job the Capildeos offered him was as a ledger-keeper, which was more suited to my mother's talents. The ledger book, surely kept by my mother, would be put away and used a few years later for another purpose. Probably it was during these years that Pa found solace in authors such as Epictetus, Marcus Aurelius and other writers associated with contemplation and self-consolation in the face of tragedy. Reading replaced sign-painting and lettering. Chain-smoking helped to lessen his anxiety, no doubt at some cost to his health. He also took up a new hobby, making walking sticks. And the experience reawakened his artist's vision.

It was also during these harrowing years that I believe my parents moved from place to place – from Chaguanas to Cunupia and Chandernagore, which was wild and undeveloped. How did my mother, who had lived for so many years in a big house on the Main Road of Chaguanas, with running water and later electricity, cope with bringing up her children in the bush? Many years later, at home in Nepaul Street in St. James, Port of Spain, in times of loose talk, she would hint at failed business ventures during those earlier years. We never questioned her deeply about these ventures, which we never really understood. By that time, in any event, they seemed irrelevant. It is in writing this personal history that certain happenings are taking shape, certain questions are being raised.

There is an almost surreal episode in a piece of fiction written by Vidia about a father and son sharing a night of terror during a particularly severe thunderstorm. The images of thunder and lightning, howling winds and rain thrashing the wooden doors and windows, which cannot be closed, are graphic. The dark night and the house situated in the middle of nowhere might have been a childhood recollection of Vidia's. It is possible that the story, even if exaggerated as written, is fundamentally true. It is also probable that Vidia chose at some point to stay with our father while our mother went with Kamla and possibly Sati back to the Lion House. And while this is all conjecture, the time and the story seem to match.

There is also a vague recollection of a short story by Pa of another night of terror and ambush in a lonely rural area. If my memory holds true, the main figure of Pa's story hides in a tree to escape the torment and the tormentor. Both stories are night stories and both conjure up images of terror and loneliness. Did Pa's story influence Vidia's? In probably his best novel, *A House for Mr. Biswas*, there are elements of both stories.

Among our belongings only two photographs exist of a young Seepersad Naipaul. One is on his driver's permit, issued when he is twenty-two. The other shows him looking rakish with a hat on, when he is about thirty. Cameras were not common in Trinidad in the nineteen-thirties and photography was largely formal. Most of the portraits in our family album were taken by professional photographers in studios. In 1933 there is the first and only Naipaul family portrait. Taken in a studio, it shows Pa standing with Kamla in front of him, with Vidia on Ma's lap. (Sati is still unborn.) Everybody is dressed up for the occasion. One suspects that Pa arranged a visit to the photographer's studio to celebrate his becoming the Chaguanas correspondent for the *Trinidad Guardian*. It is a happy picture of the young family.

Pa, Ma, Kamla, Vidia on Ma's knee, Sati in utero, 1933

# CHAPTER 2

## *Heidi of the Tropics*

During Pa's recovery years the family grew from three to five children. Penniless as newlyweds, my parents nevertheless never allowed matters such as money and job security to determine the size of their family. Large families were commonplace in those times.

Pa was five feet seven inches tall. He was always slender and he dressed well. He believed that when he slicked down his hair with a side-part, he could be as dapper and debonair as Rudolf Valentino. As his health improved, his play-acting and his vanity returned. Once more he could look at himself in the mirror.

He also moved his family out of the rural area around Chaguanas, away from the scene of his biggest crisis, out from under the immediate shadow of the Lion House – although by no means away from the power of the Capildeos, on whom he still depended.

First he moved with Ma and the children to 17 Luis Street in Woodbrook, an eminently respectable address in the city of Port of Spain. Our maternal grandmother, Nanee, had bought 17 Luis Street around 1936. She had done so on the advice of her daughter Kalawatee and Kalawatee's husband, Ramnarace Permanand. (Another daughter, Dhan, had married Ramnarace's brother Ramnarine.) The house had a malign history. The previous owners, before Nanee bought it, had been members of the family of Boysie Singh, a notorious criminal accused and convicted of killing Thelma Haynes, whose body was never found, in one of the most sensational trials in Trinidad history. Nanee must have done many *pujas* to erase the sins involved! She had lived in Luis Street on and off to look after her son, Rudranath, who was a student at Queen's Royal College (QRC), located nearby. Now she invited Pa and Ma to live in the house with their children so that she could return to Chaguanas, confident that Ma would take excellent care of Rudranath, her younger brother. We were only too happy to oblige.

These moves and manoeuvrings by Nanee Capildeo, including her acquiring of property in a residential part of Port of Spain, had everything

Pa in his thirties

to do with her keen awareness that education was crucial to the youngsters in her family, especially her two sons. Education is always important, but in Trinidad and Tobago, when we were growing up, it was an unusually complicated, stressful and sometimes anguished matter. Almost nothing was more important to the future of young people, or harder for people of limited means to negotiate. Whether they were rich or poor, or those in between; white, African or Indian – the future of almost every child seemed to depend, almost in a neurotic way, on gaining entrance to the few schools that virtually guaranteed a place of advantage in our highly competitive society. Passing certain examinations had an almost sacred significance in our lives. Around the age of eleven, winning an 'exhibition' (which guaranteed admission to a high school and also paid one's way while there) was the first major step, especially for the poor. If one got into high school, then at around sixteen or seventeen one faced the Cambridge University-administered Senior School Certificate. If you got grade one you were on the road to success; grades two and three usually indicated a dimmer future. The *crème de la crème* of the students stayed on in the elite schools to try to gain a Higher School Certificate. The SSC examination covered eight subjects; the HSC concentrated on three subjects chosen from one of four areas: Science, Mathematics, Languages and so-called Modern Studies. The ultimate aim of HSC students was to win one of the four 'island scholarships' offered by the government to study at a university abroad. (To study abroad almost always meant Oxford or Cambridge. What would become the University of the West Indies started modestly in Mona, Jamaica in 1948 as a college of the University of London. UWI became independent only in 1962.) In 1946, a fifth scholarship was established, for girls only. Previously they had competed against the boys, usually without success. To my knowledge, the only girl to win against the boys later became Sister Francis Xavier Ulrich, a teaching nun who would have a huge impact on the education of the Naipaul girls.

Our school system was a complicated and often disturbing challenge. Until 1961 (the year before the nation gained independence), the government maintained only one boys' secondary school, Queen's Royal College. QRC was superbly located in Port of Spain on the western side of the Queen's Park Savannah. It was the grandest of the row of buildings called the 'Magnificent Seven', which included the residences of the heads of the Roman Catholic and Anglican churches. A seven-year school, it took in some 500 students altogether. Its grounds and athletic facilities were excellent. Non-religious by design, it mainly served local white Protestants, upwardly mobile or established black and mixed-race Protestants – and a handful of Indians. Roman Catholics, led by the white or near-white French Creole social elite, had responded by establishing two rivals to

QRC: the College of the Immaculate Conception (CIC, or St. Mary's College, as it was better known) on Frederick Street, also in Port of Spain; and the girls' school at St. Joseph's Convent, located on Pembroke Street across from the back entrance to CIC. Though they employed some locally-born priests, it was the Holy Ghost Fathers from Ireland who ran CIC. In a similar way, the Sisters of Cluny maintained St. Joseph's. Devout Protestants responded with Bishop Anstey High School for girls, an excellent institution, also located in the capital. Presbyterianism also had its elite high schools, but Naparima College for boys and Naparima High School for girls were down south in San Fernando. The Catholics also had good high schools in the south, including Presentation and La Romain, but none to rival CIC in those years.

The government did a much better job of providing primary and intermediate or pre-high school education. Here, too, the churches complemented the government effort. Rivalry was intense among these schools for winning the exhibitions to secondary schools (although white students typically had automatic entry to our elite high schools). In high school, pupils vied for the Jerningham Silver Medal, awarded to the outstanding student at the Senior Certificate level; and finally, at the Higher Certificate level, for the Jerningham Gold Medal and one of the coveted island scholarships.

Private high schools (Progressive, Ideal, Pamphyllion and so on) sprang up in Port of Spain mainly to serve the striving black classes in the city, but were sadly underfunded and never a threat to win top prizes. But where were Hindus from the 'heartland' (especially Caroni) to go to school? It was incongruous to have devout Hindus entrusting their children to Catholic priests and nuns, or to devout Anglicans, or even to secular instructors at QRC. But in my childhood, and certainly in my family, the decision was easy. We pushed to get into the 'best' schools, regardless of religion, or the lack of religion. Pragmatism, ambition and a curious set of circumstances shaped our family's fate in this regard. Pragmatism made the boys eager to go to QRC, with its fine record of winning scholarships and creating national leaders. But for the girls, the fact that Nanee Capildeo, the virtual head of our larger family, had been brought up as a Roman Catholic, before marrying into Hindu orthodoxy, made the idea of attending St. Joseph's Convent hardly anathema. The stricter piety of the Convent school was also perhaps more comforting to devout Hindu parents in thinking about their girls' education.

To prepare for entry into the top high schools, we looked to Tranquillity Boys' and Girls' School. Located in Woodbrook in Port of Spain, Tranquillity seemed to have no rival in prestige or performance. Accordingly, Nanee Capildeo set her sights on it as the ideal upward path for her family and, as I have already related, in a shining display of her charisma, had persuaded its formidable headmistress, Miss Umilta McShine, to accept her grandchildren into the school.

Certainly, we made concessions over our Hinduism when we attended Tranquillity, and later at other schools. Like the other students, we cupped our hands under the tap to drink water when we were thirsty, though, for Hindus, drinking from a tap that everyone used was considered a form of pollution. Like everyone else, we quickly learned to respect and honour Miss McShine's strict rules, even when they appeared to differ from Hindu values and practices. We may have been separate as Indians at Tranquillity and other schools, but we lived contentedly among many people of different looks, skin complexions, religious beliefs and cultures. And we cannot say that we felt oppressed or unhappy.

Nanee took the move to Luis Street seriously. She wished to have her arrival in Port of Spain noticed. Her approach was unusual and left us in a state of controlled embarrassment, but we had no choice but to go along with her wishes. To mark the occasion she organised a memorable *puja* or religious service under a peepal tree in the Botanical Gardens in Port of Spain. (The peepal is the species of tree under which the Buddha had sat in Sarnath, not far from Benares, where he meditated and received enlightenment.) The Botanical Gardens are next to the grand Government House, where the British governor lived, and are a popular place with local strollers. We were in full view of any passers-by, although thankfully it was a weekend, when foot traffic was thin. None of us dared to stay away from what Nanee clearly saw as a statement of pride in Hinduism. Holding our heads high, we thus attempted to demonstrate to the unknowing the great way of life that our religion embodied.

The move to 17 Luis Street was a stroke of luck, although, as I have pointed out, we were never intended to be its beneficiaries, the property having been acquired mainly, I believe, to help Nanee's second son, Rudranath, who was a stellar student at QRC and widely considered to be a major contender to win the 'island schol' in Mathematics. Adding to the drama was the fact that Rudranath's older brother, Simbhoonath, the unquestioned heir apparent of the Capildeo family, had not won one of these prestigious scholarships. Nanee was determined to give Rudranath every opportunity to succeed, so she installed him in Luis Street, from where he could walk to school. She herself alternated between living in Chaguanas and Luis Street. Every week she travelled to Port of Spain to make sure he was doing well. With our father securing a permanent job in Port of Spain in 1938, and with my mother's even temperament, sharp intelligence and good husbandry well known, my grandmother decided to offer 17 Luis Street to the Naipauls as a temporary residence in exchange for their looking after Rudranath.

The offer came after our parents' brief sojourn in Belmont where the situation had not been particularly comfortable, or indeed adequate. Luis Street in Woodbrook in 1938 brought a drastic change in our lives and our fortunes. Kamla and Vidia, now eight and six respectively, had spent a large part of their early childhood in the Lion House. In Ma's absence they clung to her younger sister Tara. Pa had visited them regularly to ensure their wellbeing. He tried to strengthen them and to counteract what he termed 'Capildeo bad food' by bringing them raw eggs, but I doubt they got them. He wanted his family brought together, living under the same roof, under his charge.

In Woodbrook, we were a family at last. Vidia no longer had to cling to Kamla, but an unshakable bond had already formed between them. 17 Luis Street was a concrete house built on stilts with a separate servants' room. Spacious and uncluttered by either furniture or people, the house had three bedrooms, a gallery, a living and dining area, a pantry, an upstairs kitchen with running water, a bathroom and a flush toilet. Such luxury was very new and very exciting. Rudranath was well looked after, though by the end of 1938 there was no need for him to be in Port of Spain. With the Second World War revving up in 1939, he won one of the prized island scholarships

Pa with Rudranath Capildeo (right)

and left Luis Street, not returning to Trinidad until 1946. By that time he had earned a Master's degree in Physics and Higher Mathematics and was hailed locally as an intellectual giant.

Kamla and Vidia had started school in Port of Spain. They began at the Woodbrook Presbyterian School before quickly moving on to the more prestigious Tranquillity Government Intermediate School. Vidia shot through the infant school like a comet and by the age of ten had won the prized exhibition or scholarship that took him to Queens Royal College and a remarkable secondary school career.

Pa told me that he was always aware that we had limited time in the Luis Street house. While we were living there it seems that the entire Capildeo clan, with the exception of two of the older sisters, Ramdoolarie and Rajdaye, moved en masse to the Petit Valley estate owned by my grandmother. At some point she had bought this estate from the Maillards, one of the most respected and affluent coloured families in Trinidad. In 1893, Michael P. Maillard, one of the first black businessmen in the island's history, had founded a department store that became a major point of pride for many Trinidadians. When he sold it in 1928, he no doubt made a handsome profit. At some point his descendants decided to sell the beautiful three-hundred-acre estate they owned in Petit Valley and move to Port of Spain.

It is unclear exactly when the transaction took place, and where the money came from. I concluded a long time ago that Uncle Simbhoo was the person who suggested that Nanee buy the property. He had probably heard that it was for sale during the time he was in training to become a solicitor in the office of a man named Cameron, who owned a substantial quantity of land in Petit Valley, as did the prominent Scott family, Chinese Trinidadians who owned the celebrated racehorse, Jetsam. The Scott farm was opposite the lands Nanee bought, and I often saw the champion horse strolling in the pasture. The Maillard estate would not have come cheaply, but Nanee had the means to buy it and did so. Shrewd and resourceful, she owned several properties, perhaps a score or so. She always seemed to have enough cash on hand to make quick purchases and to maintain various large households.

The spacious, elegant main estate house had six bedrooms upstairs that allowed each family a basic space of its own. But Pa had other ideas. Not wanting to live in such close quarters with other members of the Capildeo clan, and with so much land available on the estate, he evidently asked for a plot of land on which to build a house. Nanee granted him his wish. The new wooden house built on stilts in Petit Valley was Seepersad Naipaul's first house and the family's first self-owned home. Petit Valley is the setting of my earliest memories. The scent of the freshly planed wood and

Nanee at the entrance to the Petit Valley estate house

Kamla (right) and cousin Deocooar (Ahila's daughter) in the grounds of the Petit Valley estate

cedar curls in our new home has remained with me. There are vague memories of Pa's mother visiting both the big estate house and our smaller house, about five to ten minutes away and separated by a cocoa plantation.

The Petit Valley estate of my childhood remains the most idyllic place in the world. The walk through the valley which separated the estate from the road, the aunts going along the valley to do their washing, the walk through the cocoa estate to the big house with all the cousins, the oranges and avocados in that house, not in baskets but in heaps on the floor, the cows in the savannah, an area large enough to allow cricket to be played there on the weekends by the villagers, made me a kind of Heidi of the Tropics. At Easter there was a greasy pole and believe it or not a ham at the top of it! But this excitement was for the village folk, the estate workers, not for the new occupants of the Great House.

The grandeur of the estate and the Great House with its beautifully laid out garden at the top of a plateau was stunning. The new occupants, the various branches of the extended Capildeo family, including ourselves, had not yet reached the level of sophistication to appreciate the Eden we were in. The long driveway which abutted the wide marble steps at the base of the plateau forked to the right and left to climb the incline, embrace the house and garden and reach the covered area between the back of the house and the kitchen. The double-tiered kitchen was carved into the hill. The smell of the tonka beans on the hills behind the kitchen sailed through the area. The huge clay oven on the second tier of the kitchen brought Hansel and Gretel to life.

Separated from the kitchen was a row of servants' rooms and beyond that a garage that could hold four cars. There was also a manhole. On the other side of the kitchen and quite apart was a bathhouse with a concrete tub that required steps to climb up and down into it. As children we squealed and chattered in the icy-cold water which was channelled from a cistern in the cocoa estate. Bamboo poles brought water from the cocoa estate to the kitchen and to the main house. Why the flush toilet system was never connected by my grandmother was anybody's guess. Why the bathroom was turned into a sewing room, an enigma!

The house itself had high ceilings and tall doors. On the bottom floor there were two large bedrooms and a smaller bay room in which my grandmother kept her iron chest, which we all called a *chiss*. At the front of the house the gallery ran from the bay room to the washroom on the other side of the house in an L-shape. A Rangoon vine trailed along the railing of the gallery with its pink, cream and reddish florets and incredible jasmine scent. The large living-room was matched by a large dining-room. Furniture was sparse for such a large house and the bentwood furniture from Czechoslovakia was almost lost without rugs or side tables. Between the ground floor

Vidia in Petit Valley, aged 6 or 7

bedrooms at one end and the living and dining room at the other, there was a pantry and the staircase to the upper bedrooms.

If the house remained unused and unfurnished for the grand living it suggested, it nevertheless provided an unrivalled setting for family weddings. Several grandchildren were coming of age. Arranged marriages were still the order of the day among Hindu families. As children we were ignored, rebuffed and entranced by the daylight and nocturnal wedding activities. At night the light was by Petromax lamps, as electricity had not yet arrived in Petit Valley. The house and the tents could house and sleep so many that our grandmother would have felt like a queen bee on these occasions. Small as I was, I can recall at least four very large weddings and falling asleep in the same bed every night.

For us children, the Petit Valley Estate was a haven of delight and space. Although we had our own home 'up the valley', we spent many hours, perhaps days, with our cousins in the big house where all the excitement seemed to be. The usual purges of castor oil or senna, the cure-all turmeric and milk drink, the ear-piercing, the baths, with first a scrub with a loofah, then soap and lemon followed by the soothing and healing neem plant, the weeding of the long driveway, were all part and parcel of Nanee's care-giving.

Our father must have enjoyed his privacy, away from the hullabaloo of the big house with its prying eyes and sharp ears, and the menfolk who appeared to do very little indeed. Building and living in his own house would have softened the blow of moving from Woodbrook to 'the valley'. But living in Petit Valley meant a far longer distance to work and school for himself and the children. Sati was now also at school.

The main transport was by bus, whose schedule was at best haphazardly followed. Nanee Capildeo had acquired a car, possibly a Studebaker, with its trunk opening to form a seat at the rear of the car. Other cousins were now also attending Tranquillity in Port of Spain. The car, however, proved even more unreliable than the bus and the band of school-goers found itself walking back home a little too often. Pram 2348 was how the car was called. At that time, the early nineteen-forties, mechanics were few and far between. One of our uncles became a self-appointed mechanic and earned the name Power Mousa (*mousa* being the Hindi word for maternal uncle). We would recognise him as Uncle Bhacku many years later in Vidia's book of stories *Miguel Street*, always listening to hear if the tappets were knocking.

By 1939, the news of war had replaced Edward VIII's abdication in the headlines. The advertisements by recruiters to join the war effort and serve king and country filtered into Petit Valley. At the same time the activities of Gokhale (Gandhi's mentor), Gandhi, Nehru and Mohammed Ali Jinnah were intensifying towards Indian independence from Britain. Gandhi was the focus of attention between his bouts of jail sentences and fasting. The Indians in Trinidad and British Guiana followed the events in India closely. Those without radios went to friends and relatives to get the news. The non-Indian population knew or cared little about events in India, but to the sons and daughters of indentured workers, the ancestral land was close and real. The lure of a return trip lingered in the hearts and minds of some who saw themselves on the periphery of the society in which they lived. Both Seepersad's and Droapatie's fathers had come from India. As a reporter, my father was agitated by the news on both Indian and European fronts. But there was also a disaster closer to home.

In an attempt one evening to clear the bush from encroaching on his newly built house, things got out of hand. The fire which he had lit to clear the path threatened the house. With no neighbours, Kamla and Vidia were sent to alert the family in the big house. It was already night. The two had to pick their way through the cocoa estate in the darkness, tormented by the thoughts of *soucouyants*, *la diablesse*, *douens*, *loup-garous* and other denizens of our vivid island folklore. The oft repeated story of the fear that gripped the two that night told of a nightmarish experience. The family was roused but it was all to naught. The house, our first home, was reduced to ashes.

Not long after, the Naipaul family was back in 17 Luis Street. We were alone once more, apart from a family who occupied rooms at the back of the property. I think the father worked nearby on the new American base facilities at Docksite. He and his wife had two attractive daughters, Janet and Jean Ector, older than Kamla. Later they became part of the Little Carib Folklore group, founded by the dancer and choreographer Beryl McBurnie.

If Petit Valley continued to maintain its tranquillity in spite of the war, the same cannot be said of Woodbrook, or Port of Spain in general. One could sense the change. The area of landfill at the southern end of Luis Street was the site of a new dual carriageway, the first of its kind in Trinidad. Before long Docksite, as this area was called, was being fenced and wooden buildings were mushrooming. All the green parks of the city, which were called 'squares', were being dug up with trenches. The sound of sirens and sight of searchlights playing in the night sky became almost nightly dramas. 'Lights out' meant total blackout, which was scary. Still too young to grasp the idea of war, I would cling to my father for comfort and security.

Ration cards made an appearance. One had to line up for bread, each person getting his allocation. Butter and cheese came in blue tins, mainly from New Zealand. Trinidad had no poultry farms and eggs were scarce. People who lived in the rural areas and reared cows and goats, ducks and chickens were much better off than people in the city or its suburbs. Frenetic planting of crops was part of a 'Grow Your Food' campaign and root crops became another staple apart from rice and wheat flour.

People joined the armed forces but there was no mixing and mingling. Trinidad was still a Crown colony and only people considered 'white' could become officers. Even in time of war race and colour would divide rather than unite the *pro patria* troops. However, not all white people were acceptable. Those with German roots were screened and monitored and not admitted to the draft. Some younger boys of mixed ethnicity joined the cadets as a precursor to entering the forces. All of this I would learn as I grew older. But with my father as a reporter there were stories about submarines and German intrusions into our Gulf, threatening to blow up our oil fields. Still in the age of innocence, I had no idea of oil or oil fields and their useful but combustible nature.

The same blissful ignorance related to the word 'enemy'. I was never sure who the enemy was. I could not see any difference between the Chinese and Japanese forces. Who was Chiang Kai-shek? Were the enemy white people or Chinese people? We had both kinds of people in Trinidad. There were Germans in Tranquillity and Kamla said there were Germans at the Convent. It was very confusing to a child. But their presence did not cause much of a stir, apart from rousing curiosity. Pa's knowledge and excitement spilled into my realm of consciousness and names became household names. As I grew older I would read anything I could find about Baldwin and Churchill, Roosevelt and Truman, Hitler and Goebbels, and learn a little.

Pa still rode a bicycle to get to work. I remember he used bicycle clips to keep his trousers from tangling in the greasy open chains. He sometimes wore a hat. I liked the sound the clips made as he took them off. In time, Kamla left Tranquillity and went on to St. Joseph's Convent. She too would

Pa and Kamla
in Luis Street

Vidia in Luis Street
aged 14

cycle to school eventually. Vidia walked to QRC, which was not far off, and Sati, Mira and finally I would walk to school come rain or shine.

Kamla was the big sister and she began to help our mother in looking after us. She made sure that we washed and bathed, that our hair was well kept and that we did not have lice. (The Convent checked the children's hair regularly for lice.) She took us for walks in the city so that we knew our way around town, but too often she played disappearing tricks on us to make us scared and cry. Vidia kept away from us all. Four sisters became a problem and a nuisance.

He was also close to outgrowing a medical condition that had dogged his days from early on and made life very difficult for Ma. For as long as I could remember, Vidia had suffered severe asthmatic bouts that wracked his chest and seemed to threaten his very existence. In those days, before the invention of inhalers that shot relief into lungs, children and their parents endured repeated traumatic episodes. I remember vividly such stressful episodes involving Vidia at Luis Street, and I became well acquainted with the scent of Thermogene Medicated Lint, which promised more relief than it ever delivered. A square pad of cotton-wool-like fabric soaked in medication would be placed on his chest to try to relieve his terrible breathing difficulties. His condition improved as he grew older – by the time we moved to Nepaul Street in St. James – but he was long in outgrowing asthma. (In his early twenties, when he had his appendix taken out while at Oxford, a sudden bout of asthma caused an alarm.) Hounded and haunted by these attacks, as many youngsters are, as a child Vidia could be particularly difficult to deal with. If being afflicted with asthma shapes personality and character, then perhaps it made him into a wounded animal.

Meanwhile, Pa, now back at his job at the *Guardian*, began to flirt with publishing his short stories. The pool of the literary-minded fraternity in the early forties was small and Pa was wetting his feet, but he got encouragement when he joined a small group that met at the home of Judge Eric Hallinan. A combination of passion and encouragement allowed him to write several stories about the life and people he knew best. In one of his rare shows of affection, Simbhoonath Capildeo backed him to publish privately a collection of stories of Indian village life called *Gurudeva and Other Indian Tales*. The slim blue publication with a cover showing a woman's face with an ajoupa in the background appeared in 1943, with a print run of a thousand copies. A copy sold for one dollar. The cover was done by a colleague at the Trinidad *Guardian*, Alf Codallo, who became well known later as a painter of local folklore and forest scenes. I do not know how the books were sold, but sold they were. I am almost sure there were no notices or

reviews in the *Guardian* or the rival *Gazette*. The one thousand copies sold out. Very few original copies survive of *Gurudeva and Other Indian Tales* (though Vidia edited an expanded version that came out in London in 1976, more than twenty years after Pa's death). I remember Kamla and Vidia sticking a slip of paper on the first page of each copy of the original edition, denoting 'errata'.

At the *Guardian*, Pa was assigned to write pieces about the needy and destitute. The challenges of the war, with food shortages and poor employment, brought distress to folk who did not or could not cope. The idea was for the articles to drum up public awareness and support for the less fortunate. Able to empathise with the poor and vulnerable, Pa wrote sympathetically and honestly. His work was noticed by the head of the Social Welfare Department, Dora Ibbertson, who was to offer him a job and thereby instigate a major change in his life and that of his family.

The house in Luis Street was starting to fill up. The school-goers from the Valley, finding their daily journeys tedious, began to occupy the downstairs of the house. The Simbhoonath Capildeo family had also joined others of the Capildeo clan in Port of Spain. Their children were quite grown-up when like strangers they descended on us in Luis Street. The Naipauls had to vacate the two front bedrooms for one at the back. All our belongings were crammed into that one bedroom. We could not all fit in the bedroom and the older ones, Kamla, Vidia and Sati, slept dormitory-style with our cousins on makeshift beds. My mother attempted to maintain our singularity by cooking all our meals on our one-burner stove.

Early in 1945, on 25th February, there was an addition to our family. Shivadhar Srinivasa Naipaul was born in the room called the Pantry in Luis Street. Kamla was fifteen, Vidia thirteen, Sati eleven, Mira nine, I was seven. Pa added extra names in fun, 'Shivadhar Srinivasa Gokoolnath Damodhar', and rang them out as he once did in a cartoon: 'Tunapuna, Sangre-Grande, Chacachacare, Mahatma Gandhi and back!' The sketch showed a ticket collector on the footboard of a bus. Another quirky tongue-twister of Pa's was 'Lin Yutang Kahang Tang-Bup', or getting us to chant the names of the Gods of Siam – 'Owah, Tanna, Siam' – his old irreverence emerging once more when in a good mood.

Shiva's arrival was a shock to some of us. A second son also marked a change of job for Pa. The lure of a government job was an offer difficult to dismiss. It promised security and pension benefits. It freed him from the whims and fancies of editors and owners who could sack anyone at any time. It also meant a better salary and that was very important.

Before Shiva's birth Dora Ibbertson had arranged a visit for the Naipaul family to the Bishop's House in Toco. Picturesque, rocky Toco was in the north-east of the island. Pa knew the area for he had often been to Balandra as a young man. We had never before had a vacation all by ourselves. So in this new bonding experience we staged our little concerts in the Bishop's House and tasted cream cheese for the first time. Running out of supplies in Toco, our mother ventured into Port of Spain to restock. It was already dark when she got back and had to climb the hill to the house burdened by all the baggage. I remember the relief we all felt when she returned.

As I remember it, we walked to the nearby beaches every day. Down the steep hill and along the road where mangoes were plentiful we walked in Indian file. Sans Souci was our favourite spot and it was there we were amazed at the wonderful swimmer our father was. He had learnt to swim in the Caura River where he often went with his uncle and cousins. I was always anxious as he swam out beyond the breakers. My mother, to my great relief, barely ventured beyond the water's edge.

Being a family alone on vacation would never happen again. As with all good things there was an end, and we returned to our life of school and semi-communal living.

With children of different families growing up in the same small house there were constant arguments and rows. Our father was especially aware of the readiness of the aunts to 'pelt a slap' not only on their own children, but on nephews and nieces. Pa would brook none of it and I, being a tattle-tale, constantly fed him news of the comings and goings that alerted him to the threats or occurrences. Everyone learnt one did not interfere with Bhola Mousa's children. But in the overcrowded house nothing would stop the snide comments and on-going tensions – though, in time, these generally petered out without festering.

With Pa's new job as a social welfare officer came other changes. He was asked to attend a course in Jamaica with other social workers from the British West Indies, including British Guiana. Pa had never travelled out of Trinidad. But he had a passport which had been carefully kept. Quite early in his career as a journalist he'd had the inclination to seek greener pastures abroad. The idea had come from the British expatriate, Gault McGowan, his editor at the *Trinidad Guardian*, who had supported, encouraged and fostered

Savitri, Kamla, with Shiva, Sati and Mira, circa 1946

Seepersad's style of journalism. My father had obviously more than toyed with the idea, for he had taken the trouble to get his passport. In the end he lacked the courage to take up the challenge and stayed where he was. But, for our father, the *Trinidad Guardian* was never the same without McGowan.

Pa spent six or more months in Jamaica. He was impressed with Jamaica's use of its folklore to increase self-awareness, attract visitors and stimulate craft. He liked the local songs, 'Linstead Market' and 'Yellow Bird', and would hum and sing phrases from time to time. On his return from Jamaica he brought a pair of gold earrings for our mother. Ma would get a jeweller to reproduce the style for each daughter as we grew up.

Pa on his course in Jamaica: front row, seated 2nd left

With Pa's going to Jamaica we heard of Nanee's plan to leave Petit Valley for Port of Spain. Her eyesight was failing and she needed a more manageable environment. We knew at that stage we had to find a new home. It is more accurate to say our parents and my older siblings began to think seriously of a new home. Things were so congested in Luis Street that on Pa's return from Jamaica there was no room for him there. He was accommodated in a room in a rundown house at No. 27 Luis Street which Nanee had also recently acquired. It was a particularly difficult time for the family, but Pa's new job gave him some leverage to make a move. With his job as a travelling officer, Pa had been able to acquire a motor car. The little Ford Prefect, licence number PA 1192, caused consternation and jealousy. We had a motor car but we needed a house.

In choosing a house two things were paramount: the distance from our schools and, more important, the price. I am almost certain that my parents never had a bank account. Pa summoned the courage to approach his Uncle

Pa and PA 1192

Sookdeo Misir for a loan. Once more Sookdeo Ajah did not disappoint. The loan was free of interest.

The Luis Street we were hoping to leave, and in which we had grown up, was a real hodge-podge of people. It was a street where virtually every class and creed found a home. We came to know all sorts of folk. However, while each household was generally friendly or at least polite in dealing with the others, we were not truly a community of common or shared values or aspirations. In Luis Street lived at one time a lawyer who became the mayor and then a Chief Justice of Trinidad and Tobago, and then a member of the exalted Privy Council, our supreme legal authority. At the Docksite end was a Syrian-Lebanese family that expanded tenfold just as the Capildeo clan had done. Nearby lived a young man who later became head of our army after Independence. Luis Street had cowherds, a pyrotechnician, teachers, carpenters, shopkeepers – and a brothel-keeper. There were other itinerants who were occupied or involved in activities in Port of Spain and needed a refuge for a while. As readers of my brother Vidia's fiction will recognise, Luis Street, between Wrightson Road and Tragarete Road, became Miguel Street in the collection of short stories of that name.

The house lots on nearly all the streets were five thousand square feet. Nearly all the more substantial houses carried a separate servants' room at the back. At the back of each lot there was a ten-foot-wide sewerage trace so that one was scarcely aware of the neighbours facing the next street.

Carlos, Alfredo, Rosalino, Alberto, Anna and Petra, like Luis, were the names of children of the Siegert family, renowned in Trinidad; the streets of Woodbrook were named after these children. In 1875, Carlos, Alfredo and Luis Siegert had arrived in Trinidad from Venezuela, bringing with them a family secret that would make them rich. Their father, a German surgeon named Johannes Siegert, had emigrated from Berlin to Venezuela, where he privately developed the formula for what would become known as Angostura Bitters. Manufactured in Trinidad, it is still popular around the world as a zestful addition to beverages. In 1899, with part of their profits, the three sons bought the former Woodbrook Estate, a sugarcane plantation only slightly outside the centre of Port of Spain. They then converted the cane-fields into attractive, well-designed residential tracts. The streets were set on a north-south, east-west grid, with Ariapita Avenue the main thoroughfare. The Woodbrook we lived in never flooded; the streets were swept and washed daily using water from fire hydrants. Various types of horse-drawn carts provided all sorts of services, from scavenging and huckstering to funeral-bier transporting.

Trolley buses, connected to overhead electric lines, provided the main means of urban transportation. These buses ran to the city centre of Port of Spain, from which one could take a bus, tram or train to other areas. There were several pleasant squares in Woodbrook, the result of good planning by the colonial government. Being near Docksite, the land freshly reclaimed from the sea by American military engineers for defensive purposes, we were on the water's edge of the Gulf of Paria.

To add more glamour and excitement to the environment in the early forties, American GIs roamed the streets on their way to and from their quarters at Docksite. Within their compound and behind the chain-link fence an open-air cinema often kept us spellbound. We children called all the GIs 'Joe'. Everyone was 'Joe!' and Joe was usually a nice guy. Joes chewed gum and as children we craved and sometimes begged for chewing gum and bubble gum. Roller skates became the latest fad, to Pa's disgust, because he detested the noise. The scraping and screeching broke the peace of the neighbourhood and affected his rest periods or his work schedule.

In quick time, Jewish immigrants, so strange at first and most with little English, were opening a wide variety of businesses in the city. They would prove to be itinerant. Very few stayed in Trinidad when the war ended. But they did introduce hot dogs as the first foreign fast food in Trinidad, and the Green Corner outlet opposite the Globe cinema became famous.

By the time we left Luis Street everyone had made many friends at school. Before Luis Street we only knew family. Friends and schools enriched our lives. Our knowledge of people, places and things expanded rapidly. It would not have been the same for our parents, especially our mother who was more entrapped by domestic duties, her personality shaped by her upbringing.

However, Ma found the time to attend and complete a course in sewing at the Royal Victoria Institute near the Memorial Park. My father had his job, his world of books, his creative writing, the cinema and his small coterie of literary minds as well as his children growing in knowledge.

Only eight years old, I recall the excitement of moving. I had never seen our new house in Nepaul Street, St. James. I had no idea where we were going. I knew the geography of Woodbrook and the way to the Queen's Park Savannah at the foothills of the mountains. I had never heard of or been to St. James. Later I would learn all the streets there had the names of cities or places in India. I would also learn that St. James was nicknamed 'Coolie Town'. We lived two streets away from the police barracks, where men and

Savi and Vidia aged 6 and 12

women played hockey on the greens. The Rialto cinema was a stone's throw away and the Roxy cinema not more than ten minutes away. St. James was much further away from our schools than 17 Luis Street. Whilst QRC was not far from the Roxy cinema, Tranquillity another fifteen minutes away, one had to take either a trolley or a bicycle to the Convent.

My father was forty years old, Ma was thirty-three, Kamla sixteen, Vidia fourteen, Sati twelve, Mira ten, I eight and Shiva almost two. Power Mousa was able to fit all our belongings into his van. So on 31st December 1946, we landed at 26 Nepaul Street with an old hat rack, a kitchen safe, a china cabinet, the bookcase, a four-poster bed, two smaller beds and our parents' SlumberKing bed. I have no recollection of saying goodbye to anyone or of feeling sad on leaving Luis Street. Rudranath Capildeo was back in Trinidad and teaching at QRC. The war was over. Roosevelt was dead, Attlee became the British Prime Minister, Hitler had committed suicide, the former Edward VIII, now the Duke of Windsor, had been packed off as governor of the Bahamas, and Gandhi was either in jail or fasting. Seepersad Naipaul and his family were in their own home.

A new dawn would begin on 1st January 1947.

No. 26 Nepaul Street

# CHAPTER 3

## *On Nepaul Street*

My father had bought the house in Nepaul Street from a young man and his mother named Nieves. Of Portuguese descent, Mr. Nieves worked as a solicitor's clerk. He had supervised the building of the house, where sills and frames were often crooked (I know, because I made the draperies). Apparently his aged mother was no longer able to climb the steep and uneven steps to the upper floor.

Our home, which seems so small today, was bright and beautiful and inviting. A two-storey building, the bedrooms and the bathroom were on the upper floor, while the living-room, dining-room and kitchen were on the ground floor. Upstairs, between the two bedrooms and facing the street was an open-sided gallery on the south-western corner which was immediately turned into a half-bedroom for Vidia. The wooden partitions between the rooms had woodwork grilles at the top. The windows remained open except during rain, and the winds skipped through both bedrooms. The openness of the ground floor, with its lattice panels on which a bleeding heart vine grew, mitigated the smallness of the house and allowed plenty of light and good ventilation. No part of that small, compact house was dark or claustrophobic.

Our parents' bedroom had its SlumberKing bed, with the hat-rack pinned on the back of one of its doors. A tiny desk was in the corner and later they would add a cypre wardrobe with a full-length mirror. The girls' bedroom had a tall iron four-poster with a smaller bed in which Kamla and Shiva slept. There was room for a decent corridor between the beds. We also had a bureau with four drawers to hold our belongings and a draped makeshift cupboard behind one of the doors that held our dresses, with shoe-boxes on the top. The two-tiered cotton curtains, graduating from cretonne to *broderie anglaise* over the years, allowed privacy and easy laundering. All laundry was done by hand over a washtub by our mother.

With Pa's gardening skills, through each bedroom we could view greenery: the hills and acacia tree to the north, our neighbours the Sudans' breadfruit tree to the south and our struggling plum tree to the east, which finally grew into view bearing few fruit but shiny leaves. That the property faced west into the afternoon sun was a definite drawback. But with everyone out of the house except on weekends and during the school holidays we managed the heat of the early afternoons. We had a very small yard with a curved driveway to the garage. In retrospect, the size of the plot made it easier to manage, with a tiny garden on three sides and a back area for the laundry lines.

Our arrival at 26 Nepaul Street was unforgettable. There was a hubbub of activity involving only our family. Pa and Vido had to mount the beds while Ma and Kamla were putting up the salmon-pink draperies and encasing the cushions of the Morris chairs with matching flowered cretonne. The chairs had come as part of the deal with the house.

With polished floors and matching rugs, a small table and a shining brass pot with three legs and the heads of lions, and the smell of new linoleum on the kitchen floor, we were buzzing with joy and experiencing a lightness that would carry on for days. Mira, Shiva and I had nothing to do but keep out of the way. Sati must have been doing some kind of pleasurable chore like hanging our teacups on the cup-hooks left by the previous owners. The Rediffusion box on the wall in the gallery upstairs provided news and music, and our world seemed complete. (These boxes, or closed-circuit transmitters, rented by the month and operated by Radio Trinidad, were everywhere in homes before radios became cheap and the government granted licences for other stations to operate.) With time the old kitchen table that held our pots and pans would be replaced and Ma would enjoy working on her two-burner kerosene stove. We as children were happy and carefree, but we had no idea what this, our new home, would have meant to our parents who had struggled over the years to get to home base.

In 1946, at the early age of fourteen, Vidia earned his Cambridge University-administered School Certificate with a brilliant performance. By placing among the top sixteen competing students in the island, he won himself a 'house scholarship' that paid his way to begin studying at QRC for the Higher School Certificate. Having also won the College Quiz, a well-known local competition, for QRC, his fame as a student began to grow beyond his school. A year later, two years older than Vidia but less precocious, Kamla earned her own SC honours. Without going on to the HSC level, she left St. Joseph's Convent just as our sister Sati was about to enter the school.

Our parents must have been proud of their children's successes. While no one knew anything about how Pa had done at school, we children were well aware that he had not gone to high school. We also knew that our mother had topped her class regularly and that her teachers and peers had considered her an outstanding student, one quite capable of winning a

Kamla, on her last day at school

Vidia in Nepaul Street, aged 15

bursary or scholarship to go to high school. Her parents, however, would have no part of that venture. In the Capildeo family, only boys went to high school. Our mother had never fully accepted being deprived of further education, but she surely enjoyed knowing that her Vidia was now emerging as an academic achiever who could rival the accomplishments of her brother Rudranath – to an extent beyond the reach of anyone else in the Capildeo family.

At the *Trinidad Guardian*, which Pa had just left, his prestige would have risen with Vidia's academic success (the results were published in the newspapers). Now in his new job as a social welfare officer, with no newspaper deadlines to meet, he was finding a little more time to devote to his creative writing.

We girls, ranging in ages from nine to seventeen, while progressing satisfactorily, did not match Vidia's excellence. Little attention was paid by anyone to our studies, and our parents, grateful that their girls were in two of the best schools in the island, depended on the teachers to inculcate not only academic subjects but the objectives stated on the report cards of good attendance, punctuality, conduct, discipline and the more elusive virtues of deportment and attitude to authority.

1947 went by quickly as we settled into a rhythm. Kamla and Sati took the trolley bus to school, walking through the Mucurapo Cemetery to Ariapita Avenue in Woodbrook. Vidia, now in Higher Certificate, got a bicycle, possibly the one Pa had used while working at the *Guardian*. Mira and I walked to school at Tranquillity. By seven o' clock on mornings the house was empty of children except for Shiva.

There were many things in the house to alter, to repair and build. The gate needed repairing and reinforcing. The kitchen had to be altered, the garden had to be created. Having PA 1192, the Ford Prefect, allowed the weekends to be used for both work and pleasure. The older children generally opted to stay at home while Mira, Shiva and I were herded into the car. Ma too, depending on where we were going, sometimes came along.

Apart from visits to Pa's relatives scattered in the rural areas, many of our excursions were to nurseries for plants, especially rose plants. It is on these visits that Pa toyed with the idea of building a rare orchid collection. His 'monkey throat orchid' would be the first of three orchid plants he would begin to nurture, but we all knew he was more serious about the roses than the orchids. The size of the yard did not deter Pa's ambition to have trees, though. So an avocado tree was planted next to the garage, and along that same north side of the yard an acacia would grow, quickly followed by the ylang-ylang with its perfumed light-green florets.

The colourful crotons along the fence were backed by a long narrow flowerbed at the front of the house. In that bed we would also grow onion

Mira (14), Shiva (5) and Savi (12) at Nepaul Street

lilies, a delicate white flower that stank of onions after two days in a vase. Miniature red and white carnations, pinks and Michaelmas daisies filled the beds and flower-boxes around the house. We learned quickly to pinch the stems at their nodes and plant them in the well-manured beds or boxes. The narrow bed abutting the southern side of the house held anthurium lilies propped up by blocks of rotted, spongy immortelle pieces. We did not have a hose and all watering was done with buckets and cups. A narrow trellis was built above the anthurium bed and the bleeding heart vine prospered. Our garden allowed us to have fresh flowers in our tiny living-room. This was quite unusual and somewhat highbrow, given our circumstances.

While Mira and I never seemed to have homework at Tranquillity, Kamla, Vidia and Sati always had a great deal to do after school. After tea each day, our dining table, which stands today in the same position as it did then, served as our study area. The pattern of tea followed by homework continued through the years.

Kamla and Carol Stollmeyer at the dining table. Note the bookcase and Morris chair

On working days, Pa, after his tea, would retire to his room. There on evenings he would either be at his desk or on his bed, always with his pack of Anchor cigarettes and matches beside him. Reading, typing or napping, he saved his gardening mainly for weekends. His old habit of making walking sticks faded and occasionally he would sketch or paint, more as a learner than an artist. Lettering and stencil-making for political banners for his brother-in-law were things of the past, and except for an occasional swim in Carenage, a beach area a few miles west of the city, he lacked physical exercise.

Our mother, whose husbandry extended to sewing for her four girls, encouraged Mira and me, as she had done before with Kamla and Sati, into learning to master needlework, especially embroidery in her favourite pattern on pillow cases. In the scheme of things we were simply a normal family, the house finally allowing our parents to savour their privacy and exhibit their skills.

Our arrival in Nepaul Street, while it did not cause a stir, would have been noted. Next door, to the north, Dr. Soodeen held his surgery only on afternoons. Opposite lived an old woman and her adult son who never introduced himself. To the south, and our only neighbours, were Mr. and Mrs. Sudan, the parents of four adult children, Rosie, Richard, Roy and Roderick. They were warm and welcoming. Mr. Sudan, who worked nights at a nearby pumping station at the back of the Police Barracks, soon began to make a wooden mobile with wings flapping for Shiva to push around. Later he would help me fashion a stem for a Christmas tree which I made with dyed rope and wire. Mira and I were fascinated by Mrs. Sudan's coal pot, an item which we had never had. Mrs. Sudan used the ashes, along with fibre from a coconut husk, to scrub her pots and pans. The real lure, however, was their tamarind tree and its deliciously acidic pods for making into chutney or, with sugar, what we relished as 'tambran balls'.

With the proximity of the Rialto cinema and a cart selling coconut water at the corner, Nepaul Street was a lot noisier than Luis Street. The Western Main Road, now our main thoroughfare, offered pharmacies, laundries, bakeries and a fish and vegetable market not far off. We children, though, were not encouraged to venture beyond the bakery or pharmacy. We were getting older but knew the geography of St. James far less than Woodbrook. We understood it was a rougher area. We would make very few but excellent friends in and around St. James, mainly through our schools.

Friends would expand our knowledge of people and how they lived. We had no Hindu friends in either Woodbrook or St. James and very few at school. We cooked and ate different foods. Our family did not use beef or pork and their products. We did not go to church or Sunday school. At school we learnt that we were heathens but that did not bother us. We celebrated Christmas but we were not Christians. We celebrated Divali, lighting our house and garden with *deyas* (earthen oil lamps) when no one else around us celebrated it or knew about it. We knew our boundaries in the city without having to be told them. We learned manners and a different version of etiquette from that which we had acquired through our large and extended Hindu families. Our world increased in richness and knowledge as we were fortunate to have parents who understood the need to visit and be visited.

Our parents also developed friendships outside the family. As the friendships deepened and as we grew older we came to value the importance of choosing educated and progressive families as friends. Money had no relevance in these relationships. Jules Mahabir encouraged our father in his writing endeavours and certainly would have savoured the recognition Pa received sixty-two years after his death at a conference on the Naipauls in 2016 at the University of the West Indies at St. Augustine in Trinidad. The Rampersad family and three of its daughters, Ivy, Mavis (a physician) and Velma, offered firm and committed support. The Miles family, especially Gene and Joyce, were always about and around, and our close friends Myrna and Eulah Berridge, who lived on nearby Agra Street, shared with Mira and me our teenage fantasies, dreams and goals.

We were pedalling along smoothly. The whole household seemed to focus on Vidia's push towards the island scholarship in languages. Vidia was fifteen going on sixteen and precocious, especially in his use of language. He enjoyed introducing his older cousins, especially the females, to words like 'banal' or 'trite'. He stopped eating meat but would stay with fish and vegetables. Ketchup became a new discovery and he ate it with relish. Half the dining table was used for his books and Cassell's dictionaries. Kamla, studying for her School Certificate, waned in importance. Vidia and Pa had regular discussions on various topics. In Vidia's preparations these two were bonding to the exclusion of all others. Perhaps Kamla and Sati sat at the dining table with their work, but Vidia usually stayed alone late into the night, studying. Until the end of 1948 only half of our dining table was used for our meals.

Visitors in the evenings, though they were not many, would upset the routine. Instead of greeting people, Vidia would go upstairs to announce their arrival. While shy about meeting people other than school friends, he was in general not calm in his response to many other occurrences. When a school report used the word 'promising' to describe his effort and results he ranted for quite a while. The words 'promise' or 'promising' used about him upset Vidia terribly. He would carry that precision in the use of words forever, and every now and again, even in everyday relaxed conversation, he would question one's use of a word. 'Everybody says' or 'Everybody thinks' would bring the retort: 'Who's everybody?'

Most of us at home would not have known about the vow Vidia wrote in his Latin primer to leave Trinidad in a fixed number of years. The vow could not become possible without his winning one of the major scholarships. His school report had indicated that some of the teachers thought him not quite ready to go all the way, but Vidia had other ideas. At the end of his first year of study he took the examination for the Higher School Certificate.

While the two eldest Naipaul children awaited exam results, life continued. Kamla began work at the *Trinidad Guardian*. Exactly what she did, I don't know. She certainly had no shorthand and could not type. Her salary was the princely sum of forty dollars a month (Trinidad and Tobago not US dollars).

Money for our schooling was invariably an issue at 26 Nepaul Street. Our school fees stood at sixteen dollars a term for the first child and twelve dollars for all other siblings. Fortunately, we girls could save on some textbooks. Our range of subjects at St. Joseph's Convent, as in most high schools for girls, was quite limited. Science, Higher Mathematics and History were not part of the syllabus. This limited choice made it easier to pass books down the chain in the family, usually getting to me in quite a tattered state. Apart from the set books for Literature and the daily notebooks which we called 'copy books', we needed to buy few texts. And yet these books dug deep into our family pocket. The Convent also required students to have several sets of uniforms. Apart from the everyday school uniform there was a 'dress' or more fancy uniform, a games uniform to be worn once a week, and for one year a special cooking uniform. There were no 'hand-me-downs' in uniforms or blouses.

St. Joseph's Convent paid very close attention to details. One learned quickly that failure to comply brought severe reprimands and possible embarrassment at the monthly 'House Notes'. Mira joined Sati at the Convent. I had to wait one extra year to enter, as the family's expenses and circumstances altered quickly in 1949. Sister Francis Xavier, who had readily accepted all three Naipaul sisters and two cousins before me, had gone to Oxford University to do a Master's degree. In her absence, and to my deep disappointment, I was not accepted at the Convent in spite of my excellent school record. I entered later, in the last term of the second year.

Based on her School Certificate results, which were excellent, Kamla applied for and received one of the earliest scholarships offered by the government of India (an independent nation since 1947). The scholarship was for an undergraduate course of study at Benares Hindu University. (Benares, on the banks of the Ganges River in Uttar Pradesh, is an ancient holy city now known as Varanasi.) To say that we were surprised, delighted and excited would have been an understatement. There was however, a fly in the ointment. The government of India would cover all expenses in India, but the family had to agree to pay the cost of the journey to, and eventually from, India.

We were at a time when passenger air travel was still not developed or commonplace. The journey to India would normally be via London, and almost entirely by ship. This meant more than a few weeks of travel. The cost of the journey was almost one-third of the money still owed to Sookdeo Ajah on the house at 26 Nepaul Street. Our Pa did not think he could approach him again for a loan. However, with the advice of a Mr.

Khurana, First Secretary of the Indian High Commission, who offered to go with him, Pa decided to journey 'down the islands' to Gasparee, one of the islets in the Gulf of Paria close to the mainland of Trinidad. Holidaying on Gasparee Island was our Uncle Simbhoo and his family. Mr. Khurana and our father explained our dilemma and requested a loan. In a sense, the pride of both the Naipaul family and the government of India was at stake. Nevertheless, they returned empty-handed. It was Simbhoo's mother, Nanee, now almost totally blind, a cataract operation having failed to restore her sight, who agreed to provide the money needed by her grand-daughter.

But she did so with certain conditions. One condition was that Vidia, when he began to work and earn money, would repay the loan. The other was a querulous request that Kamla must promise never to go to our grandfather's ancestral home in Gorakhpur in Uttar Pradesh, then the United Provinces. Thinking now what Nanee may still have felt about Pundit Capildeo's departure to India in the company of another woman, it is not surprising that no one, not even our father, questioned this seemingly strange request. Kamla when in India never went to Gorakhpur. But Vidia did many years later, and added some light to what he would call, in one of his more acclaimed books of cultural commentary, this 'area of darkness'.

I'm not sure that at the time we in the family fully appreciated all the possible dangers facing a young woman from overseas visiting India, when the horrific troubles attendant on the partitioning of the country were still fresh in the mind. We felt Kamla was very brave to risk her life, in a sense, in order to gain a university education. We made our misgivings known, of course, but the Indian High Commission assured us that clashes between Hindus and Muslims, as well as other factions, were unlikely to take place in or near Benares.

The problems and plans surrounding Kamla's impending departure for India were soon upstaged by the release of the results of the island scholarships examinations. Still enrolled at Tranquillity, I remember well a posse of QRC students on bicycles riding past the school, seemingly on their way to the rival college, St. Mary's. They were shouting in unison, 'Mark didn't win no scholarship! Naipaul win de scholarship!' Thinking that Vidia had won the scholarship in Languages, I was eager to get back home and join the celebration. Then I discovered to my dismay that the scholarship had been awarded not to Vidia but to Albert Mark, a student at St. Mary's. I am not sure that Vidia was even listed as a runner-up.

A rumour quickly surfaced (originating, it is said, from someone in the office of the Director of Education who had leaked the information) that something was not quite right about the decision, about the fairness of the award. The rumour was that Vidia Naipaul had achieved higher marks than Mark (the son of a respected schoolmaster in Diego Martin) but that Vidia had been passed over because he was younger than Mark and would undoubtedly win the scholarship when he took it again the following year. Irate, Pa sought the advice and help of Uncle Simbhoo. Together they planned to approach not only the Principal of QRC, but also as many members of the Board of Education as possible. A controversy began to build even as Vidia ranted and raved at home that Pa was irresponsibly dragging his name 'through the mud'. The household became silent on the subject. It seemed that Vidia would have to steel himself, accept the unfair results, and return to QRC.

Mira and I watered the plants quietly, as it was the dry season.

At a formal meeting of the Board of Education, and after a careful review of the marks, the government decided to award Vidia Naipaul an additional scholarship, on terms identical to the island scholarship, but which he would take up a year later. The announcement lacked the glory and the splash of publicity attendant on the original winner, but getting a similar scholarship assuaged the wound and fulfilled the financial need. It was during the interim year that Vidia, working temporarily in the office of the principal of QRC, gained access to certain papers and the exact scores in the examinations. He copied out the rival scores by hand. They left no doubt that although his rival had performed very well, Vidia himself had been cheated. The blame, such as it was, was placed on QRC for not adhering to some new rule involving the Languages scholarship. The additional scholarship was meant to guarantee that the student would not be punished for the school's administrative failing. The issue of the discrepancy in marks was not addressed.

Vidia's ordeal and then victory and Kamla's departure for India in August 1949 had a telling effect on every member of the Seepersad Naipaul family. Mira describes Kamla's leaving as being like a death in the family.

Kamla travelled on the *Ariguani* on 7th August 1949 to England. In London she stayed with Rudranath Capildeo and his wife Ruth, an Englishwoman. She visited Pa's cousin Basdai and her husband Carl Mootoo. (Basdai was the younger daughter of Sookdeo Misir, and Pa had grown up with her as brother and sister after Sookdeo Misir took him in as a boy.) Ration cards and indeed the limited availability of almost all goods reflected the lingering effects of the dreadful war on Great Britain. Our Uncle Rudranath, however, was generous. Thinking it almost reckless of our parents to send Kamla off to huge and unknown India with so little money, he slipped her some 'insurance' funds before she left. She seemed to take the challenges of travel in her stride.

At home, we had taken Kamla's presence for granted, and now her absence, which we all had difficulty in coming to terms with, left everyone sad. Little Shiva, who had been taught the song 'You are my sunshine, my only sunshine' and who had shared a bed with Kamla, now gave problems at night. Sati occupied Kamla's place in the bed but could not fill the breach. Even Vidia buried his face in the pillow to hide his tears. Pa was quiet in retreat and Ma tried to be stoic. No one was prepared for Kamla's going so far away. Anxiously, we awaited the arrival of the blue air-letter forms from her.

When the snapshot of herself on the boat from Aden to India arrived, we were glad to see her looking happy and lovely in her wide-brimmed straw hat. She bought a photo album in Aden for the family which is today almost seven decades old.

Kamla on the voyage to India, 1949

Kamla's departure from Trinidad marked the start of the series of the letters between Kamla and home (Pa, really), Kamla and Vidia, and later Vidia and Pa. We, the younger ones, wrote occasionally and were usually consigned to the postscript area of the letters from abroad. The publication of *Letters Between a Father and Son*, both the first (1999) and second or expanded version (2009), give honest insights into the family and its various personalities. They also laid bare the special anxieties of Pa and Vidia concerning their urge to write fiction.

Vidia applied for a place at Oxford University and was accepted by University College to read English starting in the academic year 1950–1951. During the year or so before taking up his place at Oxford, he got a part-time job at QRC as a secretary in the Principal's office, then spent some time working in the Records Office of the Red House, the seat of government, housing the parliament chambers as well as the Registrar General's office. He also taught briefly at Tranquillity boys' school. There I would see him more often in lively conversation with the boys than formally teaching them anything in a classroom. His three jobs allowed him to repay the loan for Kamla's passage to India.

Vidia was supremely anxious to leave Trinidad. It was as if leaving would bring an end to all his anxieties and stresses. But the extra year at home did him some good. He became something of a cinema buff. He went only to the 'pit' or cheapest, rowdiest section of the cinemas, where he was entertained not only by what was on the screen but also (often much more so) by the witty comments of the pit-goers. He struck up a fraternal relationship with our cousin Owad Permanand (the first-born son of Ma's older sister Dhan), who was already married. Because Owad was much older than Vidia, Pa thought he might be a bad influence on the youngster. Besides, Owad was married to Jean Asgarali, the sister of the star cricketer Nyron Asgarali. Because the Asgaralis were Muslim, the Permanand family ostracised both Jean and Owad, and expected us all to do so. Vidia stood his ground. When Kamla, far away in India, agreed with Pa who disapproved of the marriage, Vidia responded by scolding her. Considering himself a free man, he flirted with girls and began to visit those he thought clever or attractive, including one of Ma's young cousins, Golden. His regular swims in the sea at Carenage caused us anxiety when it became dark and he had not returned on his bicycle. He ordered from abroad a body-building course, called (I believe) the Ross Body-Building Program. Thus began his lifelong routine of daily exercise, even as he grumbled about having 'fat Capildeo thighs', as he called them.

Although we had a car, Vidia, like Ma, resisted all encouragement by Pa to learn to drive. Pa had tried to bribe Ma by telling her that she would be the first woman in an *orhani* to drive a car in Trinidad.

At the end of July 1950, Vidia left by air for New York. On 2nd August he boarded the SS *America* bound for England. When he was leaving us, our mother tried to get him to observe a few traditional Hindu customs. Hindus have some form of rite for nearly everything. When you are leaving your home on such an ambitious journey you are supposed to do *pujas*, to bend and touch the feet of your parents and other elders, and receive their blessing by a touch of your head, and also to swallow a spoonful of yogurt or rice pudding to show that you had been well cared for while still at home. These were village habits turned into rites. Vidia had no time or patience for such gestures. Whatever he did was reluctantly done. As he later described such a departure in his book, *Miguel Street*, he boarded the plane without ever looking back or waving, his shadow that of 'a dancing dwarf on the Tarmac'.

He would never see Pa again.

Vidia's departure did not have the same effect on the household as Kamla's had done. Pa and Ma were visibly more affected than Sati, Mira and me. However unpleasantly precocious or rude Pa had found Vidia, Pa knew he was slackening ties with a beloved son, someone in whom he believed and who believed in him. Pa was probably the only person on the island who thought that Vidia's plan to read English at Oxford was an excellent choice. (Most scholarship winners seemed to favour medicine or law, practically the guarantors of wealth and prestige at home.) The letters from first to last confirm their symbiotic relationship. Vidia would spend the rest of his life seeking to fulfil his father's hopes and dreams for them both. In choosing writing as a vocation, Vidia would allow no one and nothing anywhere in the world to eclipse his goal of becoming a great writer.

With Kamla's and now Vidia's departure from Nepaul Street, Sati, Mira and I, almost a teenager, enjoyed a kind of liberation that we had never felt before. Our two gatekeepers were not around to control, comment and restrict. Kamla had always had friends who visited, but never boys. Vidia had kept his few friends at the gate or conversed over the fence. We would eventually get to know some of Vidia's friends such as Charles John, Wilfred Cartey, 'Wags' Springer, Alloy Awai and Herbert Bishop, all Afro-Trinidadians who would go on to hold high and respectable positions in Trinidad. 'Wags' would die while still quite young and Cartey become blind too soon. But there was no fraternising. The Miles boys, Carl, Rudolf and Ainsley, were the only boys outside the extended family who entered our house regularly. They were the brothers of Gene, Joyce and little Judith; they always came as a family in their car driven by their mother. Nepaul Street was en route to the new suburb of Glencoe west of Port of Spain where they lived.

Sati, Mira and I bicycled to school every day come rain or shine. While there were various routes, we generally chose the quieter and more scenic route past QRC, eastwards around the Queen's Park Savannah, eventually turning off past Bishop Anstey High School and down Pembroke Street towards CIC and our destination, St. Joseph's Convent. We cyclists on our way to school every day knew each other but rarely exchanged greetings. As 'convent girls' we were expected not to disrespect our school uniforms by buying and eating food on our way to and from school. We were also not expected to 'lime' or chat with boys on the streets. 'Liming' is a term that developed in the fifties in Trinidad to describe spontaneous meetings and equates to today's 'chilling out'.

One day, two young men from QRC, refusing to be dissuaded by our shooing and flailing arms from the open gallery upstairs in our house, approached our gate on their bicycles. Pa was in his garden. The young men greeted Pa, who invited them in. They had come to see my sister Sati, and Pa called Sati downstairs to meet them. The two young men were Dougie Myers and Ken Lee Young. This interlude changed our lives. We realised that we could invite or welcome boys to our home. Before this, neither Kamla nor Sati, four years older than me, had ever had any of their boyfriends to visit, and we had never known who they were. Sati was the limer in the family. A spot near Bishop Anstey and near the Savannah provided a convenient location for regular liming. Both Douglas Myers and Ken Lee Young went on to rewarding careers, with Dougie becoming one of the earliest Trinidadians to obtain his seafaring licence as a ship's captain.

Meanwhile, Shiva, not yet five, was everyone's pet. We had a dog called Treve and another called Gyp. Shiva loved the dogs and Pa took many pictures of them together. He started school without a fuss, but did not understand why his school was in the opposite direction to ours. First there was a little private school organised by 'Teacher Van', as we called her, just two or three streets away, followed by the more formal St. Agnes Anglican Primary School, with Reverend Buxo as its head. Everyone in the household affectionately helped to teach Shiva his ABCs. Pa also tried to get him interested in flying a kite but Shiva was dissuaded by the rough Savannah to which Pa took him. His interest in kite-flying disappeared.

Growing up hearing the music of the steel band at the bottom of Nepaul Street, Shiva – unlike Vidia, who later claimed to detest the very sound of such music – grew to like it. Pa did not share Vidia's attitude to the steel band. In fact, I recall going with him in 1951 to interview the revered arranger Ellie Mannette, the so-called father of the modern steel band and leader of the popular Invaders orchestra. The Invaders 'pan yard' was at the top of Luis Street. Some of us were much too young to frequent the yard, but we always regarded it with fascination and a measure of pride. Living in Luis Street, creolisation was unavoidable. However, we were not allowed to roam the streets of St. James, which was a rough district

Pa and Shiva, circa 1951

Ma and Shiva, reluctant schoolboy

Shiva and dog, circa 1948

compared to Woodbrook. The one exception was during the Muslim religious festival of Hosay, developed as a sort of Indian version of Carnival in the West Indies and British Guiana (later Guyana). Then our cousins would come from other parts of the city to St. James to join us in viewing the colourful *tadjahs*, model tombs shaped like mosques and exquisitely decorated, being pushed through the streets, before being dumped into the sea.

We watched Shiva mature. Coconuts were no longer 'conkatonuts' and school became serious business. We were well aware that he had missed out on certain pleasures and opportunities from which Vidia had benefited. For example, Pa did not read to Shiva as much as he had read to Vidia as a little boy. Comparing his two sons, Pa recalled Vidia as more receptive to his reading.

Vidia arrived in England a few days before his eighteenth birthday. Maybe like Kamla he was met by our cousin Boysie at the docks or by someone from the British High Commission. In those years, an official representative met every British Caribbean scholarship student and even those arriving students who had won a place at university through the Departments of Education of their countries. We were thrilled to get a photograph of him on the steamship *America*. From then on, letters flowed back and forth from Trinidad, England and India. These letters encapsulated the news that family members wished to share. They were comforting, complaining, scolding and encouraging. On the whole, the writers showed genuine care and concern both for the welfare of the family and for the art of writing. Pa wrote regularly and his letters show how well he knew and understood all his children. Ma, like Mira and me, mainly cropped up in the postscripts and often not all Ma's messages were relayed. Sati, now the eldest of the remaining siblings, took on the role of scolding both Vidia and Kamla when the letters became too few and far between.

In his letters, Pa became increasingly obsessed by his desire to have his work published, even as Vidia seemed to be doing little to help him with this goal. Pa believed, for instance, that another local writer, Samuel Selvon, a friend who also served as an editor at the *Trinidad Guardian*, and who in 1953 was to publish a breakthrough West Indian novel in London, *A Brighter Sun*, had 'mulched' his ideas even as Selvon had sat on stories submitted by Pa to the *Guardian*. 'How can two persons be writing on the same themes and each be equally successful?' Pa asks Vidia. 'Good Lord... He had all my stories at the *Guardian* for months; then he goes and writes on the same themes.' But even as Pa suffered, he generously tried to give Selvon his due: 'He seems gifted and has made a go of his talent, which in my own case, I haven't even spotted.' Selvon was different from Pa in another respect. Although he was himself also Indian, he seemed notably more interested in 'creole' or Afro-Caribbean material than in the almost exclusively Indian folk who dominated or even monopolised Pa's tales.

Meanwhile, Vidia's whining and his constant need for money and cigarettes played on Pa's sympathies. Pa feared that Vidia, in his second year at Oxford, was on the verge of a breakdown such as he had had, although the comparison seems to verge on the preposterous. Jobless, uneducated, censured, and with a wife and children to support, Pa had faced an abyss; Vidia at Oxford on a scholarship had everything going for him. Pa did not see Vidia in that light. From his earlier pleas to his son to find his 'centre', he urgently recommended books to heal his mind and lift his spirits. He tried to cheer up his son with homespun wisdom: 'People like us are like corks thrown in water... We simply must pop up again.' Of the three major players in the published *Letters* – Pa, Kamla and Vidia – the self-effacing, anxiety-ridden Pa comes out not only as a benevolent exemplar and dreamer, but also as the man with the truly unusual talent, self-taught and wise, who, as he grew tired and felt himself growing old, sought solace and peace in his little garden on Nepaul Street, and in sleep.

Pa began to suffer from bouts of anxiety or depression. He was about to make a major change in his job and we were unaware of what this meant. Concerned about the future of those of us still in middle school and with Shiva now starting school, he would from time to time complain of stomach aches. Maclean's stomach powder became a staple in our home and that did not always bring relief. On weekends, frenetic bouts of English grammar lessons were held and occasionally a dose of Hindu mantras. Our father was never authoritarian and never struck any of us. He left the discipline to Ma and seldom ever scolded. He seemed to understand each child at each stage and allowed us a latitude and flexibility that none of our cousins enjoyed. He liked meeting our friends, both boys and girls, but mainly girls. He did not like the Rediffusion box kept on all day and definitely wanted it off at night when he would be either at his typewriter or on his bed.

This was a time when he was writing as feverishly as he could some of his longer short stories and continuing the story of Gurudeva. Quite often he asked me to write as he dictated his work on 'Gurudeva' or 'Ramdass and the Cow' and other stories. He began at this time successful and encouraging communications with the influential BBC programme *Caribbean Voices*, edited and presented by the literary journalist Henry Swanzy in London. The acceptance of several of his stories not only perked him up but encouraged him. With Vidia in England, he asked Mr. Swanzy to allow Vidia to occasionally read one of his stories, and he and I would go around the corner to a neighbour with a short-wave radio to hear the broadcast from the BBC. It always began: 'This is the BBC calling the Caribbean.' Being only twelve or thirteen, I was happy that Pa thought me clever enough to transcribe for him. As I look back over the years I realise that I became Pa's 'go to' girl, or girl Friday as some people say, because I ran many errands for him from then on. It was as special a time for me as it had been in the war days when the sirens blared and smoke and searchlights filled the skies and I was the baby in the family and close to Pa.

Sometime in 1950 Pa resigned his government job and returned to the *Trinidad Guardian*. He had been overlooked for a promotion and obviously felt he could not continue to work in the department and be happy. The change would plunge the family into hardship.

Sati was studying for her School Certificate exam. Her plans to do the Higher Certificate, a two-year course, seemed in jeopardy. While Pa was having a small measure of success with his writing and the photographs which accompanied his feature stories, this could in no way compensate for the loss in income. With Kamla in India just managing to survive on her allowance and Vidia at Oxford, there was no way to alleviate the hardship. Up to that point, in Nepaul Street, we had managed to avoid stresses in our day-to-day living. Now we girls were all teenagers, we were acutely aware of our family's worries. We wanted to help, but jobs were not easily available in one's teens. Boys, mainly boy scouts, did the 'bob a job', getting a shilling for washing cars or cleaning windows or drains. Babysitting by girls was never an option in Trinidad, and as girls we were acutely aware of the limitations of what we could do and where we could go. As schoolchildren our chances of earning were severely limited. We had not achieved sufficient standing academically to give 'extra lessons'. We tried. Sati managed, even while working for her Higher Cert, to get a job at the racetrack selling tote tickets for a few days. I bravely began to sew clothes, such as I made for Mira and myself and for friends. The little we earned kept us in uniforms and dresses. As far as I remember we never complained to Kamla and Vidia that Pa and Ma had difficulty 'making ends meet'. We were beyond seeking any more help from the wider family and simply had to learn to forgo treats like going to the cinema, college plays and even some birthday parties that required not only dresses and shoes but presents.

Pa's stories on *Caribbean Voices* reawakened in Vidia his own desire to write even before he was halfway through his course at Oxford. Pa would try to keep him on course, but Vidia's temperament and complaints bothered him. With an allowance of thirty-five pounds a month, he should have been comfortable. Most students, apart from the trust-fund students, managed on less. But Vidia always defended his use of cigarettes as a social necessity and always seemed to be lacking and needing money. Pa promised what he was unable to deliver, but food parcels were sent regularly by parcel post or by anyone willing and able to take things, such as the Simbhoonath Capildeos.

They had sold their newly acquired home in Patna Street in St. James, in which they had never lived, and left for London in the hope of settling there. However, despite his training and acumen, Simbhoo was never able to secure a professional position in England and eventually returned home. Racial antagonism would appear to have been his greatest barrier.

1951 slipped quietly into 1952. On New Year's Eve, Ma, as usual, stayed awake to hear the ships blowing their horns at midnight, while the church bells rang. 1952 would turn out to be a most eventful year in

Vidia and friends at Oxford

the family. It began with Shiva starting school at Tranquillity Boys Intermediate. While this might appear a trivial event, it marked an important transition for Shiva. At last he was going to a school where Vidia had gone and doing some of the things that we had all done. Apart from this, we awaited Sati's Cambridge School Certificate results.

Pa wisely anticipated that Sati, having missed long periods of schooling because of a skin condition that had not responded to medical treatment, would get a Grade II Certificate. In *Letters between a Father and Son*, Pa is quoted as saying that 'Sati failed for the second time'. This is an error. Another Sati in the family (the daughter of my aunt Dhan) had failed the examination for the second time. Our Sati would not sit the SC test until the year 1951. She failed to get a Grade I certificate, the highest grade possible, but received a Grade II. Nevertheless, because she was a fine student, and on the recommendation of her teachers at St. Joseph's Convent, she was accepted into the elite Higher School Certificate class of about twenty-four students, which began in January 1952. This was unlike most of her fellow students, whose high school days ended at the School Certificate level. Indeed, Sati would become the first girl among the Capildeo or Sookdeo families to successfully complete her Higher School Certificate studies.

Meanwhile, Kamla was studying for her final exams in the Bachelor of Arts programme at Benares Hindu University. She was also trying to solve Vidia's 'growing up' problems: preaching, cajoling, tempering and scolding. It was the year of Kamla's twenty-second birthday, and a personal drama was building. A young man of Indian descent from Fiji, Vincent David Richmond, seemed to be of particular interest. We learned eventually that he was pursuing a course in pharmacy at the university on a scholarship from the Indian government. We knew little else about him. A photograph showed that he was handsome, but we never learned, for example, what his religion was. Did his English names mean that he was a Christian? If so, of which denomination?

Kamla sought Pa's assistance to write to the University's Chancellor to give permission for them to meet socially. Pa never fully approved of the relationship. Somehow he knew that Richmond did not come from a prosperous family, and in addition Pa wanted Kamla to come home after graduation. Nevertheless, he wrote the letter giving his consent to the open friendship. Although there were many women at the university, their marriages had already been arranged by their parents. It was the same for the young Indian men. Courtship was not permitted and liaisons, when they occurred, had to be clandestine. Breaking the rules at university level, while they might appear ridiculous today, was considered a serious breach at BHU. However, the university authorities must have seen these two islanders, Vincent David Richmond of Fiji, and Kamla Naipaul, a West

Kamla and Vincent Richmond at Benares

Indian, though Indians, as falling outside orthodox Indian culture, and they reluctantly allowed restricted visitation.

Working hard towards her finals and dealing always with the problems of language (many courses were in Hindi), lacking tutors at times, eating different foods in a different manner, needing books in English, Kamla was finding it difficult nearly all the time. But there were also high points. She played the role of Buddha in a university dramatic production and she met Pandit Nehru when he visited the University.

Kamla's letters home, unlike Vidia's, were never of complaint but of fact. As she approached her finals, her letters, not surprisingly, became fewer. Pa would often say that he did not understand 'that girl', but he worried and cared deeply about her. Meanwhile the letters between Vidia and herself were mainly personal and almost always about Vidia. Like Pa, Kamla would try to get him to focus on the important, to keep his balance, and to manage what he termed his homesickness and loneliness – the latter having to do mainly with his unrequited relations with young women.

Kamla received a first-class degree and to our consternation, and Pa's disappointment, applied at once for an extension of her scholarship to pursue a course in learning to play the sitar. The one accomplishment no Naipaul could claim was anything to do with music. While we did not have 'tin ears', no one had ever learned to play an instrument of any kind. Hence our consternation at Kamla's wanting to master the sitar. We, especially Pa, were disappointed in the delay of her return either to England or Trinidad. Four years away seemed a long time. We also knew that the delay had more to do with Vincent David Richmond than any sitar. He had written to Pa seeking permission to become engaged to Kamla. According to him, they would marry within two years.

Perhaps Kamla had other ideas, or at the very least a sense of confusion about what she really wanted. In one of her letters to Vidia, as she was about to leave India, while she indicated that she was engaged to Vincent, she said that she was not at all sure about marriage. On 7th June 1952, she wrote: 'As you know, I have grown to hate this idea of marriage. I think it is the end of life. And I have begun thinking that marriage is concerned about all that's sexual and I don't like it.' No wonder Pa wrote to Vidia: 'I don't understand that girl.' Later, on 11th October 1952, Pa wrote: 'That girl is unpredictable: the letter dated two days earlier was asking me my consent to her engagement... Her engagement and her coming away do not click. I have told her so.'

Kamla was not the only confused person among Pa's children abroad. In response to Vidia's mutterings about homesickness and despondency, Pa hastened to book him a passage home. His own personal trials in his late twenties had made him acutely sensitive to Vidia's darker moods. But Vidia, after agreeing to come home and making plans to do so, changed his mind. Instead, he set off for a vacation on the Continent. With Kamla's doubts and delay and Vidia's change of plans, Pa was doubly disappointed. Above all, he could not quell his anxiety until he felt reassured that his elder son's state of mind was improving.

Ma at Nepaul Street after cleaning the car

# CHAPTER 4

## *Of Birth and Death*

At times, Pa was a man of sweet moods. It was one of those evenings where normally he would tease Ma by telling us a story that embarrassed her, or which she felt foolish about. We were at the dining table and he was sitting at the head of the table, where he normally sat with his back to the kitchen. Pa often ate the evening meal with us while Ma cooked and the food came hot off the stove. We were having roti, or flatbread, for dinner along with some kind of vegetable or fish. This evening was special. Suddenly Pa held up a tiny baby's vest at the shoulders. Almost dancing the little thing, he announced with a smile: 'Your Ma is going to have a baby.'

He, it seemed, was just the news carrier. It was all Ma's doing. At first, we children were stunned and puzzled. None of us had suspected that Ma was pregnant. It was just about the last news we expected. But while having another child must have been hard on Ma, who was thirty-nine, she was philosophical and accepting of the turn of events. Pa, too, knew it was 'a mess' to have a new child under these circumstances but he also accepted the news. In fact, he seemed pleased. Abroad, Kamla and Vidia had to come to terms with the surprise from home. Guided by Ma and Pa, we all soon took it in stride.

Sati, Mira and I now had new household chores. We helped do the ironing. However, Ma never allowed us to cook. She was a great cook, but she kept us out of the kitchen because she did not want us to spend time making meals when we could be studying or doing something she considered more worthwhile.

Two cousins who had stayed briefly with us, Deocooar and Phoolo Sahadeo (they were the daughters of Ma's sister Ahila), moved in with us. They helped with household chores as Ma carried her new child to term. Probably for the first time, her pregnancy was supervised by a doctor, Mavis Rampersad. On 4th October 1952, Ma was delivered of a healthy baby girl at the Port of Spain General Hospital on Charlotte Street. The pregnancy and birth were both difficult and Ma, instead of gaining weight, became quite slim. As for the baby, Kamla sent names from India, but we could not decipher her handwriting. We at home, including Pa, named her Nalini Vimla. The baby brought joy to the household. Pa always said he loved his daughters and we were old enough to see him enjoy this fifth girl. From a nickname of 'Little Nell' our baby sister became 'Nella' and today we all still call her Nella, just as we called Vidia Vido and 'Shivan' became Sewan. I have no idea if Nalini Vimla was entered in Pa's book of names, but she was certainly a joyous addition to life at our home on Nepaul Street.

Ma with Nella, 1954

Two weeks after Nella's birth, Nanee died. Soogie Rosalie Gobin Capildeo, born in 1881, had been a bulwark to at least twenty-four grandchildren and their parents, from Chaguanas to Petit Valley to Woodbrook in Port of Spain. This grand matriarch, who housed and protected all, was sometimes called 'Queen Victoria', not without reason, by the older grandchildren. She was only seventy-one when she died but we thought her so old! Following what she perceived as sound Hindu tradition, her two educated sons, Simbhoonath and Rudranath, inherited nearly all her many properties, with the approbation of her daughters, but with my father's disgust at their sheepishness. Sibling rivalry would develop between the two sons. Their tense relationship would be further riven by politics and fighting over property. When Rudranath died at the age of fifty, the brothers had been estranged for many painful years.

Nanee's death only accelerated the changes overtaking her large family. By 1952, with all the branches of the Capildeo children finally in houses of their own, the clan was irrevocably changed. Nanee, the trunk, who had held up all the branches, was no longer there to unify the various parts. Gradually each of the families with educated and grown-up children would become self-sustaining. Arranged marriages, carried out at an early age, became a thing of the past. The acquisition of elite education, advanced skills and lucrative jobs became an essential goal for virtually everyone. Competition among members of this complex group sometimes became raw.

In London, Boysie (a son of Ma's older sister Kunta) and a recalcitrant Vidia, seeking the warmth and security of their eminent academic uncle, Rudranath Capildeo, felt humiliated by Rudranath's wife, Ruth. An Anglo-Saxon, she was probably not prepared to wait hand and foot on male family members as many of us women in the West Indies might have done as a matter of course. In turn, Boysie and Vidia probably did not deign to adapt their presumptuous Caribbean ways to entrenched British customs. Vidia also resented the fact that Ruth charged him one pound a week for his accommodation (Uncle Rudranath was never a wealthy man). Each family had to forge its own way and so determine its own future. These tensions were reflected elsewhere in the clan. The shifting sands beneath our feet led to many and varied changes. The world was opening up, with travel becoming easier following the end of the ugly war. As people began to make more money, a thirst for adventure grew. Many of our cousins looked beyond Trinidad. A few fled, a few escaped, a few simply moved at their own pace to new and distant shores, immigrants once again in someone else's land.

Ties loosened. Shiva and Nella, the youngest among us, would grow up knowing very few of their cousins on either the maternal or paternal sides. At this time, our visits to Pa's relatives also lessened. With a new baby, Ma's freedom was severely curtailed. We, including Pa, were quite happy to stay at home on weekends. Also, Pa was writing more energetically, even if complaining of tiredness more often. The little garden was a source of pride and joy to him. His orchid collection had grown from three to five species.

Nella, in her first year, naturally became the focus of attention. Ma had the work and we had the fun. Nella enjoyed the nightly massages and the extended playtime that we had grown accustomed to with Shiva as a baby. Shiva, in his seventh year, was already a loner but not without attention. He became very curious about our friends and sometimes paid more attention to our goings-on than we wanted. Occasionally, he threatened to betray Mira and me by telling on us when we made disparaging remarks about our cousins or friends. We would then have to bribe him to keep quiet!

Vidia was not yet in his final undergraduate year, but was already thinking of a further course at Oxford. Pa, meantime, began suggesting how they could live and work together as writers. Pa seemed to have all the ideas for their future, all the hope of living and working side by side, as it were. In a strange way, Pa was crying out for help, while Vidia himself seemed always to need help urgently – though perhaps help of a different kind. By now, Pa had typed up more than a dozen short stories, some old, some new, in preparing a manuscript that he imagined a London publisher would want. In his anxiety to get it published, however, he probably had no idea of the extra stress he was placing on Vidia at Oxford. He, in spite of all of his encouragement of Pa's writing, continued to be uncertain about the viability for any London publisher of a book of short stories based on the lives of East Indians in Trinidad. As Vidia feared, the upshot was that he failed to get a publisher for Pa's stories.

Vidia, trying to keep up with his studies even as he was also writing stories himself, with his own hopes of publication, was simply stretching himself too thin. Socially insecure in a place like Oxford, weighty with learning and tradition as well as snobbery and elitism, he, with the rejection of his first novel, must have begun to wonder if his ambition to become a great writer wasn't an absurdity. Vidia fell behind in his university essays, his other writing faltered, and his personal relationships, especially with women, continued to be unsatisfactory. He was facing many difficulties as his final year approached. His self-diagnosed 'breakdown' only gradually improved at about this time when he met a young woman and fellow Oxonian, Patricia Hale, for whom he seemed to care deeply and who seemed to care at least as much for him.

Shiva, Savi, Sati and Mira in school uniform

At the start of 1953 in Trinidad, Sati, Mira and I were busy preparing for our cousin Shekhar Permanand's wedding. The Ramnarace Permanands lived around the corner from us in Cawnpore Street in St. James. Shekhar, the eldest son, was engaged to a friend of ours who lived in D'Abadie, a village about twelve miles east of Port of Spain. Kamal Dharrie, the bride-to-be, was the second daughter of a prominent and prosperous Hindu Brahmin family. While the parents behaved in public as if it were an arranged marriage, Mira and I knew that our cousin Shekhar had been visiting the Dharrie family's home regularly. We kept the secret.

The Hindu wedding would take two days to be completed. Shiva was chosen to be the Sahibala. This old wedding custom related to village life in India where the bridegroom, still a child, would be accompanied by a companion, normally a member of his family. The Sahibala's garb and refinements would distinguish him from the rest of the all-male groom's entourage. In Trinidad, we no longer had child bridegrooms. But the idea of the Sahibala as a young companion to the bridegroom stayed, though he no longer had any specific duties. In the marriage ceremony of old, he would sit next to the groom to receive gifts, mainly money, before the groom would take a taste of the specially prepared dish of *kitcheree* (peas and rice) as a just-married man in the household of his new in-laws. It seemed a way of collecting some of the money spent on the wedding. The parents, and not the young couple, were in the charge of the spoils! On the wedding night, while Mira and I looked after Shiva and tried to find somewhere to nap, Sati was occupied by the attention of the bride's cousin, Crisen BissoonDath. The relationship developed while Sati continued her studies at the Convent. Mira and I tried but failed to benefit from the many boxes of chocolates Sati received. She ignored our entreaties and then our taunts.

With Shekhar's wedding at the centre of attention, and the all-important Trinidad Carnival also in the air, we suddenly got news one day at school that Pa had collapsed on the stairs of the *Trinidad Guardian*. Evidently he had suffered a heart attack. He had been taken to the General Hospital in Port of Spain. With Nella only four months old, Ma was unable to visit Pa until we got home from school. We did not have a telephone so the news was slow and late in coming. When Ma finally reached the hospital, Pa was mad with her for taking so long to come.

That evening, one of Pa's colleagues brought home the Ford.

We had never known Pa to be ill. He had frequent stomach problems but never seemed to take them seriously. Pa was not one to suffer from fevers and colds, as so many people did in Trinidad. He had no chronic sinus problems. He hardly drank alcohol, and then only a little rum, or now and then a bottle of beer. I had never seen my father with a hangover. None of us knew anything much about heart attacks. We asked questions but did not learn much. Our rotated visits to the hospital brought us to a paler and worried Pa. He was confined to bed and not allowed to walk by himself even to the bathroom. He was visibly distressed and forbidden to smoke. A spittoon rested on his bedside table. It made me want to retch.

Sati, Mira and I rallied around to help Ma look after Shiva and Nella. Our bicycles made us mobile and we steadily carried needed items to and from the hospital. Visiting hours were between four and six in the afternoon, but we were allowed to deliver and fetch things at other times. Somehow we managed to keep the household going and also give Pa the special attention he needed. For Ma it would have been harrowing. Pa stayed in hospital for a little more than six weeks. Ma was surely told how gravely ill he was, but she never said anything to us about such a serious matter. The clock seemed to be standing still, but school helped to keep our lives in order.

While we awaited Pa's homecoming, Mira and I embarked on a plan to paint the inside of the house. My close friend, Gloria Youngsing, a fellow student at the Convent who was also a prefect and the captain of her house at school, as well as a noted athlete, joined us in our labours (our friendship survives, although now we scarcely meet). We chose dove grey with pink trim as a mild and soothing colour scheme, and got the job done. Then something of a miracle occurred. It came with an unexpected meeting at the hospital between Ma and one of her neighbours from many years before. Pa and Ma had been a young couple living in St. Joseph, with Kamla and Vidia as little children, when they first met this Indian woman. The old *parosin* or neighbour, meeting Ma again, saw her plight at once. She offered to send her daughter, Pinky, to help us. They were now living not far from us. Pinky could walk to our home.

Pinky was back at her mother's home after a failed marriage. She came to help us not as a salaried worker but as the daughter of a friend. As a young girl in St. Joseph, in fact, she had occasionally helped Ma on evenings to bathe Kamla and Vidia. We use the word 'godsend' quite flippantly at times, but now Pinky indeed seemed a godsend. She stayed with the family for thirty years. Her given name was Parbatee Soochit and she would come to know very well every member of Seepersad Naipaul's family. When the time came for her retirement she chose to stay with my family, with whom she had then lived for twenty-four years. Pinky died in 1984, well cared for by us and by her brother Harry, who never forsook her.

By the time he left the hospital and got home, Pa was visibly older. His soft fine hair had become sparser and greyer. He had also begun to brood. Ma, as usual, bore the brunt of his moodiness. He became a little testy with Sati, Mira and me. For the first time we could not play games in response to his calls. When he was well, his call for 'Sati, Mira, Savi' used to have each of us waiting for the other to answer.

On the second round, one of us would have to give in, or sometimes he got stuck on only one name. We knew how deeply he had always cared for us.

Over the years we had got used to, and were sometimes amused by, Pa's bouts of anxiety over our futures. Whenever a young woman, particularly an Indian woman, earned a degree or qualified as a professional in some other way, and her picture appeared in the newspapers, Pa would redouble the grammar, punctuation and comprehension lessons. We had to measure up to the latest rising star. Now, out of hospital, he no longer seemed interested in such matters. He was easily irritated. If Ma was late with his juice or his meal he would refuse to have it. At this time Ma was often miserable. She had to cope with the demands of both Pa and Nella, whom she was trying to wean. I did not have to be a mother myself to empathise with Ma's day-to-day challenges.

At the end of every month I rode to the *Trinidad Guardian* to collect Pa's pay, held in a small brown envelope. Pa knew it was only a matter of time before he was sacked. I knew that one day soon there would no envelope to collect. It was difficult not to remember Pa's jocular promises to Ma in better times: 'I'll buy a pretty brooch for you, my soosoowah! I'll buy a diamond ring for you, my soosoowah!' ('Soosoowah' was a made-up word of endearment he reserved for Ma only, never for his children.) After Nella's birth, and before his collapse and confinement in the hospital, he had asked me to buy a new dress-length piece of fabric and a new pair of shoes for Ma. I chose carefully, and both Pa and Ma approved of my choice. Ma liked the high-heeled shoes, but wondered all the same when again she would be stepping out in high heels. She made a dress from the fabric. There is a memorable picture of her with Pa. She is wearing the dress and the shoes. They are in the yard at the edge of the narrow garden on Nepaul Street.

Ma's life with Pa had never been a bed of roses. He had not had a single conversation with Ma before marriage. He had observed her and fallen in love. This was not unusual for the time. They both carried the same nickname in their respective families, Bhola, 'the quiet one'. Ma lived up to her name but Pa could move from calm to explosive in seconds. With such different personalities, they managed more to complement each other than to combust. More often than not, Ma stifled her opinions. Her restraint or pragmatism led to a household with few quarrels and not much screaming or shouting to awaken the neighbours. Pa and Ma shared an understanding that was private and intimate. Their snide comments aimed at one another were momentary and normal for two smart people. As children we could easily guess at their true feelings for each other. But we could never cross the threshold of their bond.

During the early, wandering years of their marriage, Ma was stoic as Pa's

Ma in her new dress, with Pa in the yard at Nepaul Street

anxiety to stand on his own two feet steadily increased. Ma did not rush back, as many of her sisters did, into the arms of her mother, although Pa when in a bad mood often accused her of wanting to do so. Pa hated being separated from his young children, but the Lion House had provided badly needed financial stability at times, if not total happiness for all concerned.

As I grew older I began to wonder about the husbands of so many of Ma's sisters who allowed themselves to become part of the extended family household for quite long periods. How did they live? Who provided food? Who provided clothing? In a recent interview, a cousin of mine, about my age, Suren Capildeo, called these uncles 'lazy bitches'. While this remark is gender-inaccurate, he was most probably echoing the sentiments of his father, Simbhoonath. The irony is that Suren, with the exception perhaps of one uncle, could hardly have spoken for even five minutes with these uncles in his lifetime or their lifetimes.

Living in a different time and being first-generation children of indentured immigrants, my uncles' Brahminical upbringing did not prepare them for the world in which they found themselves. Authoritarian attitudes and strict codes of conduct stifled both parents and their children. My father's vision to be his own man, to paddle his own canoe, distinguished him from them all, including his two educated brothers-in-law, Simbhoo and Rudranath. And now that the time had come for him to enjoy the fruits of his vision and his labour, here he was, confined to bed and with his life threatened.

The mail was slow. Even airmail letters in the early fifties were slow in coming. Apart from telegrams for very good or very sad news, communication moved at a snail's pace. By March the news of Pa's illness and bleak prognosis had Kamla in a dilemma. She had become engaged to Vincent Richmond and they had made plans to marry and live in Fiji. Kamla hoped to get a job there and send money home. Having some natural misgivings about such a bold move, she tried to put the onus on Ma to decide whether she should forgo marriage and instead come home. Ma wisely advised her to marry Vince and go to Fiji. Pa, feeling somewhat better after time and loving care at home, resumed his correspondence with Kamla as well as Vidia, but appeared to take no part in Kamla's decision about Fiji.

We learnt that Vincent had been apprehensive about Kamla's return to Trinidad. Such a move would surely put an end to their plans for marriage. However, Vincent never offered to come to Trinidad. Not a wealthy person or from a wealthy family, and perhaps as an older and educated son, he no doubt had family obligations, a feature not uncommon among East Indian families. The history of Fiji, with its plantations and indentured labour, was similar to Trinidad's.

With negative responses to her applications in Fiji, but positive replies from schools in Trinidad, Kamla decided to come home. While the Hindu organisation, the Sanatan Dharma Maha Sabha (SDMS), which sought to provide schools for Hindu children, could not match a job vacancy to her qualifications, the Presbyterian school authorities were positive in their response. The new secondary school in St. Augustine needed someone with her qualifications. A little light appeared in the tunnel for us. But did this offer then dim, or even put out altogether, the light for Kamla and her happiness with Vince?

Kamla's impending departure from India pleased Pa and excited us so much that we neglected to reflect sufficiently, if we reflected at all, on the immensity of the sacrifice she was making, and the depth of her sorrow in leaving Vincent behind. We had no idea if Vidia had influenced her decision. He, more than anyone else, could sway Kamla in making important choices. In 1948, when she had left us for India, we were all still very young. But she had always been caring and nurturing where we younger children were concerned. Vidia, on the other hand, always seemed to be anticipating problems at home involving Sati, Mira and me. In fact, we were doing well at school, all in the top classes and giving Pa and Ma little or no cause for anxiety.

Sati had been the third child but then became the middle child as we grew into a family of five. Pa used to refer to her as *maghilkee* – meaning middle child. Middle children are sometimes notable in families for wanting or having their own way or not following the status quo. While we paired off in the family – Kamla and Vidia, Mira and I – Sati remained alone and wanted to be alone. Her friends remained her friends and not our friends. Sati liked to read. While she was no dull bookworm, she remained the most avid reader in the family. Now in her final year of secondary school, while she never neglected her studies, there was no slacking off in her affection for Crisen BissoonDath. Pa and Ma gave their consent for their engagement while she was still at school. The rest of us were more than a little shocked by Sati's choice. Crisen was the second son in a family that ran a dry goods store in the small town of Sangre Grande in eastern Trinidad. He didn't seem to us especially attractive. His skin was none too good, and Mira and I use to say that he had 'vesicular' cheeks. Toiling in the family store, he remained largely uneducated while two of his brothers went off to become doctors and another became a teacher. Still, Sati had made her choice.

Pa began to write even more regularly. Spending quite a bit of time with him as his main assistant, I was very aware of his moods and his grumblings. I would write as he lay on his bed and dictated his thoughts, helping him to recall where he'd left off when he lost concentration and lamented his lot in life. While this experience made me a much better writer, both in composing essays and studying literature, and got me good grades at school and at university, I never quite realised at the time my luck in gaining this valuable experience.

In August, Kamla returned from India. Her arrival home brought great joy and relief to the household. She had stopped off en route in England, where she visited Vidia and met his girlfriend Pat, who presented her with a bouquet of yellow roses.

The household was a buzz of excitement at Kamla's arrival. Only Vidia was missing. Baby Nella was now ten months old and Shiva eight years. When Kamla left home in 1948 Shiva had been only three, Sati fourteen, Mira twelve and I ten. Every one of us would be different from the siblings she had left behind. Pa, though greyer now, still looked well. In fact, his looks belied his fragility. Ma, just forty, was probably the person who had changed the least of all. Kamla, slender and stunning, with impeccable carriage, was at her beautiful best. She was twenty-three. Wearing saris brought back from India, she looked like a screen star. All her saris were striking. She would wear the simpler ones and nevertheless be outstanding wherever she went. She also brought back a wooden box filled with glass bracelets that glittered and shone on the bellies of what looked like wooden rolling pins.

She quickly adjusted to the changes facing her as an adult in Trinidad. Kamla had never taken driving lessons. Now, with Pa laid up, she would be compelled to learn to drive. It was Pa, though, who eagerly drove her to St. Augustine Girls High School for her interview with Constance Wagar, a white Canadian educator who was principal of the new school founded by the Presbyterians as part of their mission in Trinidad. Kamla came home with a job offer and a starting salary that equalled Pa's pay at the *Guardian*. Pa had written a lengthy article on the leading Presbyterian educator, Elodie Bissessar, a few years earlier. She had impressed him so much with her carriage and her diction that we got a little tired of hearing her praises being sung. This woman had risen to become principal of the Government Teachers Training College in Port of Spain. Now he began to feel he had produced his own version of Elodie Bissessar. Kamla was just a graduate teacher but he was very proud of her, and doubtless relieved that her income would contribute handsomely to the family's support.

For at least three months, stretching from June to some time in September 1953 (when Kamla received a reduced monthly pay cheque for working part of that month), our family had no regular income at all. Ma would surely have had help from others. Abel Cardoso, a Portuguese grocer, had allowed her to buy goods on credit. Ma kept her books diligently. I discovered one day that her good friend Ivy Thomas was also helping her quietly. (Ivy, who was married, was the eldest of six Rampersad girls, including the prominent doctor Mavis Rampersad, whose father was a prosperous dry goods merchant on Henry Street.) Ivy would sneak twenty dollars occasionally from her house money to ensure that Ma could buy milk for Nella. But most people would have been unaware of our difficulties. Ma stifled her pride, even as Vidia, without empathy, complained that Ma's letters were all about money.

Strange and haunting are the strains of a sitar. Every morning, as Kamla tried to resettle in Trinidad, we awoke to the lingering notes and soothing melodies of this instrument, which was new to us. For Kamla, suffering from nostalgia and, no doubt, a sense of lost love, the music and playing would have been meditative and soothing. For us, it was enchanting. As a child in the Lion House, until the age of six, Kamla had heard prayers recited every morning and again before lamplight in the evening. In Nepaul Street, we had no such rituals. Prayers, if and when said, were private and silent. Her youthful memories of Chaguanas, reawakened in Benares, now reasserted themselves unobtrusively at home. They made the start of each day more solemn, at least to Pa and Ma and herself.

While Sati used the rest of the vacation to pound away at her books, Mira and I whiled away our time drawing, sewing or painting. Mira was recognised as the artist among the girls. As we had friends nearby, we spent a lot of our time together, with even an odd cricket match or two thrown into the mix. Kamla succeeded in getting her driver's permit. She was looking forward to her new job in St. Augustine and she would drive herself to work in PA 1192.

For a while it seemed that all was well and going to be well.

Nella's first birthday was coming up on 4$^{th}$ October 1953. Nanee's one year *bhandara*, a feast and prayer in remembrance of the departed, was planned for 3$^{rd}$ October in Luis Street. Pa worked a little in the garden, felt tired and not very well. He lay down on the rug in the middle of the living-room. Nella crawled to him to do her usual blow-on-the-belly, spit-filled game. Pa asked me, Why did I not dress Nella in the little yellow and white number that I had made for her birthday? We were all going off to Luis Street for the event, so I agreed. As we were about to leave, Pa suggested to Shiva that he stay at home with him that day. But Shiva did not want to stay and we all left for Luis Street. The plan was that Mira and I would come back on our bicycles between three and four in the afternoon to get Pa his tea.

Between the appointed hours Mira and I cycled home. We found Pa in bed cringing in pain. I immediately went to the Hippolyte Bordes, a young, attractive couple with three young children who lived in the house opposite to us, and used their telephone to call Dr. Mavis Rampersad. Mira stayed with Pa. I may have alerted Ma and Kamla in Luis Street, but I cannot recall.

On getting back home after the phone call I found Pa in his bed, still in great distress. Mavis responded in quick time and Pa was given an injection. Mavis took Mira into the bathroom and must have said something to make Mira laugh. 'That damn girl is laughing and I am in so much pain,' Pa muttered. Those were his last words. Mavis, Mira and I were the only ones at his bedside as he breathed his last. I stared at him, touched his hands, kissed him on his forehead, and never looked at him again.

When Ma and Kamla and others arrived and their weeping began I experienced an out-of-world hollow-gut feeling. Sixty-three years later, I find it normal to shed tears when writing about this. Pa always had a soft spot for me and I always knew it. Mira always felt protected by Ma and I felt protected by Pa. Three hours later, with Nella in her birthday dress, I was back in Luis Street. I would stay there until after the cremation.

On 4th October 1953, Seepersad Naipaul, husband of Droapatie Naipaul, née Capildeo, was cremated on the bank of the San Juan River, which flows into the Caroni River basin and empties finally into the Caroni Swamp. He was forty-seven years old.

Pa was among the earliest Trinidadians to be cremated. The spot is not used as a cremation site today. Instead, the main site was relocated to the banks of the Caroni, less than a mile from the Swamp. As for the cause of his death, Professor of Medicine Surujpaul Teelucksingh told me that Pa was the first person to be documented in the Port of Spain General Hospital as suffering from coronary artery thrombosis. On the way back from the cremation, Kamla had to be brought to Luis Street. She who had witnessed so many cremations on the banks of the Ganges in Benares and sent pictures home, had several fainting spells.

By late afternoon we were all back home in Nepaul Street. Our school friends Myrna and Eulah Berridge had kindly swept and cleaned both our house and our small yard and put all the furniture back in place. A garland of orchids taken from one of Pa's more common species was hung over his portrait. Pa had commissioned this portrait in 1951 from a local artist, Errol Gaston Johnson, and had paid him fifty-two dollars for it. He had hoped to get one done of Ma also, and had envisaged their portraits with pictures of Kamla and Vidia on either side. It was an extravagance when money was tight, and was considered by Vidia an undertaking of pure vanity. Now it remained our daily reminder of our father as a man of a simple background and a most unusual talent.

On Pa's death Vidia had sent a cable. It said: 'He was the best man I ever knew.' Succinct if not original, it encapsulated the father-and-son relationship over twenty-one years.

Pa's death and cremation had happened so quickly that I remained for some time in a state of shock. It took more than a week for me to fully accept that he was gone. At home, the sitar music stopped. The instrument was placed in its sack. It would not reappear. It was as if the past had to be erased to dull the pain and start afresh. The void of man and music could not be filled. No one spoke about our loss. We did not know how each other felt. In going to collect the ashes at the cremation site the following day, Mira had picked up a vertebra, not turned to ash, and brought it home. We returned it with the ashes to the watery river bed.

Crisen, Pa, Sati; sitting, Phoola with Nella, Shiva and Mira, 1953

# CHAPTER 5

## *After the Sitar Music Stopped*

With Pa gone, for a while we all behaved in strange ways. I buried myself in sewing white dresses or black and white dresses for us all. We would wear these for a couple of months as symbols of our mourning. Kamla was the sole breadwinner and took on the mantle as manager of the household. It was a burden which would eat into her resolve as time went by. She must have felt all her hopes and plans for her marriage dashed. Sati, now less than eight weeks away from her HSC exams, as usual followed her own path. Shiva came under heavier scrutiny. Ma, needing to recover from many months of stress, was very quiet. She was, however, warm and welcoming to our friends, who provided a welcome diversion. Besides, Nella, now just a year old, needed her constant care.

School was the panacea for us all – all, that is, except Ma, who must have welcomed the opportunity to reflect and suffer in silent hours of solitude. Each of us was wrapped in a shroud of sorrow. Pa, who had guided us with subdued approbation, Pa who had intermittently galvanised us towards lives of achievement and purpose, taunting us by emphasising the achievements of others, was gone. He was no longer smoking, teasing, whistling, reading, typing, writing and gardening in his pyjamas or long trousers. The garden would gradually begin to reflect his absence, in spite of our efforts. We knew that we had to work as hard as we could and live up to his expectations. For some of us, there were also financial debts to be paid.

The house in Nepaul Street was always very small, but we did not think it so. When we moved in, at the start of 1947, we were six children along with Pa and Ma. Like most homes that we knew, there was only one bathroom and toilet. Very few families had the luxury of refrigerators, washing machines and dryers, and electric or gas cookers. The automatic dishwasher was almost wholly unknown. Until we were teenagers, however, we did not realise that we were poor. We were possibly the only family in Nepaul Street who owned a motor car and PA 1192, Pa's Ford Prefect, still stood in the garage. We never felt cramped for space. The upstairs-downstairs arrangement made our sleeping quarters a private area. The living area downstairs was adequate, inviting and well-kept, with polished floors and smart rugs and fresh flowers.

Early in 1954, Sati, awaiting her HSC results, got a job as a teacher. She had had some practice. While Pa was ill and unable to work, our Uncle Simbhoo had promised Ma fifty dollars a month in exchange for Sati living in Luis Street and tutoring his elder son, Deven. Now, as a teacher in Spring Village Hindu School run by the Sanatan Dharma Maha Sabha, her income provided the means to build something of a trousseau for herself. She and Crisen BissonDath were still intent on an early marriage, though Ma would not permit the wedding to take place until six months had elapsed after Pa's death.

On 18th April 1954, the marriage took place under Hindu rites at 26 Nepaul Street. The neighbours had kindly allowed space in their yards to accommodate the wedding tents. Pa's meagre insurance money disappeared into paying for the event. Sati put every ounce of her energy into the preparations. It seemed as if from December to March 1954, apart from her teaching, she did virtually nothing else but sew sequins on to her wedding sari. Looking back on that event I am amazed that, given our thin resources, we could ever have entertained the thought of a fairly large wedding or handle all that it involved. It must have seemed one sure way of moving forward after Pa's death.

Sati and Crisen's wedding

With Sati's marriage, we were now five children at home with Ma in Nepaul Street. Nella slept with Ma in the SlumberKing bed and Kamla reclaimed her bed.

Recreation at home was limited to board games, especially Scrabble. We played so intently and competitively and loudly, forfeiting play for errors, that Ma often threatened to 'pitch the Scrabble board in the yard'. Monopoly was never our game, and we had outgrown Snakes and Ladders, except when we played it with Shiva. Whoever won at Scrabble became 'the champion'. This was not an honour for long; it usually meant an instant challenge to a return bout. Dictionaries were not allowed except for word challenges. Very few words in today's Scrabble Dictionary were known. The *Oxford Dictionary* was our Scrabble bible. Shiva, in spite of his tender age, grew in skill quite quickly and soon became a regular player in our games.

As Kamla's driving skills improved and PA 1192 was still in reasonably good condition, we began to do something that we had never done before. Instead of going as we had done with Pa to Dhein's Bay in Carenage for a swim, we occasionally went to Maracas after school. Going to Maracas Bay was a lot more exciting than going to Dhein's Bay. The road to Maracas was still relatively new and the experience novel to most Trinidadians at a time when private cars were fewer and there were no route taxis. The road built by the Americans during the Second World War allowed Maracas Bay to replace the popular beaches at Teteron Bay and Macqueripe on the north-west coast of the island which were still restricted areas because of war measures which had not yet been relaxed or reversed. (The British government had agreed to lease the north-western peninsula to the USA in exchange for warships and the protection of oil-laden ships sailing from Trinidad to assist the Allied Forces in the war.) Driving to Maracas Bay from Port of Spain took thirty minutes. We followed the Maraval River basin northwards, gradually climbing to the foothills of the Northern Range. Here the romance of the drive began. Leaving the valley and clinging to the scarp slopes, the new road wound around the Spurs, forested with slim-trunked trees, ferns and lianas. Occasionally we came across freshwater springs gurgling out and escaping over the bare rocky patches. Excellent water for making tea, we learnt. On the opposite side the treetops provided a carpet of green, exploding with patches of bright yellow when the pouis were in bloom or orange/red when the immortelle or flamboyant trees flowered. The downward slope to the beaches revealed a different vista, with glimpses of the sea and a few small, forested islands off the shore. Being greeted by the crescent of golden sands was in itself a tonic for tired minds at the end of a school day.

This new adventure was only a part of the changes that came into our lives. The installation of a telephone at about this time, at Kamla's behest, revolutionised our ability to communicate with the world outside Nepaul Street – and got some of us into trouble. Too much talk and not enough work, according to Ma. Kamla also bought Ma a New World gas stove. Overwhelmed, Ma treated the stove almost as if it were a piece of furniture. Today it stands in the house in pristine condition, in spite of the complete burnout of the burners. Ma was never much of a baker, but this stove allowed Ma's good friend Ivy Thomas an excuse for long visits, especially just before Christmas. The regular interruptions in electricity that plagued the city made the gas oven even friendlier for making cakes. Leila BissoonDath, Sati's sister-in-law and one of our best friends at the Convent, came to live with us to avoid daily travel to and from Arima. She was a top student at the Convent and would go on to win the girls' island scholarship and later marry Simboonath's son, Deven Capildeo.

After tea each day, a new routine started, gradually at first, around the dining table. Kamla was in charge of a study group that quickly grew larger. Some boys, friends of ours, who needed help with their school studies joined. I generally sat out of the group, assessing the response of all and wondering why some of them had such difficulty to learn and to recall. These gatherings, which ended before dusk, made the atmosphere at home livelier. Everyone called Ma either 'Ma' or 'Ma Naipaul'. The following year, as they anxiously prepared for their School Certificate examinations, Ma would remind them of the precise timetable of the tests. One morning she was even able to alert, just in time, one of them who had almost missed his physics exam.

The study group was a great success. While grades varied, Mira and Leila (our boarder) had brilliant results and moved easily into the Higher School Certificate classes. They earned Grade I certificates, with distinctions in seven subjects.

Sati, Mira and I would always be grateful for the kindness of the Sisters of Cluny at St. Joseph's Convent, especially Sister Francis Xavier Ulrich. She personally encouraged us and kept us in school when Pa was ill and out of work. In an age when most girls left school at the Senior Certificate level, each of us stayed on to do the Higher Certificate. The remarkable thing is that we were not Roman Catholics. The school deferred the payment of fees until we could afford them. (We would settle all our debts before I left the Convent in 1957.) The generosity of the Sisters provided each of us with the launching pad for tertiary education, which in turn secured a future of financial stability for us all.

If there is anything that makes Seepersad Naipaul's family truly unusual as a group, it is the fact that we all, with the exception of Sati, who chose to take another road in life, earned university degrees. Given our circumstances and given the age in which we lived, this achievement was rare. Pa, weakly educated himself, had set the challenge. Ma, Sister Francis Xavier of the Convent school and Kamla saw us through at least until the elite Higher School Certificate level. Sati, for reasons she never gave, refused to join or follow me at university. After she left her teaching job at St. Augustine Girls' High School, as she did eventually, she chose to stay at home and read – she never stopped reading – as she brought up her family.

Gradually Kamla shed her saris for dresses. She rekindled friendships and also made new friends. Her beauty, unaffected stylishness and pleasant, outgoing personality, as well as her sharp mind, drew others to her. After school, the house always seemed to be abuzz. People seemed to like coming to the Naipauls of Nepaul Street for tea. Tea could be anything from crispy fried fish and hot 'hops' bread, fresh from the nearby bakery, to breadfruit chips and coconut turnovers, and of course tea brewed properly in a teapot. A red-haired, elderly white woman – I believe her name was Mrs. Myers – and Doris Fong, a schoolteacher associate of Kamla's at St. Augustine's, fancied themselves tea-leaf readers. They provided us at times with amusing entertainment and teenage excitement about fantasies of love.

Family life continued to recover from Pa's death. At the age of three-plus, Nella began to read and read quite well. We would show her off to our friends. Shiva at ten was plodding along, but pleasantly so. Or so it seemed. We had assumed that he was making excellent progress at school until we discovered one day that he had been skipping his classes regularly. This type of truancy was called *l'école biche*, or 'breaking biche'. Generally these episodes were treated as amusing times one could laugh about, especially when they concerned teenagers. But Shiva was not yet a teenager. Ma or Kamla, I am not sure who, decided to remove him from Tranquillity, where he was comfortable despite his truancy, and where so many of us had been students, and send him to the less prestigious Eastern Boys Government school in the heart of Port of Spain. Old Mr. Romilly, Vidia's former teacher, was headmaster there and was trusted to secure Shiva's academic future. But the move was a minor disaster. Shiva, plucked out in midstream from Tranquillity, had no friends in the new school. He also found the environment rough. He hated the school and reacted by taking very long walks home. This fresh piece of rebelliousness ended quickly when he was spotted by a cousin one day. Fortunately, Shiva got back on stream and did well enough to enter QRC in January 1956. It would be his school for the next six years.

Then, early in 1955, Vidia suddenly announced that he was now married to Pat, his longtime English girlfriend. He chose to give us the news in the form of a 'by the way' postscript to a routine message sent in an air-letter form. Squeezed in at the end of the letter, it read something like this: 'As you may have guessed, I am married.' None of us had guessed anything of the sort, and nobody knew anything of the melodrama connected to the marriage. Pat's father had strongly objected to it. Since he knew that Vidia was at Oxford with Pat, his objection must surely have had to do mainly or exclusively with Vidia's race or colour. Perhaps he also thought them too young for marriage. Both were twenty-two and financially insecure.

In hindsight, the news must have devastated Kamla. Having given up her beloved Vincent Richmond to return to Trinidad and help her family, now that there was no longer any possibility of Vidia coming back to lend his support, she must have felt trapped and perhaps even cruelly tricked by fate. From that time onward, she would suffer from recurring bouts of emotional turmoil and distress. Nobody she met in Trinidad seemed to measure up to her memories of Vincent Richmond. No atlas could bring Fiji closer to the Caribbean. At the age of twenty-four, Kamla had seen her karma determined by money and the vast expanse of ocean between her homeland and Vincent's. Letters from the other side of the world, already few, dwindled further and then ceased altogether. Finally one day she turned over her engagement ring to Ma to be refashioned by a jeweller. This, a final dissolution of the pledge of marriage.

The mid-fifties era was an exciting time to be alive and to feel grown-up. In 1956 I entered the Higher School Certificate class on Mira's heels. Her subjects were Spanish, French and Geography, while mine were English Literature, French and Geography. Our classes were separated by a simple partition and her friends also became my friends. Elvis Presley had begun to rock the music world. The old crooners such as Sinatra and Crosby and their melodious and romantic songs and one-tile dancing had to make way for the much more robust rock-and-roll, with its flips and dips and skirts flying. Rock-and-roll was in vogue and Elvis an absolute idol.

Politically, the era was also a time of thrilling change. Fidel Castro was about to overthrow Batista and introduce radical socialism to Cuba. Whether she was a saint or sinner, Eva Peron in Argentina was ill and needed our prayers. In Trinidad and Tobago, Dr. Eric Williams had emerged as the new messiah. Educated at QRC and Oxford and unquestionably charismatic, he would touch an Afro-centric nerve in Trinidad that had lain relatively dormant for many years. There had been eruptions of racial and ethnic pride tied to politics from time to time, but when they occurred excessively they had been quelled by the might of the police and armed forces and the supremacy of the law courts. In 1956, Dr. Williams began in earnest to lead the march to free the island from British colonialism. In addition to his racial appeal, he had the backing of a large part of the intelligentsia, who were looking for a local leader who was both educated and inspirational. And Dr. Williams matched their progressive expectations. With his guidance, for example, women became more active and important than ever before in our politics.

Trinidad was not unique in the Caribbean. In Jamaica there were the cousins and political rivals Norman Manley and Alexander Bustamante. In Barbados, there was Grantley Adams. Guyana featured Forbes Burnham and Cheddi Jagan, allies who would soon become antagonists. In the smaller islands, such as in Grenada, there was T. Albert Marryshow. In one way or another, they seemed to be leading the West Indies away from colonialism.

In Africa too, new leaders of the people were emerging, such as Kwame Nkrumah of Ghana, Jomo Kenyatta of Kenya and Julius Nyerere of Tanzania. All of these leaders and changes could be traced back to 1947, when India sent home the Raj after decades of agitation and often brutal repression. Men such as Gandhi, Nehru and Jinnah presided over the founding of a new state. That the new state then degenerated into bloody partition that led to the founding of Pakistan was telling, but seemed to deter no one in the rush toward independence from Europe. The disintegration of the British Empire accelerated, and the British Commonwealth of Nations began to emerge.

Ironically, many colonies around the world would take India as an example, even as the epitome, of the successful liberation of a people from European colonialism. This long-distance view of India was true of parts of the Caribbean. What few people seemed to realise was that India's independence had been wrung out of Great Britain by dint of blood and tears and the murderous effects of subdivision and the loss of ancestral lands. The radical move towards independence in India existed long before the people of the West Indies began to agitate for it. But the 'East Indians' in the West Indies had always paid attention to what was going on in the land of their origin. They knew and could identify the names and photographs of the major players in the Indian struggle for freedom. They knew how self-rule had been followed by the realities of independence in 1948, by bloody instability and the Hindu-Muslim conflict that had devastated entire parts of the subcontinent and wrecked its idealism. I think that many people in the West Indies saw only the glamour of the freedom struggle, not its realities.

Nevertheless, with the climate of political change so stormy in appearance, Dr. Eric Williams was well poised to make his mark on the history of Trinidad and Tobago. In the heart of the city lies the public park called Woodford Square, mere yards from the Red House, where Parliament or its latest version met. Once the haunt of eccentrics and vagrants, and well populated at one time by Indian beggars, the square became central to Dr. Williams's strategy. He renamed it 'The University of Woodford Square'. Wearing dark glasses even at night, and sporting a hearing aid which he sometimes turned off conspicuously when he did not wish to hear what someone said, he held his audiences spellbound with his passion and well-crafted oratory. Here the masses would learn of the inequities of British colonialism and the insecurities and limitations imposed by it on the people.

The message, while drumming up support effectively enough, did not tell the whole story of our history and culture. Colonialism provided many topics for discussion. To be a colonial was to be in some respects inherently second-rate, subordinate, submissive and subservient. Dr. Williams, awakening black consciousness, merged it with the idea of victimhood as well as with the twin historical enemies of emancipated consciousness: slavery and colonialism. This stirred up the fervour of his followers among the masses, as well as among many educated voters who had studied abroad and had felt the ignominy of being treated as inferiors. But others saw the situation differently. Many descendants of Indian indentured servants, having outgrown and rejected that form of colonial life, and seeing their future in Trinidad in more promising ways, tied to small businesses in particular, were wary of political change based mainly on racial grievance. Other minorities also felt threatened by what they saw as the politics of retribution and revenge. These minorities included the descendants (including those of mixed ancestry) of French, German, Portuguese, Chinese and Lebanese settlers among others, who believed they had also helped to build the country through decades of hard work, sacrifice, frugality, business shrewdness and so on. Typically, they felt insecure and provoked by Dr. Williams's brand of nationalism.

Emotions became so charged over politics in 1956 and the years that followed that even in school, among old and dear friends, it became difficult to have a decorous conversation about the subject and to weigh its merits and demerits. In our sixth form, arguments raged among the students with plenty of zeal and usually without reaching any conclusions. The merits of universal adult suffrage were a favourite topic. It often led to bouts of screaming and shouting. For people with limited knowledge of the past and of the world, Dr. Williams had brought, along with all the truths and facts he enunciated, a crucial divisiveness in our country along racial or ethnic lines. This divisiveness still exists today in Trinidad and Tobago.

For the mainly uneducated man in the street of African descent, it often seemed that the only rightful inheritors of Trinidad and Tobago were the descendants of the former slaves, although slavery had occupied only a relatively brief period in the history of the islands. To their descendants, their ancestors had given their blood, sweat and tears to build the economy. Everyone else, particularly the Indians, was somehow an interloper who had been duly rewarded for his or her labour. Now these interlopers formed the backbone of the group of recalcitrant minorities who they saw as determined to throttle the progress of the black majority. Fifty years or more since independence, which came in 1962, these ethnocentric impulses and divisions are still strong.

I can say that as Indians we had no problems on the streets of Port of Spain, or anywhere else in Trinidad for that matter, following the arrival in 1956 of the Afro-centric People's National Party (PNM). Of course, we hardly walked the streets, but drove in Pa's good old Ford Prefect or took the buses. Open and threatening racial divisiveness of this kind would rear its ugly head only after the PNM lost the Federal elections in 1959, following three years in power. It is true that Vidia, in 1956, saw this matter differently, especially after the PNM victory in September. On 29th September, according to his biographer Patrick French, he wrote to his wife Pat in England that the PNM ('a Negro party') victory 'has not only made it embarrassing for any non-Negro to walk P.O.S. streets, but has got every other community very worried'. Trinidad might well become 'hell to live in'. He called the black professionals supporting the party 'noble niggers', but explained that 'the noble nigger is really a damned nasty nigger ... The galling thing is that these very people who are so offensive over here go to England and whine for tolerance! Even children hurl abuse at you in the streets. You should see it. You will find it most revealing.'

Nevertheless, the feeling of new freedom crossed all the fissures in Trinidad. Earlier that year, the brilliant young calypsonian, Sparrow, became an overnight sensation with his song 'Jean and Dinah', encapsulating the mood of the country. The new was displacing the old and the overriding emotion was one of sudden, decisive liberation. The young and up-and-coming professionals, who some years later would be referred to derisively as 'yuppies', emerged as an energetic, even inspirational force. Despite political and other differences, a general feeling of hope prevailed. Restaurants and clubs such as Tavern on the Green, the Normandie, the Lotus, the Crab Hole and the Penthouse became popular and fashionable nightspots. These haunts gradually replaced the old clubs that had been built squarely on ethnic difference and concepts of racial and ethnic heritage and privilege. These had included the India Club, the Chinese Association, the Portuguese Club, the Yacht Club and above all the Country Club in Maraval, which was dominated by whites.

This was the Trinidad to which Vidia returned for the first time since leaving as a boy of eighteen in 1950. He was alone. Pat stayed back in England.

Vidia's return brought a sense of excitement for Kamla and a great deal of curiosity from the rest of us. Kamla had met him in 1953 on her way back from India. She had seen him again in 1955, when she spent the long July-August school vacation in London. Thus Kamla was the only member of the family to have seen and been with Vidia between 1950 and 1956.

Ma with her seven children and Crisen, 1956

For Ma, who had received some scorching letters from Vidia before and after Nella's birth, there may have been some apprehension. He and Kamla had both written accusing Pa and Ma of irresponsibly begetting children for them to mind, and complained about the burden that was being placed on them to look after the family. At that time, Pa was neither sick nor dead. Now Ma was alone. Her love for Vidia and her pride in his achievements had never dimmed. Her feelings for him were unconditional. The many years of asthmatic bouts he had suffered during his childhood and into his early teens, when she had been his main nurse and attendant, made him especially vulnerable and precious in her eyes. She had always given him special care and attention. Now she was eagerly anticipating the arrival of her son, a grown and married man at the age of twenty-three. As would almost any other mother with her son under similar circumstances, she was almost ecstatic to have him come home.

For Kamla, her brother Vidia's arrival meant having a companion to see and understand, if not completely share, the responsibility and demands of the household. It was also an opportunity for her to shine in his light, to be the hostess of the hour, and show Vidia off to her many friends. His first published novel, *The Mystic Masseur*, a comic tale of Indian life in Trinidad, had received generous critical acclaim in Britain. (*Miguel Street*, a collection of short stories based mainly on Vidia's experience of boyhood on Luis Street in Woodbrook, was written first but published second.) When the book appeared in 1956, and before he finally returned, I can testify, without reserve, to the rich sense of pride and joy we all felt in it and him. While the world would have been unaware of Vidia's ambition to be not simply a good writer but a truly great writer, all of us still at home knew of his grand ambition and took *The Mystic Masseur* as a token of his and our secret hopes and dreams.

Sent a precious early copy by Vidia, we tucked it away reverentially in the bookcase when we were not reading and rereading it. We lingered over the reviews. We would also learn, from Vidia's testy letters in response to our praise, that some reviews which we found good annoyed him, especially because he did not want to be 'pigeon-holed' as a Caribbean or an exotic writer. He wanted his work to stand on its merit anywhere and everywhere. But each favourable review and each new literary award thrilled us.

In 1956, then, Vidia was returning amid some local and even international recognition. Meeting his new fans and going to new places interested him, although he had occasionally to be rescued by Kamla when the event did not turn out to be what he had hoped. At a small party in Nepaul Street we met the young and already acclaimed poet and playwright Derek Walcott of St. Lucia, now living in Trinidad. In 1948, as a schoolboy of eighteen, Walcott had astonished Vidia and other lovers of literature at QRC by self-publishing *25 Poems*, an accomplished volume of verse.

Derek went on to found a locally important drama group, the Trinidad Theatre Workshop, which met in Beryl McBurnie's Little Carib theatre on White Street in Port of Spain. His wife, Margaret Maillard, was a friend of Kamla's from their Convent days. Margaret's family had once owned the beautiful Petit Valley estate bought by Soogie Capildeo, where I had imagined myself for a while as 'Heidi of the Tropics'. Mutual respect and admiration existed in those days between Derek and Vidia. The sparring between them, which turned ugly on both sides, would begin many years later.

Sati, now living in a small place called Guaico near the cocoa town of Sangre Grande, was away from the daily hubbub in No. 26 Nepaul Street. She and Vidia were both newly married, except that Sati now was the mother of a one-year-old son, Neil. (Vidia would remain childless.) Vidia, who was quite interested to see how Sati was faring in her self-imposed rusticity, went to see her. He discovered that she was quite happy. In addition to keeping her teaching job at a nearby private high school, St. Catherine's, she had become close friends with Crisen's cousins, the Mahases. This friendship meant a great deal to Sati and contributed to her sense of contentment.

Vidia had known Mira and me as children, but his interaction with us now was oddly limited. He never played a game of any kind with us, certainly no table-tennis or a little cricket, which we liked and he once liked. He must have formed opinions of us as we were growing up, but these we never learned. So both Mira and I were meeting Vidia essentially for the first time as grown-ups, as we thought of ourselves. We found his response to us disappointing and even disheartening. Generally, Mira and I felt good about ourselves. We were not unattractive, we had done well at school, we spoke well, we dressed well, we had decent friends. In certain ways we were different from one another. I was always bolder than Mira and tended to respond more quickly to any situation. Mira, meeker, if also funnier when she wanted to be funny, withdrew more readily to stand behind me. Practically anyone who knew us would attest to this assessment. But somehow, no attribute or achievement of ours found favour with Vidia on this visit. He seemed to think that we would amount to nothing. Whatever negative criticism Kamla had fed him about us, he had digested it all. He had an 'I'll brook no nonsense' attitude that annoyed us. Our father had never behaved in this way. Vidia seemed so different from Pa! So Mira and I avoided him as much as possible. We breathed a sigh of relief whenever he and Kamla went out.

While Kamla remained the loving sister, hostess and protector, Shiva was often left in a daze. Eleven-year-old Shiva, so proud of this almost mythical brother come to life, a father-figure replacement, could recite chunks of *The Mystic Masseur* in honour and in awe of Vidia. Sadly he would

Vidia at home in 1956 with Shiva, and below with Sati, Mira and Kamla

gaze at a brother who demonstrated little affection and less tenderness for him. Children pay a great deal of attention to their surroundings and people, and know when they are disliked. We – Mira and I – had already learnt this about Shiva, and were wary of the effect of Vidia's coldness on him. Shiva's image of Vidia would scarcely change over the years. While he admired the work and was in awe of Vidia's achievements, he was not charmed by the man.

Shiva entered QRC in 1956, while Vidia was in Trinidad. His principal, Mr. Haynes, was the last Englishman to hold that post. Over the decades, QRC had maintained a fine tradition in scholarship. Vidia had been an island scholarship winner there, as had been his uncle, Rudranath Capildeo. Indeed, both names were painted on the roll of honour on a wall in the Great Hall. Numerous other cousins had also attended QRC. Going to this excellent college was a notable success for Shiva and a fresh boost to the extended family reputation for excellence in school. One might have expected Vidia to take Shiva on a walk, before term started, to visit the venerable school, to introduce him to his old teachers and the principal. But nothing like this happened. Vidia was not prepared to play the role of big brother or surrogate father, as Kamla was actively doing as our big sister. So Shiva was not taken for a swim in the sea at Carenage, to a cinema show, or even for an outing to an ice cream parlour. These things did not cost a lot of money and would have made Vidia's visit more memorable and endearing for his brother. Neglected by Vidia, he began to wilt. Mira and I saw what was happening and tried to protect him as best we could. To get away from home, Shiva began to creep down the street to hear a new steel band that was being formed.

When Vidia's visit ended, we were relieved. Life at Nepaul Street returned to normal. Through it all, Ma had remained as solid as a rock but always in the background, in spite of several harangues from Vidia that must have hurt her. Ma was strong. I well remember Mira or me bursting into our home with our School Certificate results. Seeing Ma we would blurt out in excitement: 'Ma, I got a first grade!' Ma would simply smile and say, 'Good, *beti*.' But she would also continue doing whatever she was doing. No hugs, no special congratulations. So placid, as if you were bringing her news she already knew. The only time we got a somewhat lively reaction from her was when we said we hadn't done something well. Then she might say: 'I don't know why anything should be so hard, if you did your work. You have the books, you have the teachers, and you have lights!' (By which she meant electric lights, which she did not have as a child.) She had made do with so much less in her youth – in her life.

The following year, Mira successfully completed her Higher School Certificate and took a job at the Seismic Research Station. I entered the Upper HSC class. With the money I had received for winning a house scholarship, and also a generous cheque from my schoolfriend Carol Stollmeyer's mother for making a few outfits for Carol, we were able to pay the arrears on our school fees. (Carol was the daughter of Andre Stollmeyer, whose brothers Victor and Jeffrey were famous cricketers. She lived on Jerningham Avenue just off the Queen's Park Savannah, and we had become great friends in our Senior Certificate year.)

After Vidia's visit, and noting Kamla's increasing anxiety to move on with her life, Mira and I began to hatch our own plan to secure university education. My first year in the HSC classes had shown that I was ready for that big step. I enjoyed my studies and for the first time felt that I could really excel as a scholar. My grades in Geography, Literature and French were higher than normal and these gave me the impetus to try to win the scholarship. Should I be good enough and lucky enough in this endeavour, then Mira and I planned to go abroad together. With work and study we planned to go forward whatever the outcome. One had to be young to be so brave-hearted. We formed no alternative plans.

We were surprised but delighted when we learnt that Kamla had been granted leave of absence from her job at St. Augustine's Girls. She needed a long vacation. From September 1953 to July 1957, Kamla had been the sole earner in our household. While she had taken breaks every year in the long July-August school vacations, she obviously felt that she needed a much longer holiday. Her plan was to go to London, where Vidia and Pat were living.

Vidia and Pat were still finding their feet. While Pat was teaching, Vidia had begun to review books and write occasionally on other topics for the newspapers. Over the next few years his books would begin to tumble out with regular frequency. But his sales yielded comparatively little money, and living in London was expensive. Nevertheless, it was at this time that he began to send us ten pounds sterling every month through Barclays Bank. With Kamla away, we managed on Mira's income and what was left of the ten pounds after bank charges.

The long August vacation was the perfect time to devote oneself to study. The Cambridge University HSC exams were held in December and without school I could schedule my studies differently. With this in mind, early in August I went to San Fernando to spend a weekend with my long-time and dear friend Indra Samaroo. She was now married to my cousin Romesh Mootoo. Romesh was a medical student in Ireland and they were home on a holiday. Uninvited and unprepared, I reluctantly accompanied them to someone's twenty-first birthday party. At the party the Mootoos introduced me to a very young-looking doctor who occasionally attended their first-born child, Shani. Melvin Akal was in general practice. That introduction to him dramatically altered my life and its direction. If any of our tea-leaf readers had claimed to foresee the changes through the dregs in my teacup, I would have laughed them to scorn.

From being a persistent admirer Mel became an ardent suitor. His affable and gentle nature endeared him to all in our household on Nepaul Street. The Akal name was a well-known name in Port of Spain. There was a school in Woodbrook called Akal School that Kamla and Vidia had attended for about a week or two before they left for Tranquillity. Born on 7th May 1929, Melvin Akal was the fifth of six sons of Lionel Lewis Akal, a brother of its principal. At twenty-five, Melvin's father himself became a school principal, at another Akal School located in San Juan, just outside Port of Spain.

Long before I met Mel, my good friend Gloria Youngsing had told me of this interesting family who had lived near them at one time in San Juan. Both brothers came from a Presbyterian family who lived originally in Arouca. They had attended the fledgling but quickly respected Naparima Training College run by the Presbyterians in San Fernando. When Lionel Lewis Akal became principal, his school had about twenty-five children and two junior teachers. Their job often included going to people's homes to collect pupils and take them to school. Most of these children came to school every day with bare feet. Forty-two years later, when Lionel Akal retired, the school had a population of about four hundred students. Lionel married Viola Robinson and together they brought up six sons and two daughters. All the sons attended QRC. Competing for the island scholarship in the Science area, Mel had placed fourth. At Leeds University in England he had read Medicine. While there, he won his university colours as a member of the cricket eleven.

On my first date with Mel to meet a group of his friends, I became aware of another link between us. Mel had close ties to the prominent Mahabir family, and especially to Rodney and Claudia Mahabir. Through Pa, I had come to know Jules, the head of the family. Jules Mahabir, as I have pointed out, had been Pa's close friend for many years. His wife was Minnie Mahabir. (She had been a Mahabir before the marriage.) Rodney was the youngest of their three sons. The oldest was Dennis, and in the middle was Winston. The Mahabirs were a fascinating family. They illustrated better than most people the fluidity, versatility and adaptability of Indian and Hindu culture in Trinidad. Of solid Hindu origins, they had become devoted Presbyterians. Through Presbyterianism, and their resulting superior command of English along with their implicit cosmopolitanism, many Indians had risen in the world in Trinidad. The Mahabirs' grandfather, David Mahabir, was the first Indian to become a government-employed court interpreter, a crucial position at a time when certain forms of crime, tied to poverty and homelessness, but also to domestic violence, dogged the

Indian population. They were a family of sophistication and learning, well known in debating circles in Trinidad. In addition, the brothers were all handsome. Their parents formed a wonderful team.

Dennis, who was mayor of Port of Spain, joined the PNM. Thus he became one of the leading Indians (few as they were) in the party. No doubt he joined with the hope that an educated man like Williams would have been able to knit the various groups who were thrown together in our country into a more understanding and tolerant society and develop a national conscience as we approached self-government. The educated and younger professionals, people like the Mahabirs, were anxious for the country to shake off the restraints of colonialism and move forward. In the end, however, Dennis had to separate himself from the PNM. A generous man, he gave me his copy of *Gurudeva and Other Indian Tales.* I had never owned a copy before, and I treasured the gift. Incidentally, Dennis was the only Mahabir, apart from his parents, to end his days in Trinidad. The rest all succumbed to the brain drain that left Trinidad the poorer for their departure.

Winston, the middle son and an island scholarship winner from QRC like Vidia and Eric Williams, was erudite and suave. He became Minister of Health in Dr. Williams's first Cabinet. (Mel had taken over Winston's medical practice in San Fernando before he met me.) Winston, too, climbed on to the PNM bandwagon, no doubt because he, like Dennis, thought that Williams was truly progressive, inclusive and fair-minded. However, he was gone after five years. He left the government and the country and emigrated to Canada. There he would write a book called *In and Out of Politics*.

Rodney and Claudia Mahabir had shepherded Mel on his arrival at Leeds University to begin his medical studies in England. (Rodney was in his final year there as a medical student.) At their first meeting Claudia had removed Mel's hat, got him to shave off his virgin moustache and suggested firmly that he should never again wear the green suit he had on. She also taught him to dance – and lost her flat in the process, presumably because of complaints about the noise. Mel was forever in her and Rodney's debt. As head of the students' union, Rodney had introduced Mel to many of the professors whom he might otherwise have taken years to meet. This, together with their close friendship, made their reaction to meeting me important to Mel and also catapulted him further in my direction.

While Mel courted me, I continued my studies and worked hard towards my exams in December. However, although my results were very good, I did not get the one and only island scholarship for girls for which all the students were competing. Instead, I was offered what was called an additional scholarship through St. Joseph's Convent. This was a viable alternative to the open or island scholarship, although there were certain conditions. The offer had to be accepted or rejected by 31st March 1958. Also, I had to sign a pledge to return to Trinidad and Tobago to work for the government for a number of years, or repay all the costs involved.

I baulked at the possibility of incurring what seemed to me a huge debt. I was simply unsure of where my future lay. I was aware that the mortgage on 26 Nepaul Street had still to be paid. Also, Mira needed my financial help to get to university and I was determined to give it. While my life remained on hold, or so it seemed, Mira was busily seeking admission to a university in Britain. She got over the hurdle of matriculation and was now awaiting replies from the universities to which she had applied. Our plan to study and work would require us to be together in roughly the same place in Britain. My situation was confused. I needed to examine my options. I had my whole life ahead of me. I was only nineteen. My disposition did not allow me to shake off or ignore the state of our affairs at home. I was also not committed, as yet, to the idea of marriage. I had always assumed that as long as I got the additional scholarship I would leave Trinidad with Mira. Instead Mira left on her own to study at the University of Leeds.

Mira (2nd right) posing under Pa's portrait before leaving for Leeds – with Sati, Nella and Savi

During my time of indecision, Ma's typical silence on matters that obviously troubled me was amazing. Both Ma and Pa always indicated that one should make one's own choices. The only bit of advice Pa had ever given me about marriage was straightforward. One must ask oneself: 'Do I want this person to be the father of my children?' In writing this, I recall with amusement one of Pa's female cousins who encouraged him to 'marry off the girls'. When she was leaving, Pa made some pointed remarks about the suggestion. Then, as soon as she had left, we learned another wise lesson, when an incensed Pa swore at 'that bitch!' Why didn't she marry off *her* daughter, who 'can't do a damn thing', to some worthless man? Once again we saw Pa's passionate desire to help us succeed at our studies and make as much of our lives as we wished to make.

The 31st March deadline was at hand. Then, with time running out for me, I received a letter from Sister Francis Xavier offering me a post as Senior Mistress in Geography at St. Joseph's Convent in San Fernando. Senior Mistress meant that with my Higher School certificate only, I would be completely in charge of teaching Geography to Forms IV, V and VI (the HSC class). Sister Francis's unwavering faith in me and her courage were inspiring and flattering. This offer, together with Melvin Akal's pledge to leave Trinidad for postgraduate studies, proved to be the tipping point. I gave up the scholarship.

In August 1958, exactly one year after our introduction, I married Melvin Akal. Kamla had returned to Trinidad at the end of July. She came back in time for my marriage at the Registrar General's Office at the Red House in Port of Spain. The occasion at the Red House is a topic that warrants little mention as it reminds me of my early morning panic on that day and my horrible hairstyle. I also recall the dour or even sour faces in the Registrar's Office, where stacks of musty folders were piled on a desk. I saw the curious people peeping through a doorway at the nervous bridal couples, and also heard some loud, typically Trinidadian witticisms about who was probably or obviously pregnant and who was not. It was not romantic! When the Registrar asked me for two shillings as his official fee for the ceremony, I almost burst into tears. I wanted to kill Mel. Over my mild objections, he had insisted that we have a simple, quiet wedding. I have never quite forgiven him.

Moving south along the old Southern Main Road that skirts the Gulf of Paria, one passes through the heartland of Caroni, beyond the settlements of Chaguanas, Couva, Claxton Bay and the oil refineries of Pointe-à-Pierre to the town of San Fernando. San Fernando was then still merely a town, although it was the industrial capital of the island. It would officially become a city only in the mid-1980s, when our friend Romesh Mootoo became its mayor.

Mel and Savi at the Registrar's office and after

For me, moving to San Fernando meant going to live in a strange, new place. Even newer and stranger was the fact that I was starting another phase of my life's journey, as the wife of someone I had only known for one year. For Mel, it was different. He had already lived and worked as a physician in San Fernando for about three years. Coming from St. James, with not a clue about the lie of the land, I left it to Mel to decide where we would live. For some reason, he chose to rent a house on what turned out to be a busy thoroughfare. No. 191 Pointe-à-Pierre Road became our first address.

The driveway into our garage was at a steep angle from the main road, and near to a busy and more or less blind corner. At that busy corner, a side road led to the fairly new, up-market housing development called Vistabella, which fringed the Gulf of Paria and offered panoramic views of its coastline. Pointe-à-Pierre Road led directly to the Public Library Corner at the top of High Street, which was the main commercial centre of San Fernando. Lots of taxis plied the route, so transportation into town was quick and easy.

With the school term starting in the first week of September we had barely a month to settle in. We needed that month. Our rented house lacked storage cupboards, and it also needed fresh paint as well as new draperies to allow some measure of privacy, because the houses next door pressed close to us. Guided by our friends Zeinool and Jaffo Hosein, we tackled these various tasks. We did so even though we had no idea how long we would be staying in Trinidad before moving on to Great Britain.

The house was small, even humble, with only two bedrooms, but it was more than adequate for our needs. The front bedroom, for example, was large enough to be subdivided into a small room for emergency medical treatment, with a door opening on to the front porch. Our living and dining room ran parallel to the bedrooms. An L-shaped corridor separated the kitchen from the bathroom. The back door opened on to a flat, unkempt tract of land. We never quite managed to convert this area into a proper lawn, although we used it fairly regularly for small barbecue parties. One of Mel's earliest and most profitable investments was the purchase of a German Pfaff sewing machine for me. With the machine, I not only made my clothes but also all the draperies, bedspreads and tablecloths we needed. The furnishings were minimal. With a stove, a refrigerator, some pots and pans and a set of cutlery we were ready to face the world. (Mel brought with him his old bed.) Our cheap kitchen table would eventually be replaced by the cypre-topped dining table which, like the sewing machine, is still in use.

My new job started in September 1958, the last term of the academic year. The Cambridge University-administered tests leading to the School Certificate and Higher School Certificate were held in November through to December, with results released the following March. With nervous students facing these crucial exams and as a new teacher, I had to spot and pick topics that might ensure that both the SC and HSC classes covered enough ground. By the start of the new academic year I was assured and comfortable and the students responded by performing well, making my job enjoyable yet still challenging. Sister Francis monitored my marks with the results and gave me the encouragement that spurred me on.

Meanwhile, at home in 191 Point-à-Pierre Road, we seemed to have little in common with our immediate neighbours. On one side, the old Seventh Day Adventist couple whose house mirrored ours lived quietly and conservatively. On the other side, a family that included several young men and their friends learning to play the tenor pan seemed content and persistent, if not exactly gifted. The blind street corner and heavy motor traffic did not encourage walking around in the neighbourhood; besides, I was very pregnant.

On 24th May 1959, Mel and I welcomed our first-born, a son. We named him Ashvin Rai. Two weeks later, disaster almost struck when our baby survived a dash to the hospital. Dr. Dan, a pulmonary specialist there, deftly prevented his death from asphyxia. Both baby and parents were traumatised. I could see that Mel, being both Ashvin's father and a doctor, was at least as anguished as I was. The following day we collected our son, took him home and tried to relax as parents.

Ashvin Rai in San Fernando

As it turned out, we lived and worked in San Fernando longer than anticipated. For the next two years, Shiva and Nella would come from Nepaul Street to spend nearly all of their vacations with Mel and me. Sometimes Mel's nephew, Kenrick Thomas, came along as a companion. Dinner then was almost always the same – fried fish and hops bread, with an occasional order from Charlie's Black Pudding or a 'Marsang Takeaway' of Chinese food. At some point, I inherited Pinky from Ma, and our cooking improved to the point where Mel could restart his Wednesday lunches with one or both of the Mahabir brothers.

It took a while for me to settle into marriage. Rather naively I had thought that it would be an easy extension of courtship. I was not aware that my marriage would involve so many other people. At times I was almost panicked into thinking that I had made a terrible mistake. Fortunately for me, my older and rock-steady husband, along with the stern demands of my job, kept me afloat. The job, while challenging, was amazingly satisfying and the results equally gratifying. The students, not very far off in age from my own, were disciplined and responsive. Quite a few became my friends for life and a few still call or visit. By teaching in San Fernando I was able to support Mira at the University of Leeds (Vidia paid her university fees). My longed-for university career would be deferred. But my determination to get a university degree did not wane.

Meanwhile, in Nepaul Street, the tempo of life had changed again. Mira had left for England by ship, and stayed in London with Vidia and Pat before leaving for Leeds. At No. 26, there were now Ma, Kamla, Shiva and Nella. Shiva was thirteen and at QRC, and Nella was six and at Tranquillity. Asserting her seniority, Kamla insisted on making every major decision for the children, or so it seemed. Her decree that Shiva should elect to do the science subjects, rather than languages and literature, or other subjects, was met by his stony resistance. His response was to fail the science subjects outright. Under Kamla, Nella was corrected and scolded perhaps too often. This brought tears to Ma's eyes at times and put some fear of Kamla into Nella, a fear she never quite lost. But the fact was obvious and compelling that Kamla loved us deeply and cared about our future.

Living apart in San Fernando, I saw my visits to No. 26 Nepaul Street confined to weekends, when we had the opportunity to spend time with Ma, Shiva and Nella. In this way a special closeness developed among us.

Nella, Savi, Sati, Crisen and Shiva at Maracas Bay

As often as we could, we took Shiva and Nella to Maracas Bay. Shiva, growing up, liked going to the horse races on the Savannah when Sati and Crisen came to town. Kamla also had a busy social life, but kept different friends. I still made all her dresses.

Apart from family interests, our social life in both Port of Spain and San Fernando proved entertaining, novel and enlightening. At the centre of our social circle were Rodney and Claudia Mahabir and their friends. Apart from a few unmarried males and females, these friends were young professionals with young families, although everyone was at least a decade older than I was. My first date with Mel had introduced me to Carlyle and Barbara Kangaloo as well as the Mahabirs. The Kangaloos would become our pedro-playing partners in San Fernando, between baby-feeding times. They already had one set of twins and would go on to produce a family of seven children, including a second pair of twins. Their children would grow into accomplished adults. Two of them, Wendell and Christine, would occupy high offices in our land. Also among our happy, optimistic and accomplished social circle were the Lairds, the Richardsons, the Achongs, the Mitra Sinanans and the Tsoi-a-Sues. Colin and Jeanette Laird were a young couple who, on their return from London, lived on St. Clair Avenue opposite QRC. Colin, an Englishman, had lived most of his adult life in Trinidad with his Trinidadian-born wife of mixed heritage. He was a brilliant architect who designed Queen's Hall, still considered a jewel of a theatre by most of our people. The Lairds had three young children, all under twelve. Willie Richardson was in the Foreign Service. He had recently returned to Trinidad with his wife and their son. They were gracious people of African heritage. The Mitra Sinanans were a well-known couple from large and extended families. Mitra was already a renowned lawyer locally, but the larger Sinanan family boasted many other lawyers and also doctors. Mitra and his wife had two daughters close to my age. The Tsoi-a-Sues lived not far away from us in San Fernando. Monica was very house-proud and I learned quite a bit from her about housekeeping.

Of all our friends, however, the closest and most supportive in our early days of marriage, and until their deaths, were Zeinool and Zobida 'Jaffo' Hosein. They and their children provided for me, in particular, a home away from home. Zobida, or Jaff as we usually called her, was an excellent cook and very warm, although strict with her children. She was the elder daughter of the Rahamut family, well-known merchants in San Fernando. Zeinool, a cousin of Mel, often accompanied him to Port of Spain in the early days of Mel's courtship.

So many of our friends of that time have died, their children scattered all over the world! This global spreading is not only a pattern for the children of the first generation of Indian immigrants who came to work on the plantations (people Dr. Williams once scorned as 'a bunch of transients'). The continuing flight through emigration and the brain drain of peoples of all races and ethnicities out of Trinidad and Tobago suggest that Dr. Williams could be seen as the person mainly responsible for this damaging exodus. Determined to hold on to power, he became almost paranoid in looking for enemies. This trait made many people, including some of his most ardent former supporters, eventually apprehensive about their future. Those with the means, and many with the finest brains, fled the island in the hope of finding greener pastures elsewhere. This flight has not abated in the fifty-five years or more since Independence. Now the brakes are being applied by the so-called First World countries. Stringent rules applying to visas and tougher requirements for immigration limit the choice and number of possible destinations. New routes and new ways of escape will have to be found, sometimes with traumatic consequences.

# CHAPTER 6

## *A Season of Changes*

At Nepaul Street, the household was starting to get used to my marriage and life with Mel in San Fernando, as well as to Mira's absence in the UK, when Ma sprung a surprise on us all. It would be the first of a few changes in 1959, one swiftly following the other.

Ma, who had never worked outside the home since her marriage in 1929, took a job with her brother Simbhoonath at his quarry in Petit Valley, at that time still a semi-rural area outside Port of Spain, but already much changed from my girlhood days when we had lived there on my grandmother's estate. Now, with her new job at the quarry, Ma left the house at dawn and returned at dusk. The quarry lands lay on the opposite side of the valley from the Great House and cocoa estate, both of which had been abandoned after Nanee's death. (The estate had been inherited by Simbhoonath, who passed it to one of his brothers-in-law to be developed into residential plots. No effort was made to have the Great House occupied or rented and it simply rotted away.) Ma's job required her to check the trucks and their loads, to take a note of the transactions and to check on the state of all machinery in use. We all had to get used to her new vocabulary, which included D7s and D9s, tractors and crushers, overburden and blue metal, and all the various machine parts that had to be serviced, repaired or replaced. Suddenly and quickly our quiet Ma, usually in the background, occasionally murmuring remarks, was becoming chatty and authoritative. At the quarry she would don her hard hat and wellingtons, and climb ladders to peer into the trays of the trucks. She could tell at a glance how many yards of material the trucks were taking out. Ma loved her job. The men had to respect and answer to her, and that included the often fiercely independent truck drivers. At work she knew the idlers from the good workers and she never seemed to mind the dust and the noise.

Ma was also in charge of buying and transporting sticks of dynamite to the quarry. This meant that permission had to be sought and given by the police to purchase and transport explosives. She became so well-known over the years that pretty soon she was being invited to the annual Policemen's Ball. I'm not sure if she ever accepted but I would not be surprised to learn that she did attend at least once. About her salary Ma remained tight-lipped. At first, because she was so secretive, we began to suspect that her pay was embarrassingly small. But the job made her financially independent and more secure than she had been for years. Also, she clearly was happy.

For Shiva and Nella, and even for Kamla, this was a drastic change. The tea sessions at home, while they did not end, became very different. No more hot crispy fried fish or breadfruit chips. Not easily placated, Shiva always felt that the coconut turnovers which became a regular feature had been fobbed off on him. When my first son was born I had to make do without the presence and guidance of Ma. She had become a busy woman with a twelve-hour workday.

As usual, the long school vacation allowed Kamla to travel abroad. On the day the vacation started, Ma would put Shiva and Nella on a bus and send them to San Fernando to stay with me. One morning, when Kamla was away in Jamaica, the telephone rang. It was not a patient looking for Dr. Akal, but Kamla calling to say that she was getting married. Would I look after choosing a wedding sari and a matching blouse for her? Her husband-to-be was Hari Tewari, a businessman and a member of the family that had befriended Pa years before in Jamaica, when he had attended the course in Social Welfare. Ma had never travelled outside Trinidad, nor been on an aeroplane. But she was as intrepid now as she had been as a young woman when she first came to live in Luis Street and decided to do a sewing course at the Royal Victoria Institute. She packed her bags and set off for Jamaica. Her visit came as a surprise to Kamla, who was expecting my husband, Mel, to arrive instead. But Ma was warmly welcomed by the Tewari family, whom she had met in Trinidad many years before.

Kamla was, of course, a most beautiful bride. Her wedding album, which has now vanished, handsomely captured her beauty and the lavish celebrations provided by the Tewari family. Ma herself also looked happy and lovely in the photographs. Kamla and Hari were to live in Jamaica, where Kamla taught at the elite Wolmer's Boys School.

Life in 26 Nepaul Street became a shadow of what it once was. Only on weekends would the house spring to life. Ma would be at home and my son Rai kept the household busy.

Being the only two adult Naipaul sisters left in the island, Sati and I developed a new closeness. In growing up, especially during our teenage years, Sati had treated Mira and me as humbugs, pests. Yet I knew her friends and always got along well with them. The two brothers-in-law, Crisen and Mel, also got on well. As a merry foursome we began to spend a lot of our free time together, especially over the holiday seasons at Easter, Christmas and Carnival.

On Carnival weekend, Nepaul Street was brimful of people. Ma never minded the crush. Anna Mahase, who later became a dynamic and successful principal of St. Augustine Girls' High School, would arrive on the Friday of the long Carnival weekend with a live chicken, its feet sticking up in the air and its head down in a bag. That chicken became our dinner on Monday evening. It would be curried, and Ma made chicken pelau every Carnival Tuesday.

While the friends staying the weekend with us changed over the years, Anna Mahase remained a constant. Carnival fêtes had sprung up in many well-known clubs and places such as the popular Bel Air Restaurant and even in a hangar at Piarco Airport. These fêtes, or dance parties, had begun as economic ventures to acquire funds to run the steel bands and subsidise costume-making. The dates of the fêtes seldom clashed, except very close to Carnival itself, and we were able to go to such fashionable settings as the Chinese Association and the Perseverance, Cosmos, Portuguese and Bel Air clubs. Carnival had become not simply two days, the Monday and Tuesday before the start of Lent, but a season unto itself. In the crowded house at such times, Anna always chose to sleep with Ma in the SlumberKing bed. She knew that Ma would be up early every morning, and she then would have the bed all to herself until whenever.

In those days there was nothing of the street carnival as we know it today, with its beads and bikinis, bulging bodies, flailing limbs and coarse sexual gyrations. Costumed bands with historical themes were the order of the day. Veteran band leaders such as George Bailey ('Back to Africa'), Edmund Hart ('Flag Wavers of Siena'), Cito Velasquez and Stephen Leung, as well as outstanding individuals such as the European-born Wilfred Strasser with his clever *trompe l'oeil* cameos and other truck-borne representations, were joined eventually by younger, equally exciting creative minds such as the artists Peter Minshall and Wayne Berkeley. A large band then numbered in the hundreds, not thousands as they now do, and they hit the streets urged on by traditional dance bands or steel band orchestras. Spectators eagerly lined the streets, or went to the Grandstand at the Queen's Park Savannah to fill the bleachers set up temporarily to accommodate hordes of onlookers.

This was Trinidadian imagination and freedom of expression at its best. Apart from these larger bands, there were numerous minstrel bands and individuals taken from local folklore, wonderful characters in the form of towering bats, blue devils, dancing *burrokeets*, *Dames Lorraines*, the Devil of the tropical forests, or the equally scary *La Diablesse*. Amerindian characters, most of whom presented themselves as 'chiefs', with imposing, feathered head-pieces, fought the elements and ambled and danced their way in the face of the stiff breezes that sometimes tunnelled through the streets.

Perhaps above all, I loved to see the bands playing what we termed 'sailor mas'. Undoubtedly influenced by memories of World War II, the players typically wore white trousers and white jackets with military braid and buttons and scores of medals and ribbons on their chests. These outfits, topped by elaborate headpieces, were often extravagantly worked with sequins and jewels. Faces were generously whitened with talcum powder, and the players held up threatening tins of talc to use as they pleased on bystanders. This common practice gave rise to a Trinidad saying: 'You can't play mas if you 'fraid powder!' This is much the same as saying, 'If you can't face the heat, stay out of the kitchen!'

Unfortunately, Carnival also meant occasional clashes between rival steel bands, which could be bloody and disruptive, if tame, in truth, compared to today's standards of urban violence in Port of Spain and elsewhere around the world. Ma would always remind us to avoid dangerous areas in the city when she knew we would be 'chipping' down the road as the sun began to set and we made our way back home on evenings.

With Kamla's marriage and departure for Jamaica, and with Ma's job at the quarry, the house at 26 Nepaul Street had thinned out to a point that seemed almost like desertion. Shiva and Nella, returning from school to an empty house, had to fend for themselves until Ma returned in the evening. Shiva found solace in books, but Nella, at seven years, naturally felt more than a little lost. Their situation, in spite of the difference in age between them, bound them for life. That was perhaps one of the few truly positive elements in their young lives.

In 1961, we in Trinidad met Vidia's wife, Pat, for the first time. Vidia and Pat came as guests of the Trinidad government. Dr. Williams, no doubt with the encouragement of Winston Mahabir, hoped that Vidia would spend six months at home and later produce some sort of writing on the Caribbean. It was a generous offer that included a monthly stipend and the use of a motor car. Vidia needed to get a driver's licence.

Vidia and Pat lived at Nepaul Street with Ma, Shiva and Nella. The house, quiet during the day, would come alive late on afternoons. Our normal weekend stay in Port of Spain was curtailed during their visit. During the six months, Vidia also travelled to Guyana and Jamaica. Pat took a job at Bishop Anstey High School in Port of Spain, where she taught mainly Latin. Bishop's, as it is commonly known, is a girls' secondary school of the highest repute, catering mainly to Protestants. Like its main rival, St. Joseph's Convent, Bishop Anstey has maintained the standards that made it deeply respected in the old days.

Pat was petite and pretty. Mild-mannered and soft-spoken, she quietly and yet zealously guarded her privacy. It was difficult to get to know her. She spoke very little of herself, her family and her general background.

Nepaul Street, 1961: Savi, Ma, Vidia, Nella, Sati, Seromany (Dhan's daughter) and Pat

Nepaul Street, circa 1961: Sati, Savi, Kamla, Pat

With her teaching at Bishop Anstey we discovered that history had been her main speciality at Oxford, although I never learned the name of the college she attended there. She seemed very fond of an aunt in Gloucester and had one sister, Eleanor, who was a bit of tomboy, she said. Eleanor evidently did not like Vidia. In this respect she was like her parents. Pat said little more about her family or herself. Years later, we would learn that she had always kept a diary in which she recorded at length many of the feelings she bottled up in public. But she herself was liked. I still meet people whom she taught in Trinidad and who speak fondly of her. She certainly was kind, if also careful, in dealing with Shiva and Nella.

The only negative aspect of her stay in Trinidad, at least the only one that we knew of, was that she believed that the insomnia that would haunt her for years to come began there in our house on Nepaul Street. While I thought that this might have been because of the tropical heat, to her it seemed a combination of cocks crowing at all hours and the general noises of the neighbourhood. No. 26 was close to the Rialto Cinema and even closer to people living around us who seemed never to switch off their Rediffusion box. The noises affected Pat, just as for me the metallic scraping sounds of the pre-dawn scavengers were almost unbearable. Our box was not kept on all day, although some of us looked forward to the hourly news broadcasts or enjoyed the music, from the American Top Twenty hit parade to *Indian Talent on Parade*. The latter was the first, brief programme of Indian melodies to be aired on the radio in Trinidad, starting in 1947. Hosting this programme was Kamaluddin Mohammed, later a PNM government minister.

Pat's presence and her mild exhortations, his frequent travels and the presence of our spouses, when they were around, made Vidia a lot more subdued than on his 1956 visit. Besides, the Mahabir brothers, old friends, kept him busy and curious. Pat and Vidia accepted the hospitality not only of the Mahabirs, but also of many of our friends. He was not always perfectly gracious and relaxed. One visit to Mayaro from San Fernando, on the other side of the island, on a dark night of intense rain, with Vidia an erratic but insistent driver, cannot be erased from my memory. We both survived – he to write, and I to tell the tale!

As we were all working, Pat and Vidia visited Sati and Crisen and Mel and me on weekends, or during the school vacations. We used these occasions to cover the four corners of the island, but never made it to Tobago. Mel, happily, recorded on camera most of these trips and we managed to preserve quite a few pictures in spite of our movements over the years.

After Pat and Vidia left for Jamaica, Shiva and even little Nella were glad to see him go. They liked telling a story that seemed to bring them great cheer. It was about Vidia and our dog, Bhupendra of Peachly Nagar. We called him Bhuppie for short. (He had been thrown in as lagniappe when a man paid us a hundred dollars for PA 1192, Pa's old Ford Prefect.) Bhuppie was a dog of mixed breed. He must have had some large measure of terrier, with his bushy brown hair. Strangers visiting the house often found Bhuppie sitting upright next to them, particularly when they sat in one of the low, cushioned Morris chairs in the living-room. We liked Bhuppie, and Bhuppie seemed to like us – but not all of us.

It seems that one fine day Vidia decided to take Bhuppie for a stroll on the Queen's Park Savannah, across from QRC. Although he always wore a collar, Bhuppie had never been on a leash, but Vidia, a switch in hand, insisted on restraining him with one. Apparently in quick time, and much sooner than Vidia had anticipated, the walk turned into a run, then into a rout. With switch in hand but with no sign of leash or dog, a tousled-haired Vidia, sweating, exhausted and battered, returned home alone. Muttering and swearing about 'that blasted dog', he vented his anger and ranted on and on about our failure to instil proper training and discipline into Bhuppie, who was now lost forever through no fault of Vidia's. In the middle of this harangue, Bhuppie strolled into the yard, nonchalantly trailing his leash behind him. He was not even panting. Going straight to his bowl of water, he lapped it up. When he was done, he glanced at Vidia, bared his teeth and growled, curled up into a heap of fluff and fell asleep.

Shiva and Nella were old enough to see the funny side of this episode. They believed it was just retribution for trying to teach an old dog new tricks.

Left alone once more in the house, Ma, Shiva and Nella were forging a new and strange existence. Ma was forty-six, Shiva was fifteen and Nella eight. Ma tended the roses and the red bougainvillea that was now climbing up the ylang-ylang tree. The anthurium patch was in need of attention, but the bleeding heart over it on the narrow trellis Pa and Vidia had built was flourishing. What a difference that light vine made at the back of the open wooden lattice in our living and dining room.

In early August of 1961, after years of saving and planning, Mel and I finally fixed our departure from Trinidad. Mel was giving up his practice in family medicine and we would leave San Fernando. Our house in Pointe-à-Pierre was stark and basic and, like my old home in Nepaul Street, faced west and got the full blast of the afternoon sun, which often made it like an oven. We had tried weakly to create a lawn and plant a few shrubs, but water was a severe problem. Coming from Port of Spain I found it difficult to adjust to the scarcity of water. San Fernando, the nation's second city and its so-called industrial capital, supplied water to its citizens between six and eight on mornings and between four and six on evenings. Our landlord refused to install or let us install tanks because, he claimed, he would thus have created 'a precedent'. We adopted the position that we were camping until the time we would leave for Great Britain. The lack of water was one of the main reasons we spent our weekends in Port of Spain. I was not sad to leave that house. We had spent three years since the day of our marriage trying to fulfil our family obligations. At least, we believed so. Now we had to move on with our own plans.

Mira had completed her BA in Languages at Leeds University but wasn't ready or eager to come back to Trinidad. When she learnt that our destination was Edinburgh, she applied to Moray House there to do a postgraduate degree in Education. Mel's own objective was a postgraduate course in dermatology to complement his family medicine practice. I would embark on a degree course at Edinburgh University. This course would take three or four years to accomplish. We left Trinidad with our two-year-old son Rai and our faithful Pinky, who now lived with my family as nanny and housekeeper. We also shipped our Humber Hawk motor car and my precious sewing machine. On board the ship we met quite a few Trinidadians, including Lenore Dorset, whom I knew well from our days at St. Joseph's Convent. The voyage took ten (not always smooth) days. When it was over I was happy to get back on terra firma. Disembarking at Southampton, however, it took many hours to clear the car and our considerable baggage. During the drive to London, I discovered to my horror that Mel the physician was not a competent map-reader. After various missed turns we arrived in Streatham to an anxious Vidia and Pat. We stayed with them and were also reunited with Mira, who was staying with Ivy Thomas's daughter Maureen. Vidia was nervously awaiting the publication of his most ambitious novel to date, *A House for Mr. Biswas*.

Moving on to Leeds, where two of Mel's brothers lived, we had a short and unsettling stay there before facing the challenges and tribulations of finding accommodation in Edinburgh. We finally secured a ground-floor apartment at No. 41 Bonaly Road, opposite a public park. Our landlord, a Mr. Zykrovitch, was a Polish immigrant who checked on us regularly. He needed to be sure, it seemed, that our two-year-old son was not wrecking his furniture. He never thanked us for keeping the apartment in a much better state than we found it. On the other hand, we never let him know that Mira was staying with us and sleeping on his pull-out couch in the living-room. We also ignored other occupants of the building who objected to our Humber Hawk being parked in front of the building. The nearest garage was ten minutes away on foot. Otherwise we were good tenants. The rent was always presented two or three days before its due date.

At the end of a year Mel had completed his course, and I had been invited by the faculty to join the programme leading to an honours degree in Geography. During the year we had hardly moved outside Edinburgh. We did not have a telephone and were barely in touch with Vidia and Pat. We wrote to Ma and Sati and Crisen and heard from them regularly. And we were delighted when we received a Christmas cake from our good friend Monica Tsoi-a-Sue, although Hogmanay, and not Christmas, was the big celebration in Edinburgh. Also keeping us at home was the fact that for several months we seemed to be virtually snowbound.

As a city Edinburgh is imposing. The Castle on the Hill, overlooking, it seems, everything; the glaciated Arthur's Seat not far off, and the historic and beautiful Holyrood Palace in the centre of the city give Edinburgh an ancient and almost magical feeling. The old and distinguished university, with its steps hollowed and polished from use over the ages, was a daily reminder of the special quality of the area that was our temporary home. The weather was certainly memorable. Edinburgh is indeed the Windy City, and I often found myself back where I started in trying to turn a corner. The slippery cobblestones and driving sleet compelled me to buy a pair of sensible boots. The distance to cover between buildings and lectures made me more fleet of foot than I had ever been.

Being older and married, I was a safe friend for many young men at university. But there were a few as old as I was, or older, whose journey to the university had taken even longer than mine, and I found them particularly interesting. I remember Schuyler Jones in particular, who had lived in parts of Africa and Kabul in Afghanistan for years and had published a book called *Under the African Sun*. His main interest was anthropology. He hated Geography, which unfortunately for him was compulsory in our course. His magnificent pictures in *National Geographic* magazine were his ticket to the university, perhaps assisted by his wife Lis, who was an architect. Another friend, Phillip Di Ciacca, to whom I never got to say goodbye, would have been in a quandary about how to dispose of my briefcase, which I left behind with all of Mel's love letters in it!

At the end of his course, Mel set about finding a job. This proved far more challenging than we had both anticipated. (We recalled now and then how Uncle Simbhoonath had been compelled to give up his attempt to settle in England because he could not find suitable employment despite his legal skills as a solicitor.) Outside our courses, we had made few Scottish friends. Attempts to explore a few places did not bring us any joy. Our life threatened to become staid. Mira had successfully completed her course at Moray House and was undecided what to do next. The cold weather sometimes seemed too much for us. Mel became seriously concerned about our son Rai not having sufficient time out of doors.

With the new academic year approaching, Mel began to show signs of agitation. As a non-Scottish national he could not find a suitable job in Scotland in spite of his experience and qualifications. When he eventually got a job offer it was in England. This meant living away from us. Within two weeks of the English job offer, he made up his mind to return to Trinidad as I continued my studies at Edinburgh. He would travel with Rai and Pinky; our motor car and my sewing machine would be shipped back later.

Alone now in Edinburgh, I began to look for new accommodation. Eventually I got lucky and found an apartment in a classy neighbourhood. My landlady was one of the earliest female graduates of Oxford and had lived in India for years. My walk from her house to the university was across the Commons and very pleasant. She expected me to be more 'Indian' in knowledge and attitude than I was or could be, but therein lay the topic of many good and long conversations over cups of tea.

Nevertheless, by the middle of my second year, I found myself becoming more and more uneasy. The prospect of having to travel back and forth to visit my young son and husband in Trinidad became untenable. I had also begun to change my mind about further studies in Geography. I began to think of Law as an alternative course. I spoke to the head of the department, Professor Watson, and explained my predicament. He was sympathetic. I said my goodbyes to him and to two of my fellow Trinidadians at Edinburgh, Ken Ramchand, who would publish the first systematic study of the West Indian novel, and Mahadeo Bissoon. I left quickly and flew to Jamaica to spend a few days with Kamla, who now had a son, Ved. I came back home to a very happy husband, a welcoming family and a little boy whom I had to coax into cuddling again. Mel had returned to San Fernando and to his old medical practice and got into gear pretty quickly. Fairly soon, we slipped into our pleasant old routines, but in a country that was going through historic and in some respects ominous changes.

## CHAPTER 7

### *And May God Bless Our Nation*

For most of the people of Trinidad and Tobago, the attainment of independence from Great Britain on 31st August 1962, along with the composition of a new national anthem to replace the venerated 'God Save the Queen', promised an illustrious new beginning for our islands. For other citizens, however, it was more of a mirage and even a threat than a harbinger of success. The most pessimistic among us predicted our unsteady morphing over the coming years into an uncivil civic limbo, unless we looked squarely at our inadequacies as a culture and addressed them boldly. Were we prepared to do so?

Most of us naturally looked above all to our elected leaders, as well as to our teachers, notably our university faculty, for our critical civic leadership. However, our elected leaders had already demonstrated telling signs of inadequacy, especially in the sad, swift collapse of the Federation of the West Indies, founded in 1958, but also in the ugly political tensions that had roiled Trinidad leading up to the formal conference that ended in Independence. An ill-advised referendum in Jamaica, won by anti-Federation forces, had gutted the infant Federation. As for our educators, the Jamaica-based University of the West Indies survived this collapse, but in a new form that suggested both dynamism and a new insularity. Guyana pulled out altogether and founded its own school, but regional UWI campuses opened in Trinidad in 1962 (the same year UWI itself became independent) and in Barbados in 1963.

Were we now on the right path? We needed expert guides to help us become, for the first time, our own masters. This task was never going to be a simple one. And yet some people – certainly our demagogues – claimed that it was both simple and easy. Colonialism had long bestowed privileges on the favoured few, especially local white people and British expatriates. It had kept buried, or tried to bury, the ambitions and the talents of the majority. Our political leaders were seeking to assure us now that new laws and practices would throw out what was archaic and unjust and ring in the modern and the fair. The civil service, for example, which some observers had once seen as the playground of foreigners with varying degrees of skill and experience, was to change. With Independence, such people would have to go. Our people would take over. And our lives would thus improve immeasurably.

The former colonisers indeed departed, to be replaced for the most part by native sons and daughters. But Trinidad and Tobago presented a complex set of challenges that could not be resolved easily. Most of the other islands of the Caribbean had populations that were not wholly homogeneous; Trinidad, however, was probably the most heterogeneous of them all, and therefore probably the most difficult to control. Ruled but largely neglected by Spain from 1498 to 1797, when the British conquerors arrived, its Spanish people had been radically diversified by the official Royal Cedula for Population, which in 1783 invited Catholic immigrants in particular to settle in Trinidad. The Cedula encouraged the arrival of French or French-Creole people, along with their slaves, as well as other people neither French-Creole nor slaves. Many of these newcomers had been displaced by the violence of the Haitian Revolution and by other disruptive events elsewhere in the Caribbean, and later by violence in Europe, as in the case of royalists fleeing the French Revolution. The Cedula regenerated Trinidad.

Thus bolstered, the plantation economies, absolutely dependent on manual labour, fostered first the importation of enslaved Africans, then waves of bonded immigrants from other parts of the world. When slavery finally ended in 1838, the problem of finding workers for the cane fields and the still relatively lucrative production of sugar grew acute, as the former slaves in effect boycotted the plantations. Less than a century later, the Trinidad population almost defied description and categorisation. No single group was truly uniform in and of itself. Each was marked by subtle internal differences in class, colour, caste and sub-caste, as well as by religious and other separations, despite the large umbrellas held aloft in the name of Roman Catholicism, Protestantism, Hinduism and Islam. Among the various subgroups making up 'our nation' were not only descendants of the original Spanish, who were fast fading as a recognisable entity, but also an almost maddening variety of factions that identified themselves as in one way or another fundamentally English, French, German, Portuguese, Syrian, Lebanese or Chinese (not to exhaust the list). Also disappearing were the increasingly mixed-race remnants of the Carib and Arawak peoples who had inhabited the islands before the arrival of Columbus.

With the dawning of Independence, the largest group of all in our population comprised people of West African descent, the emancipated descendants of the slaves. Marked by sharp divisions of education, religion, colour and class, this group was in many ways dominant while in other ways suppressed. Because of their musical creativity, displayed especially in the homegrown calypso and, even more ingeniously, the steel band, but also because of their colourful language and personal style, they tended to define what it meant, in the minds of many people, to be Trinidadian. But they were not without rivals among the various populations in Trinidad. Comprising the second largest group were those almost equally born in adversity, though part of a system that was, unlike slavery, individually finite. They, too, were blessed with natural gifts and, in addition, possessed settled historical and religious traditions. These people were the descendants of the indentured servants brought from India starting in 1845, in the only truly successful scheme among the several attempts by our former European masters to replace the pool of African labour lost when slavery ended.

This mélange of humanity made up the 'Rainbow Country' that Archbishop Desmond Tutu of the Republic of South Africa would later call us when he visited Trinidad, to a fully justified hero's welcome, in 1987. But if the good archbishop meant the words as a compliment, as he surely did, they masked social problems almost impossible to solve completely. These problems would bedevil Trinidad in the decades that followed Independence in 1962.

Money, remarkably for what many must have regarded as a lowly 'Third World' country, was among the least of our problems. Our natural pitch lake at La Brea in the south, oil fields developed mainly in the twentieth century and unusually rich offshore natural gas fields found later gave Trinidad and Tobago a unique economic advantage and attracted foreign investors. Compared to many other former colonies, we were rich.

The colonial government had been paternalistic. They governed by the rule of law, mainly British law. The law was supreme. Rules guarding all institutions deemed important were codified, gazetted and available to the general populace after being publicised through the government printery. A hierarchical sense of order was maintained in politics, economics, law, government, health and education. Religion, although not codified, appeared to follow suit. Anglicanism and Roman Catholicism were at the top, and Africa-centred 'shouter' cults near or at the bottom. Non-Christian religions, notably Hinduism but also Islam, had put down deep roots but undoubtedly were seen by people with the most social prestige as exotic, anomalous and persistently disruptive.

The only institution where one's status, role and responsibility were not codified to the same degree was the family. Households based mainly on the model of the nuclear family, limited to parents and their children, thrived mainly among the wealthy or the newly emerging professional classes. Otherwise, most people were part of extended families. This was certainly true of our Hindu society. It seems equally a fact that among Afro-Trinidadians, men quite often left behind them single-parent households led by mothers and grandmothers who bore the brunt of domestic burdens.

These men – with often devastating consequences for the young – seemed largely to ignore Melville Herskovitz's dictum that 'no child should be born into this world without a man, and one man at that to call father'. Social and economic distress would plague these single-parent, matrilineal and often overcrowded homes.

It was in this climate, around the late 1950s and the early 1960s, that the new breed of politicians in Trinidad and Tobago faced the task of earning the same degree of trust that the colonial government, for all its flaws, had once inspired. The task of these politicians was simultaneously to fulfil the needs of a pluralistic, volatile society and also to keep the peace.

By this time, the name Capildeo was synonymous with politics – oppositional politics – in Trinidad. If many viewed it with approval, many others viewed it with contempt. The difference depended on one's political affiliation, which in Trinidad largely involved whether one was of Indian or of African descent. The fact that my mother had been born Droapatie Capildeo, and my father had married into her family, meant there was little chance that we Naipauls could be anything but pro-Capildeo in politics. For us, this fact was both inspiring and a shadow over our lives.

Among my earliest recollections was the period when my mother's brother, Simbhoonath, entered the local political arena in Chaguanas. He was not yet twenty, but he had been born to lead. His father, Pundit Capildeo, had built the imposing Lion House as a kind of minor princely citadel on the main road in the heart of Chaguanas. At that time, Hindus in the region regarded the pundit as perhaps their supreme community leader. His birth as a Brahmin, his knowledge of Hindi and Sanskrit, his habitual service to other Indians and his evident prosperity in a world generally hostile to Indians undergirded his prestige. Simbhoonath was only eleven when his father died in 1926 in India, but his mother, our grandmother Soogee, acknowledged him at once as the titular head of the household. She would be his loyal regent. To underscore his pre-eminence, despite the fact that he was the eighth-born among her children, she made sure that Simbhoo was called 'Dada' (Big Brother) by his nine sisters. The household catered to him at every turn. A photograph on display of Pundit Capildeo and Simbhoo, the latter wearing the *mohan mala* or sign of esteem, indicated to all visitors that his father had considered him, his first son, as his main heir. Two other sons, Rudranath, who was four years younger than Simbhoonath, and Omkarnath, were born after Simbhoo. Sadly, Omkarnath died as a child, but the patrician Capildeos now had the proverbial 'heir and a spare' to fulfil their family destiny.

Simbhoo and Rudra, my uncles, grew into authoritative young men under Soogee's vigilant eyes. They basked in the devotion not only of their mother and nine sisters and but also of most other people within and outside Chaguanas. As the town grew in size and importance, it became the centre of commercial, religious and governmental activities in Central Trinidad. With such a background, and even before people began to conceive of island-wide political parties in raging conflict, these two scions of the Capildeo family were admired by people, mainly but by no means only Indian people, as young men born to lead.

Simbhoonath attended Naparima College in San Fernando before moving to QRC. He had the books of Hindu scripture his father had left behind but, perhaps because he did not have his father at home to guide and push him, he turned from preparing to be a pundit to entering instead the field of law. He established a name for himself as a lawyer and a politician, starting at the age of nineteen in Local Board elections in his home town, Chaguanas. This town would be his political base, and later that of his younger brother, when they became household names in Trinidad.

Rudranath, who had all his secondary schooling at QRC, had a dazzling career there. His academic achievements, capped by winning an island scholarship, led on to three degrees in mathematics and physics at the University of London, including a doctorate, and then to faculty appointments there. In 1956, he also studied law successfully in London. He lived there for many years before political changes brought him back home. At first, he seemed to have an eminent place assured for him outside politics, when, in 1959, Dr. Williams made him head of the new Polytechnic Institute in Port of Spain. However, this post proved inadequate to his sense of his and the nation's needs. In 1960, he was elected leader of the Democratic Labour Party (DLP), which had been founded from a merger of Bhadase Maraj's largely Hindu PDP (People's Democratic Party) and other older and mainly white-oriented conservative groupings. After the DLP, led by Maraj, defeated Dr. Williams's PNM in the Federal elections of 1958, Bhadase Maraj, simultaneously trade union leader, religious leader of the Maha Sabha, business man and politician, succumbed to pethidine addiction. Rudranath Capildeo, still in London, was elected leader in his place – as an intellectual challenger to Williams. From 1960 to 1967, he was Leader of the Opposition in Parliament, though still as much in London as Trinidad.

By 1960, politics in Trinidad involved racial issues no matter one's basic attitude to race. It wasn't always so. In the early 1950s, when the Crown was still dominant, people with ambition to serve their communities vied against one another without appealing to race pride. Leaders such as Adrian Cola Rienzi, Uriah 'Buzz' Butler and Captain Arthur Cipriani – men of Indian, African and European descent – enjoyed widespread respect without seeking to exploit their ethnic or racial backgrounds. (Racial identity was not totally irrelevant, which is perhaps why Krishna Deonarine changed his name to Adrian Cola Rienzi in becoming the respected founder of the Oilfield Workers Trade Union and the Sugar Workers Union.)

In postwar Trinidad, the colonial authorities moved cautiously to include a diverse spectrum of local people in electoral politics. The legislative council, headed by the British governor, included both elected and nominated members. As a child going to Tranquillity I can recall the election posters supporting men such as Raymond Quevedo, better known as the calypsonian Attila the Hun. Figures as different in their racial backgrounds as C.B. Mathura (Indian), Norman Tang (Chinese), Hugh Wooding (African) and Patrick Solomon (mixed, if mainly African), sought election either to the Legislative Council or City Council. These were persons of substance, tolerant of people different from themselves and devoted to the idea of Trinidad as a cosmopolitan and harmonious society. In fact, the idea of Trinidad as the epitome of both racial harmony and racial diversity became the core of Trinidad's idealistic vision of itself as a society.

However, this idea was breaking down by the mid-1950s, when my Capildeo uncles entered politics at the national level. Rudranath's entry followed his older brother's, but by the mid-1950s politics was clearly a major part of our larger family life. Pa's role, while he lived, had been modest. I remember him doing his bit, mainly by stencilling long strips of white cotton with the motif of a star in red paint, which may have been Simbhoonath's political emblem at one time. He painted the banners and left them to dry in the long room of 'the old upstairs' in Chaguanas. Otherwise, Pa stayed out of politics. (Vidia's knowledge of countryside electoral politics in Trinidad, satirised in some of his fiction, was acquired mainly after Pa's death.) But our mother did not have to voice her opinion or her feelings about the various campaigns and hustings over the years. She always acted as if Simbhoo's political career was ordained. Probably, Ma followed Pa's lead in voting during elections in Port of Spain, but Simbhoo's career was her prime concern. (As far as I know, our parents never voted outside of Port of Spain.)

By the end of the 1950s, Trinidad politics had become deeply racialised. Heated arguments in my Higher School Certificate years at the Convent put a spotlight on the few Indians in the Upper Sixth and Lower Sixth forms. Some of these students were not sufficiently confident in the new environment to object openly to Dr. Williams's insinuations against the Indian community (his supporters were typically less subtle), but I was perhaps the most vociferous of us all in facing the full force of the Williams converts – or fanatics. (After his first major electoral setback in 1958, in elections for the ill-fated West Indies Federation, Dr. Williams infamously called Indians 'a hostile and recalcitrant minority'; his supporters echoed his dismissal of us as 'transients' who opposed social progress and unfairly controlled the cinemas, gas stations and the magistracy, among other sectors.) I would often cross the partition between the forms to argue with anyone if I felt my sister Mira or someone else needed backing. In this way, my political instincts and knowledge were honed.

While I have no proof of it, I am also certain that at a later date, Shiva, too, must have had to engage people at school against the diatribes of Dr. Williams. The families of some of his best friends at school were diehard PNM supporters. They considered Indians, especially the Hindus who were in the majority in the countryside, hopelessly backward and typically illiterate. Ironically, these pro-PNM friends would soon be among the first to emigrate to North America when Williams fell from grace without falling from political power. (He died in 1981, still in charge of both party and country since his initial electoral victory in 1956, but with his prestige and authority undoubtedly diminished.)

I believe that Vidia's animosity, or what people wish to see as his animosity, towards Trinidad is more related to his ambition to be a writer than anything else. The island offered no scope for entering, much less progressing, in this field. Nearly every writer he admired, every book he regarded as well-published, every first-class journal, was located outside Trinidad. He needed to have an opportunity to create his destiny and that destiny lay beyond the shores of our island. Vidia was also astute enough to see people as they really were and to write truthfully, if often scathingly, about them. Dr. Williams had pronounced him 'a dishonest writer' after the publication of his book about the West Indies, *The Middle Passage*, which Williams had helped to fund; and the Schools Broadcasting Programme repeatedly aired to schools a programme featuring a local poet who portrayed Vidia as practically schizophrenic. Shiva, thirteen years his junior, would himself be ill-received at UWI St Augustine. It is not the case, in my view, that my brothers have or had an original animosity towards the island of their birth, as many people seem to assume. It is much more the case that Trinidad was not as receptive as it should have been to their profession or to their dedication and talents.

As for the question about how much my uncles Simbhoonath and Rudranath achieved in Trinidad and Tobago politics, the answer is debatable. Simbhoo was earlier in that field but Rudranath certainly reached further in attaining top positions. Outmanoeuvring his brother, he had become Leader of the Opposition, before burning out as a political leader. He had nurtured even more passionately than Simbhoo a fearful vision of future racial conflict in Trinidad. This perspective came from his being both in and out of Trinidad for long periods. After living in Britain, what he saw in Trinidad when he came back here disturbed him more than it ever touched Simbhoo, who perhaps had become inured to the indignities of Trinidad life. In 1961, during a blistering election campaign, Rudranath witnessed mob behaviour on several occasions. There were PNM-inspired gangs called Marabuntas, tyre-slashings, open fights and snakes let loose at public meetings. PNM supporters not infrequently upset and looted Indian vendors' stalls, and some of the vendors tried, largely in vain, to retaliate. The police seemed indifferent to injustice if the victim was Indian. But Rudranath lost the election that year mainly because of a fit of pique, or righteous indignation, at a huge rally in Port of Spain. That day, 15th October 1961, he advised his followers to arm themselves with cutlasses. 'You will be called to arms,' he told the gathering. 'Wherever the PNM holds a meeting, you will have to break it up.'

In May 1962, in London at the Marlborough Conference that worked out the basic terms for national independence among the Trinidad and Tobago politicians and their advisers, Rudranath found himself in bitter disagreement with the Deputy Leader of the Opposition, Ashford Sinanan, and his colleague Lionel Seukeran, both of them Indian. Sinanan and Seukeran claimed that racial tension and racial discrimination did not exist in Trinidad and Tobago in any significant way. Rudranath countered by presenting the view of a group of concerned citizens of Trinidad and Tobago, written in what was called 'a memorial'. These citizens, who had paid their way to London for the meetings, had petitioned senior members of both the Conservative and Labour parties, as well as Rudranath Capildeo and Hugh Fraser, the Under-Secretary of State for the Colonies. The group, which included Kenneth Lalla, H.P. Singh, Lennox Deyalsingh and Jang Bahadoorsingh, belonged to the so-called Indian Association of Trinidad and Tobago. Their position was clear. While they backed independence, they also sought safeguards for all minorities. Proportional representation along racial lines should replace the Westminster system of government. Proportional representation would also apply to employment in the Public Service, the Police Service and the new Regiment or national army, all of which employed few Indians. Uncle Rudranath believed that he had verbal assurances from Eric Williams, the PNM leader, that these changes would be implemented. He signed the formal agreement.

But Dr. Williams was in fact totally opposed to proportional representation. This difference dogged Rudranath's footsteps in his position as Leader of the Opposition after Independence in August 1962. The following year, he effectively quit politics in Trinidad. Although he remained nominally Leader of the Opposition, he returned to his academic position teaching at the University of London, where he had earned his doctorate in physics. In 1967, unable to obtain further leave from his legislative responsibilities, he saw his Chaguanas seat declared vacant. The next year, it was won by the veteran politician Bhadase Maraj, now recovered from his illness, fighting as an independent.

The brothers by now were deeply estranged from one another. In 1966, Simbhoonath had lost his own seat representing Couva, a Hindu stronghold, in parliament. His political career was also over. On 12th May 1970, still unreconciled to his brother, Rudranath died in London of kidney failure, perhaps related to a form of cancer. He was only fifty years old. Ma was distraught. She had been much more concerned about the personal rift between her brothers than about their political differences, or their loss of political power. She never lost her love for them. Both men had been her playmates in their happy childhood together growing up in the Lion House in Chaguanas.

With the new red, black and white flag of Trinidad and Tobago raised on 31st August 1962, the urgent task now was to turn into reality the spirit of compromise and enterprise that had energised the Marlborough Conference. But who were the people to lead us? Where were our philosophers, our guiding men and women of letters? Who would ensure that enlightened democracy took root, and that high expectations about education, science and culture would be instilled in the young?

Unfortunately, consolidating power seemed to be the main goal of the ruling PNM party as led by Dr. Williams. The treasury, under his control, was the pot of gold at the end of the rainbow-people he ruled. No appeal to the electorate could be more emotive than ethnicity. Nothing could be more divisive in a plural society, where the two largest groups challenged each other for control. The population itself began to change. A voting majority for the PNM was built largely by turning a blind eye to uncontrolled immigration, mainly from the smaller, African-dominated islands of the Caribbean. Squatting by these newcomers on politically strategic state and private lands became the norm. This largely illegal influx guaranteed success at the polls, even as it crucially affected the cultural fibre of the nation.

Every institution became overburdened. And with this overburdening, emigration to the metropolitan world beyond Trinidad accelerated. At first it was to Britain, where substantial numbers of relatively poor but enterprising people had sought greener pastures, starting in the early nineteen-fifties. Emigration would continue in wave after wave for a combination of reasons. Insufficient school places, mistrust of the protective services, inadequate and downright poor health-care, inequity in jobs and promotion, racial aggression and antagonism, nepotism and corruption, violent crime and a culture of virtual impunity – the list went on. Dr. Williams had switched off his hearing aid. He was deaf to all criticisms, even those from within the PNM. Those who did not like his policies or his pace could 'get to hell out' of Trinidad and Tobago, as he more than once said.

Many of Dr. William's earlier protégés fell out with him and withdrew from leadership. Some did so quietly, but others did not. The brain drain continues long after his death. Race remains the main bogeyman fighting progress. And the pernicious shift system in schools, which he introduced in the mid-sixties to facilitate the now overcrowded education system, and which has cast so many of our young people adrift, is compounded today by trafficking in illegal narcotics and the appeal of radical, militant Islam. Who among us are optimists today?

With our return from Britain, and perhaps even more so with the return of Mira, who moved back into 26 Nepaul Street, life brightened in Ma's old household. Mira settled in quickly, although she was not entirely happy to return to Trinidad. Nevertheless, she found herself a secure position at St. Augustine Girls' High School, once a fledgling school but now recognised as a first-rate institution. She became the third Naipaul sister to teach there and the first one with a degree in Education. Life improved further for her when a chance meeting with Amar Inalsingh, a family friend, blossomed into a romance. Mira and Amar's engagement was announced at our fifth-anniversary wedding celebration in San Fernando. It was the first celebration Mel and I had ever hosted. Dennis Mahabir eloquently made the announcement and proposed the toast.

Amar, known by his colleagues as Carol Homer Inalsingh, was a medical doctor interested in oncology. A small family luncheon for the Naipaul and Inalsingh families was held at Nepaul Street. The marriage ceremony was conducted by the eminent Reverend Roy Nehall. (Reverend Nehall, after a short stint in the Senate of Trinidad's Parliament, soon emigrated with his family to Canada.) The only non-family at the luncheon were Rodney Mahabir and his second wife, Micky. They were in charge of the champagne. I was in charge of the meal. A few hours later the newlyweds boarded the French liner *Antilles* and left for Britain, where Amar was to pursue post-graduate studies in radiography and oncology in London before returning to Trinidad to take up a position at Port of Spain General Hospital.

Mira and Amar eventually moved to the United States, where Amar established his own cancer clinic in Florida. They have three children: Aruna was born in England, Nisha and Anil Amar in Trinidad. All three are qualified professionals. We meet each other as often as we can. The cousins, through the wonders of twenty-first century technology, see and speak to each other as often as they wish. Such technological change has redefined the idea of emigration and immigration, citizenship and ancestral loyalty, community and foreignness.

I went on to have two more children: a second son, Kiran, and a girl, Siri. With Siri not yet a year old I entered UWI to attempt to complete a degree. There was no faculty of Law in Trinidad. Going to Barbados was out of the question. In two years I had a degree in English and Sociology. I had acquired the insurance policy I needed in the event of the unexpected. The year was 1968. When the Head of the Sociology Department, Dr. John McDonald, invited me to undertake a part-time job as tutor in Sociology I was surprised but soon excited. I believed that here, at last, was my sure route to postgraduate work, which I craved. But alas, the government of the day not only took me away from my substantive post at my alma mater, but refused to second me to continue a work-study programme at UWI. I went full circle and took up a post at Tranquillity Secondary school. Another teacher, who was also sent there, left after a couple of weeks and returned to UWI to pursue a course in Foreign Affairs. Joining the Diplomatic Service, he rose to the post of High Commissioner while earning a degree in Law at the same time. There is an old Indian saying: 'Gopaul luck is not Seepaul luck.'

My years in Tranquillity were, however, deeply satisfying. I have a plaque in my home for 'Outstanding and Dedicated Service' given to me by the Past Pupils Association of Tranquillity. In December 2015, thirty years after I left my job there, Mel and I were invited by the graduates of 1985 as guests to their Christmas dinner. I think I may have done more good there than I would have done at my alma mater. The past pupils of St. Joseph's Convent school in San Fernando had bestowed on me a similar honour many years before, but severe flooding had prevented me from attending that function. I always regretted that.

My return home from Scotland had meant a great deal to the entire family, but especially to Nella and perhaps even more so to Shiva. I had left Edinburgh in time to ensure that Shiva completed his School Certificate examinations and entered the Higher School Certificate class. Confident in his ability, I helped him to cover the Geography section of the Higher School Certificate syllabus, but his marks in History were disappointing. QRC had suffered from the loss of many skilled veteran teachers during the drive by the government, without adequate preparation, to provide secondary school places for virtually everyone. Unlike St. Joseph's Convent, Bishop Anstey and St. Mary's (CIC) in Port of Spain, QRC would never recover its former glory.

With Anna Mahase's help, we spoke to Father Pedro Valdez, the Trinidad-born principal of CIC, who admitted Shiva to his school. Shiva studied hard, with brilliant results, and won the island scholarship in Modern Studies offered by the government. His subjects were History, Geography and Economics. The Holy Ghost Fathers at CIC took care of instruction in the first two subjects, while Shiva was aided in the third by perhaps the leading economist in Trinidad and Tobago, the esteemed Frank Rampersad of the national civil service.

In 1964, at the age of nineteen, a still boyish-looking but slightly stoop-shouldered Shiva left by ship to follow in Vidia's footsteps to University College in Oxford. At not quite six feet, he was taller than both Pa and Vidia. Shiva had many of Pa's mannerisms, and a wonderfully mischievous sense of humour. He tended to be absent-minded, as well as a little lazy at times.

Cups of tea would collect around the Morris chair on which he sat to read and Ma would then have to humour him into clearing the mess. She was patient with him. He once flooded the bathroom by leaving the house with the shower still running. When he returned home and called out for Ma, she had a mild question for him: 'Did you bring the boat, son?' They both burst into laughter when he realised the point of her question. Towering over her, he loved to hug her and to display openly the depth of his genuine affection for her.

Shiva was affable and warm. He could also be competitive in certain areas. He and I vied for years within the family for the position of Scrabble champion. He would gloat and tease so much when he won that I really did not mind losing. He loved writing. In 1962, he had won an island-wide essay competition for secondary schools on the subject of Trinidad's new political independence. The seeds of being a writer had already been sown. About Vidia he had some sentimental ideas. He used to think rather warmly that they would be like the Huxley brothers.

Shiva read widely and voraciously. He knew a lot about Mao, Bertrand Russell and Jung. I was out of his league in that sphere. Before he left Trinidad, he took a job in Clifford Sealy's small but seriously stocked bookshop on upper Frederick Street, not far from CIC. At the end of a week he had to pay Mr. Sealy, rather than have Mr. Sealy pay him: Shiva had spent more on books than he had earned as a helper. He had also lost his bicycle while working at the bookshop. He thought that the chap with his bike was kindly taking it out of the sun!

Spending so much time with Shiva during his formative years, I feel that I had my finger on his pulse. In crucial ways he had been deprived. He had never experienced the infant joy of having his father, or anyone else, read to him. Pa was in Jamaica during his infancy, and on his return from Jamaica we were cramped and unsettled in 17 Luis Street. When we moved into Nepaul Street, settling in as a family and sharing the same space were novel experiences for us all. While we did not ignore Shiva, and he did not lack love and care, he would grow up mainly in an atmosphere of study and scholarship. Almost every day, he heard the sound of a typewriter being pounded. That atmosphere, his personality and, I suppose, his genes made him the person he grew up to be.

Gentler in nature than Vidia, swallowing disappointments rather than reacting to them with aggression, he tried to evade stress instead of confronting its source. If he were like Pa, that suppression of anger would erupt at some point later. Usually, someone as placid as Ma would pay the price. But here I hazard a guess only, because my own feeling is that Shiva was innately very much like Pa. To me, Vidia always had so much of the grit and tenacity of Ma, and although he hated his 'fat Capildeo thighs', he showed he had also inherited the Capildeo's overweening faith in them-

Shiva (4th from left) celebrates his scholarship with the Inalsingh family: Amar (left), Sati (2nd left) and Crisen (right)

Shiva leaves for England, left to right: Simboo Capildeo and his wife, Savi, Mel, Mickey Mahabir, Nella, Rai, Shiva, Ma, Sati

selves. This faith gave them the arrogance they displayed at will, and masked their true feelings in their *namastes*, the ritual greetings among Hindus that acknowledged caste superiority and inferiority.

Following the birth of Kiran, my second son, Mel and I began to build our own home in a promising new housing development called Valsayn Park, located near the old capital city of St. Joseph east of Port of Spain. I was twenty-six then. Now I am almost eighty. We are still there. The years since we moved into Valsayn span most of my adult life. Now when I see how difficult it is for young people, even those who are well educated and established professionally, to own their own property, I realise our foresight – and our sheer good luck – in taking this bold step while still newlyweds and young.

For me, perhaps much more than for Mel, it was a bold step. I had lived as a child in 17 Luis Street in Woodbrook. For a while I had been 'Heidi of the Tropics' on Nanee's estate in Petit Valley. At 26 Nepaul Street in St. James, I had become a teenager. In all that time, especially during the war years, I had usually been part of a disparate set of people. On Nepaul Street, I knew one of our neighbours fairly well, and in those years I made a few very good friends at school; but much as I loved the house that my father had bought for us, I cannot say that we ever became or saw ourselves as part of a community in St. James. At the age of twenty, I had moved to San Fernando as a newlywed. There I had shared a good life with certain people whose kindness I will always recall with pleasure. But I never really knew my neighbours. We had exchanged polite greetings but, as far as I can recall, never had a genuine conversation with any one of them.

Now I moved into Valsayn Park, a new housing development, as a wife and mother of two sons but also as a working woman still needing to complete a Bachelor of Arts degree at the St. Augustine campus of the University of the West Indies. The birth of Siri, my third child and only girl, would cause me to defer my entry into the university by an additional year. However, it also gave me precious time to build and then settle into our new home at 3 Woodlands Road in Valsayn. That home would become the centre of our universe for over fifty years. When we approached Mel's bank for a loan to buy the land, it rejected us, although he was a doctor and I was also employed. Needless to say, we felt crushed. Then we decided to walk across the road and try our luck at the newly opened branch of a Canadian bank. The people there not only quickly gave us the loan but also invited Mel to become the branch's 'official' doctor. We bought one of the plots at Valsayn Park and I began to sketch a plan for our house.

Our piece of land was in a cul-de-sac with a roundabout at the eastern end of Woodlands Road. On this short end of the street there were six other plots. Houses, complete with families, already stood on the three plots opposite to ours. As our home went up, we started to get to know the families nearby. They were glad to see new people moving in. Valsayn was as yet underpopulated. Most people reached out to one another, because everyone was basically new to the development. Our house, when it was finished, stood alone on the south side of the street. We looked north to the hills, with the whitewashed monastery of Mount Saint Benedict up above and our home within earshot of its morning chimes. In the dry season, we took cautious note of the blazing bush fires. In April the golden-yellow blooms of the poui trees dotted the hills. Short-lived though these blooms were, they heralded the start of the rainy season. Then mist and clouds would often veil the monastery. Almost overnight the hills became once again bluish-green. This beauty kept us going during the difficult early years of the development.

The fact that our house would have two storeys raised eyebrows while it was being built, but that was what I wanted and Mel was satisfied with my reasons. I wanted two storeys instead of the flat, California-style 'ranch' design favoured by most of the other residents. I also chose its floor finishes, its windows and virtually all its other main features. We needed an architect to do the drawings and give the exterior a harmonious facing, and Mel hired the accomplished Hayden Franco to work with me in this capacity. We also found an able builder in Mr. Rajkumar. People often speak bitterly of building their house as a living nightmare, but our team worked to time and budget and with little or no stress. Fifty years later, we have no structural flaws and fully enjoy the physical comforts of our home. It was Hayden Franco's idea that we include a swimming-pool in our plan. While this idea gave me a few qualms at first, we agreed to it and I have had no regrets. After numerous earthquakes the pool still serves its purpose both for its look of comfort and luxury and as a ready means of pleasant exercise. Mel swims almost every day.

I designed the house so that when you came through the front door you had a full view of the garden. I took the idea from Nepaul Street, where the sight of the flowering vine behind the wooden lattice mitigated the pressing smallness of the house and suggested space and openness. As Pa did at Nepaul Street, I paid close attention to our garden. I am truly proud of it. Our garden reflects years of tending, even if it has endured many phases and changes. Gone are the delicate roses and gladioli we once cultivated. Now we have mainly tough shrubs, along with a few sturdy exotics. At first the fire ants and the leaf-and-petal-toting 'bachacs' presented a constant menace. We won that war, but we have had less success dealing with the gorgeously green young iguanas that wreak havoc when they find anything to munch on. Add to these factors the ill effects of rough weather caused by El Niño and La Niña, my age and slowing pace, and Mel's chronic lack of interest in digging and planting, and it is amazing that I can still say we have a beautiful tropical garden at No. 3 Woodlands Road.

In August 1964, just after Shiva left Trinidad for Great Britain, we moved into our new home. Our elder son, Rai, was five. Kiran, our second son, was not yet two years old. While Rai might have preserved a few vague memories of San Fernando, I think our children know only our house as their home, and our garden as their only garden. Our daughter, Siri, was born the following year, 1965. She arrived on my birthday, 3rd April. Apparently she was sent to remind me that birthdays should be celebrated. (When in 2004, Siri's only daughter Kira was also born on 3rd April, we felt this was an omen of some kind, although so far we have not unravelled its meaning.)

We moved into Woodlands Road with very little. We had a large Persian rug, as well as the few items of furniture we had acquired in San Fernando. For a couple of months, while our kitchen was being finished, we cooked on a hotplate and in an electric wok. We ate at the same dining table, with its beautiful surface made of our native cypre wood, which had been our first purchase after marriage. We still eat breakfast and lunch on this table. It is now fifty-seven years old.

On the site of a defunct coconut estate, Valsayn Park was not paradise, though on the whole the development was decently planned. The speedy Churchill-Roosevelt Highway, built by American military engineers during the war, divided the new development into North Valsayn and South Valsayn. On both sides, the paved roads were laid out on a grid system. The streets ran east-to-west, with two entrances and exits running north-south on either side of the highway. On both sides of Valsayn there were large plots for sale of about a half-acre in size (around 22,000 square feet) and smaller plots that each covered roughly 8,000 square feet. In North Valsayn, the smaller parcels were excised from a site that had been cleared to host an International Scouts Jamboree in the 1950s. 'Jamboree' remained the name of this area, just as 'Realsprings' remained the name for the smaller plots on the eastern side of South Valsayn.

Located about eight miles east of Port of Spain (a fifteen-minute drive under ideal circumstances) and a similar distance from Piarco, our international airport, Valsayn seemed perfectly placed. The plots themselves were affordable, going in those early years for fifty cents (in local currency) per square foot. The development attracted both older folk and also many young couples who, like us, wanted to raise their families away from the crowded city. For people who worked in the various industries sprouting up along the Churchill-Roosevelt Highway (including rum distilleries, beer factories, cigarette manufacturers and makers of household products), a home at Valsayn Park meant a short commute to work. It was also conveniently close to the University of the West Indies at St. Augustine. In the early 1960s, UWI seemed to be on the brink of rapid and substantial expansion in Trinidad.

Alas, with every passing year, commuting to and from Valsayn became more difficult. Getting to Port of Spain in fifteen minutes became more of a vague hope than a reality. As privately owned motor cars began to flood the island, traffic lights had to be installed to accommodate vehicles from other settlements along the highway. Taking children to and from school in Port of Spain became a constant challenge and frustration. The planners had tried to anticipate these problems. They had reserved what they imagined would be adequate open spaces for the development of businesses and the construction of a school. But efforts to develop a suitable school complex proved to be inadequate, no match for what was available in Port of Spain. Recreational areas were also a problem. Instead of having one large open area, which could be developed as a public park, the developers had left a few vacant half-acre lots scattered throughout the area for the residents to maintain. On the brighter side, Valsayn would eventually boast the first successful shopping mall in Trinidad. This was an important feature for those of us who ran households.

Another major nuisance was the profusion of sandflies and mosquitoes on the old estate. At dusk, biting sandflies made outdoor entertaining virtually impossible. We grew lush lawns and sprayed pesticides religiously, but the mosquitoes and sandflies persisted. What with the nipping insects and other bugs and the worsening traffic problems, Valsayn became too much for some people. Families moved into and then promptly out of the development. Within five years of our arrival, more than half the people we had met there were gone. Properties were always on the market. It would take almost a decade before land and house prices began to rise and for enough vacant plots to be sold and houses built to make the development the success it unquestionably became.

Those of us who had stayed put when others fled endured the nuisances as best we could. In fact, we developed a stronger sense of community than Mel and I had ever known in the past. We improvised. Until the shopping mall was built we looked out for each other as various trucks and vans brought goods and services to the area. For almost fifty years, I have had fresh shrimp delivered by a man called simply 'Kaks'. Gardeners were in great demand, and they were on the whole as reliable as they were forward-looking. Former young workers, now living abroad in Canada and the United States, drop by occasionally to reintroduce themselves to us as virtually unrecognisable mature men who clearly have done well in life.

Later, I would look back and see that Valsayn Park, of which we were a part, was a small but telling chapter in the social history of our young nation.

When we bought our plot and built our home, Trinidad and Tobago was still enjoying the first thrill of Independence. The future was anybody's guess, but we were, on the whole, optimistic. We, the people, would determine our future. And we attracted a vital cross-section of the national community. True, our neighbours at first seemed to be predominantly white people. We certainly did not know that this would be the case when we bought the plot, and over the years the racial composition has changed. Now the area is mainly Indian. One of my disappointments has been that although Valsayn Park is close to the UWI campus, it has never been home to the professors. UWI provided them with housing independently. We did, however, attract a fascinating array of individuals and families who brought joy into our life and gave it a depth and breadth of humanity for which I've always been grateful. I'll never forget these people.

Obliquely across the street, on the north-eastern corner of our cul-de-sac, lived the Ferreiras. The head of the household, and without doubt the flashiest figure in the neighbourhood, Max Emilienne Ferreira was not only a well-known estate agent but also the nationally acclaimed host of many cultural shows and pageants. Tall and handsome, he was still a heart-throb and epitomised a certain kind of Trinidadian cultural heritage and social style. His French Creole roots ran deep. I remember how his aunt, Tante Thérèse, as we called her, used to come to the Convent when I was in the HC class to help us improve our French pronunciation. She spoke to us only in French. Max was no less impressive. In addition to his French and Portuguese family background, he had begun his working life in the oil fields of Maracaibo in Venezuela, before returning home to venture successfully into real estate. He knew local history well. With his snooty mannerisms, so typical of the dominant French Creoles, his delight in language and languages, including our local French *patois*, his endless stories, his lively comic sense, his love of calypsos, his habit of denouncing groups of people as yahoos (especially his Portuguese brethren, whom he branded *vasges*, meaning low-class or vulgar), Max entertained and edified us endlessly. He loved books and enjoyed quoting Schopenhauer, although Balzac was clearly his favourite author. With my smattering of French I enjoyed bantering with him in that language over the years.

Odette, Max's wife, was warm-hearted and charming. She never carried a grudge and had the ability to forget or overlook frailties. Her jitterbug dancing had attracted Max, and many a lady was left in distress when they got married. House-proud but easy-going, she became one of my closest friends and a confidante. The cosmopolitan Winston Mahabir, who had the joy of owning a champion racehorse like the Ferreiras' Aurelian, declared Odette to be the purest and truest Creole in the land. Her colourful and spicy use of language made him laugh so hard at times that he cried. Odette had the charm to meet anyone in any stratum of society. She was not a great cook and would never become one. Her grocery cart, with its pre-cooked and packaged foods, always contrasted with mine, which was usually loaded with items for cooking and baking. But she was industrious. As the children grew into adulthood she opened a wine shop, a venture well ahead of its time for Trinidad. As with her cooking, however, she never quite mastered the pronunciation of her French labels.

With six children, two girls and four boys, and later with the acquisition of a monkey called Jake who lived in a huge cage around a tree, the Ferreira household was always busy. Nilsa, the eldest, was not yet sixteen when we came to Valsayn and Christian, the youngest, only about four. Apart from Christian, who went to school with us, education was not considered a priority. Max eventually sent the three older boys to boarding school in England with the hope that the colonel in charge there would drill some discipline into the handsome miscreants. With this unorthodox household, and with our shared enthusiasm for horse-racing, we enjoyed thirty or more years of genuine camaraderie. We had the occasional argument but many more celebrations. When the Ferreiras finally moved out of Valsayn, they encouraged us to follow them into a trendy new development west of Port of Spain. But we declined.

Directly opposite to us lived the Hutchinsons with their only child, about three years old. Once, with some concern, we watched from across the way as Beverly, their daughter, seemed intent on climbing the wrought-iron pole that led to their roof and their television antenna. Somehow she managed to escape injury. Workmanlike and quiet, both husband and wife seemed bent on minding their own business. Despite various overtures, only young Glenda Ferreira among us could claim to be their friend. Following disruptive, even traumatic Black Power marches in Trinidad in 1970, and after six years of being our ever-so-distant neighbours, 'Hutchie' and his family returned to his native Barbados. Their departure was only one example of the exodus of talented, good people of all colours and ethnicities and levels of income who gave up not simply on projects in community like Valsayn, but on Trinidad itself as we veered and stumbled into our future.

But it was not long before another young couple moved in, and with a flourish. The Hendersons had given each other a Shetland pony as a wedding present. Their family grew to include three children, and the idea of the pony was to prepare their offspring later to ride a horse. Hugh Henderson is a gentleman-sportsman who, like his neighbours, enjoyed horse-racing, cricket and similar activities. A true son of the soil, he first worked for two of the larger industrial companies near Valsayn, then became an adviser to Prime Minister A.N.R. Robinson in the NAR government when it came to power in 1986. When that government fell in 1991, and after an attempted coup by the Black Muslim-inspired Jamaat-

Al-Muslimeen (one of the most traumatic episodes in modern Trinidad and Tobago history), the family exited to Canada. We would not see the children grow up. But Hugh and Jeanine, his charming wife from the celebrated de Verteuil clan, returned to Trinidad when their children reached university age. Their elder son, Douglas, chose to return to Trinidad to live with his own young family, while the other three children remained in exile in Canada. We do not see them often enough but we enjoy the occasions when we do.

When the Frasers, another large family on our street, sold their home to Gerald Montes de Oca, Mel and I soon realised how lucky we were to acquire as a neighbour this most excellent man. Homegrown but a veteran traveller, he was well-respected as the CEO of one of the oldest industrial firms making household goods in the nation. He acted as vice-chairman of the Board of Directors of BWIA, our island's airline (it became Caribbean Airlines), and then managed for many years Valpark Plaza, our pioneering shopping centre. Gerald accomplished even more in life than my brief synopsis suggests. In fact, he was cherished throughout the island. Although he belonged to a devout Roman Catholic family that produced several priests, he honoured me, a Hindu, by asking me to become godmother to Gary, his only son. Gary grew up almost as part of our household. Today he is head of his own family in Denver, Colorado. His mother, Raj, remains a close neighbour and a cherished friend.

In sharp contrast to the piety of the Montes de Oca family, but no less inspiring in its own way, was the Ghany household. The Ghany parents and children lived ten houses away from us at 23 Woodlands Road. The children who lived in that house were the offspring of Noor and Andrea Ghany. Noor was Indian; Andrea was of mixed French ancestry. Both had been married before, and each had previous children. Their household in Valsayn included seven girls and two boys.

After leaving San Fernando, I had taught at the Convent school in St. Joseph, at the foothills of the Northern Range and near Valsayn. During that year I had met two of the Ghany girls, Hafeeza and Koraisha, who were not yet in the Senior Certificate class. Popular with the staff, they were always eating or bringing things for the teachers to eat. They introduced themselves to me on the memorable day when the school lined the Eastern Main Road to await the arrival of the Prime Minister of India, Indira Gandhi. They knew who I was. Their brother Iqbal was a medical doctor who had been at QRC with Mel. Within days we received an invitation to dinner to meet the rest of the family.

If the Max Ferreira family was unorthodox, I need to find a more graphic word that can do justice to the various members of the lively, warm, kind and fascinating Ghany family. Noor, the head of the household, had attended QRC and was a friend of the prime minister, Dr. Williams. The son of a prominent family in nearby Curepe, Noor was the subject of a certain amount of gossip. It was said that his brother Nazir, a lawyer by profession, had a sideline trade in providing white women from England as concubines or *nika* ('wives') for Muslim men who could afford them. ('Nika' is a form of Muslim marriage which, while not legal, is morally and religiously acceptable.) The gossip did not end there. Noor himself had fathered seventeen children. He was also a tireless entrepreneur, among the first to bring Indian films to Trinidad and the first to import Mazda motor cars from Japan. At one time he was our sole importer of cheese.

Despite these colourful connections, the children in the Ghany household were brought up to love and respect their siblings. They were a close-knit bunch. Zaleena, the eldest, was already married and living in Canada but the others lived in Valsayn. All the girls shared their mother's exuberance. Through her, they also became excellent cooks of a variety of foods. In fact, they flourished, while their poor brothers had a harder time. Obviously smothered by the girls, the boys struggled to find a path that would lead to secure, lucrative jobs. Glowing with their mother's *joie de vivre*, the girls met life's challenges head on. Seldom daunted by unhappy turns of events, they were fortunate to attract mates even after some of their own early marriages failed. They turned out to be good mothers and attentive grandmothers. They learned to survive in a competitive world by deploying qualities and abilities they would not have learned in HSC classes, or in college.

As in San Fernando with Zeinool and Jaffo Hosein, our first and very special friends in Valsayn were much older than we were. The Walkers and the Johnsons were related by marriage. Ralph Walker was the older brother of Norma Johnson. It is interesting that these two couples, with very different interests and personalities, would prove to be so influential on a couple as young as we were then. Both the Walkers and the Johnsons had children who were around my age. Yet we spent hours of our free time in common pursuits and beneficial activities.

Ralph Walker was a gentle and devoted husband to Rhoda, whom we all called Dilly. The father of two sons who were still abroad when we first met, he was a self-made man. He owned and ran the pre-eminent furniture business in Trinidad, Lumber Industries Limited. An early morning riser, he liked taking solo drives just before sunrise, during which time he would stop for a roadside coffee and bites of black-pudding at places he knew well. A quiet man, unable (or so it seemed) to laugh out loud, he had a mischievous smile and teasing eyes behind his spectacles. Always respectful and thoughtful, and perhaps meek, he almost seemed to be someone of whom others could take advantage. Then, just after celebrating his and Rhoda's thirty-fifth wedding anniversary, he fell seriously ill and died. He was sixty-three.

Rhoda Walker, his wife, was no stranger to sorrow. In my opinion, she was the only true 'duchess' in Trinidad, a poised woman of impeccable manners. She came from a family that had owned oil-rich lands. As a child, she must have seemed truly blessed by good fortune. Then one day, while she was a young boarder at Bishop Anstey School, the news came that her entire family had died in an explosion in the oil fields. How she survived such a shock is almost unfathomable to me. But survive she did. Clearly she had already learnt enough from her mother and her sister to pattern the rest of her life on theirs. Always perfectly dressed, she paid attention to detail as no one else I ever knew. Slow and deliberate, she took no half-measures. She was excellent company. Together, year after year, we would go together to horse-racing and cricket matches; we even toured South America together, after Ralph's death.

While she could not change her style or adapt easily, Rhoda did not expect others to be like her. She knew and loved good food, even if the *Cordon Bleu* course she took did not turn her into a great chef. Her Christmas gift-wrapping was such a sight to behold that I was forced to try to improve on mine (her gifts were always hand-delivered in a golden mesh basket). Her birthday was on Christmas. Every year we spent Christmas morning after breakfast with her. Indeed, Christmas was never the same again for me after she left her exquisite home in Valsayn, perhaps the best home ever designed by our friend Colin Laird. After living for a while in an apartment in Port of Spain, she too left Trinidad for good. With her elder son, Gordon, she emigrated to Ireland. Most of her grandchildren live there.

James Henry Jeffrey 'Sonny' Johnson was a bit of a rebel in his own family. His wife Norma (Ralph Walker's sister), with her much stricter upbringing, tended to be stoic. She reminded me of Ma, my own mother. She and Sonny were almost opposites. Norma once declared that Sonny had married her in order to 'become a bachelor'. (My husband, Mel, quipped to Norma: 'Norms, you made a mistake. You shouldn't have married Sonny. You should have leased him!') Norma's tart statement – and some even more snide, directed at others – let us know that behind all of her stoicism and hard work was a humorist and a pragmatist. Sonny came from a large family. I had known his niece, Deanne, from our class at St. Joseph's Convent and we had remained good friends. A pillar of the elite Queen's Park Cricket Club in Port of Spain, Sonny spent most of his leisure hours at its clubhouse. He was probably there, playing not cricket but poker, when each of his seven children was born.

As time passed, he became a close friend of our venerable Chief Justice, Sir Hugh Wooding. Under Sir Hugh's influence, he became a high-ranking member of their Freemason's Lodge. As for Sir Hugh himself, Mel and I got to know him (another QRC man) when we spent the better part of three days in his company on our way to Jamaica one year. After our plane broke down in Puerto Rico, it took the airline all that time to fix the problem. One of the most distinguished men in Trinidad and Tobago, with a legal career dating back to before 1930, Sir Hugh held court over meals and drinks and made the enforced interlude enlightening, pleasant and memorable.

Sonny Johnson was a provider of specialist foods and wines, with his three eldest children, Carol, Derek and Jeffrey, working with him in the business. Brash, loud and fleet of foot, he had married well; he enjoyed life, whereas Norma seemed mainly content to be efficient at it. Efficient she was, and more. Most of the recipes I use today at Christmas are from Norma (except for our Christmas cake and sweetbread – more like a Dundee cake – which I got from Dilly Walker). Norma, who looked after her family well, enjoyed a good rapport with both her own children and her children's friends. Sonny and Norma, when their children had all grown up and left home, found the house and its grounds in Valsayn too difficult to manage. They moved to Port of Spain.

At least they stayed in Trinidad. So many friends and relatives gave up on it. In this respect, the year 1990, the year of the Muslimeen attempted *coup d'état*, attended by looting and killings, marked a turning-point for many people in Trinidad. Violent crime increased rapidly. Old neighbours fled Valsayn and the island. When new tenants moved in they installed not only electronic burglar alarms but also 'burglar-proof' iron grilles that defaced most of the houses and turned them into virtual prisons. Doorbells warning of visitors became mandatory. Fences grew higher, as did insurance premiums. But money seemed to be no problem for certain buyers, who demolished older homes to make way for new mansions.

The tempo of our lives in Valsayn changed. We who were young when we first came more than fifty years ago have become forced to be more reclusive in our old age. No more can we saunter across the street to check the limes on Gerald's tree for our iced daiquiris. No neighbour now stubs his or her toes, as more than one did many years ago, running across the street to see if the car in our driveway was really on fire. Jake the monkey can no longer escape from the Ferreiras in order to swing nonchalantly from our chandelier. Andrea Ghany will not be rushing up the street with a kettle of boiling water to make sure that our children had a warm beverage before leaving home for their exams. Odette Ferreira is no longer there to learn how to make *dhal* and *paratha* and other Indian delicacies that were new to her. Young Gary Montes de Oca will not sniff inquisitively near our covered pot and then guess exactly what I was cooking for dinner. The bell has tolled for many of our neighbours. We are left with memories of a past generously shared and richly enjoyed.

Living among such colourful and kind persons and families, Mel and I never lacked inspiring, intelligent fellowship. We consider ourselves lucky to have shared the decades living at home in Trinidad with these people on the former coconut plantation, once bedevilled by sandflies and mosquitoes, that became our beloved Valsayn Park.

At Valsayn: Savi, Ralph and Rhoda Walker, Sati, Jaff and Zenool Hosein

# CHAPTER 8

## *Ma and her Children*

Nella came to visit the weekend we moved into our house on Woodlands Road. The following weekend she moved in for good. There was no way she could stay in Nepaul Street with Ma working hard and in charge at the quarry. Nella was just twelve years old and already at St. Joseph's Convent in Port of Spain. She needed our company. Besides, she had always been a big sister to our children, and Mel and I were happy to have her. She and Siri shared a room and the boys shared the other bedroom. In the boys' room we kept three beds so we always had a spare for guests. Downstairs was our 'en suite' bedroom cum library.

Because Nella was now living at No. 3 Woodlands Road, Ma came more often to spend weekends and holidays. However, while No. 26 Nepaul Street was no longer the main place for large family gatherings, it remained the family house. Many visitors to the island stayed there. My sister Mira and Amar lived there with Ma for several months, maybe even a year, on their return from Britain with their daughter Aruna. There they awaited completion of the renovations to the property they had purchased in the Cascade, one of the river valleys leading down to Port of Spain. While with Ma, they prettied up No. 26. They remade the kitchen and had tiles installed in place of its rotting wooden floor. During one of his visits, Vidia replaced the old wooden staircase which led to the upper floor. So No. 26 was being kept in shape, although the old garden wilted.

Nella and Rai travelled to Port of Spain to school. Rai, starting at Tranquillity, was then sent to the Convent Junior School, Maria Regina, to prepare for the eleven-plus exam. Traffic on the main thoroughfares to Port of Spain became more and more of a problem, settling into a daily crisis that has not yet been resolved. Getting to school on time required the children to be on the road by 6.30 am. As a result, our housekeeper Pinky and I had early starts to each day. Mel, too, had to leave for San Fernando around the same time.

Fortunately, we had some help around the house in addition to Pinky. Just before I started my course at UWI, Winston Mahabir recommended a pleasant and honest young man who needed a job and a home. Ralph Roopchand became gardener-cum-chauffeur and executed his duties to

Rai and Nella

Kiran greeting Ma

Siri and Ma with parrot Hanuman, c. 1973

perfection, so that I look back on those days as almost halcyon. When, after some years with us, he was offered a job as a chauffeur by the local office of the United Nations, we urged him to take it, although we knew that we would probably never find another Ralph Roopchand. He kept in touch with us as long as he lived, but sadly did not live long enough to see his son qualify as a medical doctor. Ralph knew every member of the Naipaul family and all respected and liked him.

When Shiva left for Oxford in 1964, Vidia and Pat, as well as Mira and Amar, were also in England. For most people, admittance to Oxford or Cambridge University is like being given a master key to a secure future. Vidia, however, had left Oxford ten years before, apparently without any fond memories of his time there. Anxiety and hardship, along with his mettle and tenacity, or a sense of privilege, drove him toward achieving his grand design to be a great writer. Shiva's stay at Oxford seemed to have left him more disoriented than when he entered.

In those days, as perhaps even now, Oxford University seemed to pose unique challenges. Someone like Shiva faced even greater problems than most undergraduates. There was the disadvantage of knowing oneself to be a colonial, an alien from another world, in a system seemingly dedicated to emphasising one's inferior and alien status. As such, one soon understood that one was off the social register, inherently disqualified from membership in the ranks of the elite, the pedigreed, the boys' club, the trust-fund upper crust. To be known as a scholarship student was in itself an impediment and a constant embarrassment. The foreigner or provincial newcomer had also to learn the elaborate jargon developed over the generations to manage such basic matters as meals, vacations, parties, classes and examinations. The elusive dress codes, the often intricate etiquette governing the use of the various 'quads' and 'stairs', the snobbish culture of sherry parties and teas both 'high' and 'low', learning the proper use of various types of helpers and servants unheard of in most other university systems – all served to underscore the demeaning sense in many foreign and ex-colonial students of embodying 'the Other'. The culture shock was enough to throw almost any such young man off course, no matter his best intentions and intelligence.

Vidia, wishing to save Shiva from some of the pitfalls he had encountered, instead brought added pressure, rather than soothing enlightenment, to bear on him. Shiva himself seldom complained about either Vidia or Oxford, but instead brooded silently on his unhappiness. He could not expect much help from Mira and Amar. They lived in a tiny apartment in Putney, so small that even storing a pram for little Aruna posed a problem.

Shiva was on his own. And no one in the family living in England could help him when he suffered a traumatic shock in his first year at Oxford. At university with him was another young Trinidadian, a former classmate and friend at QRC, Stephen Moosai-Maharaj. Stephen was a self-assured, intelligent young man from a well-known and respected family. As an honoured Head Boy at QRC, he saw himself as a natural leader, with a bright future in Trinidad politics. Oxford was supposed to top off his academic and social preparation for the brilliant career to come. The academic terms at Oxford University are very short. During the vacations the 'quads' are virtually deserted. Shiva and Stephen, having no homes in England to go to, were among the handful of students still in residence during the Easter vacation. One day, the college authorities asked Shiva to identify the body of a fellow student found dead in his room. Evidently the student had died in his sleep. To Shiva's horror, the body was that of his friend Stephen Moosai-Maharaj.

For Shiva, the shock was severe. As an individual, Steve had seemed to have everything Shiva did not have: he had been poised and confident, ambitious but certain about his future. Now, Steve was no more. The post-mortem showed he had inhaled his own vomit. Medical authorities ventured the opinion that overindulgence in alcohol could have caused severe irritation to the stomach. Not accustomed to drinking much alcohol, Stephen had perhaps imbibed too much on this occasion and died. Stephen's father and other members of his grief-stricken family were on their way from Trinidad. Shiva would have to meet them and help them negotiate the painful, complicated situation. The waiting seemed interminable. The whole episode caused him to lose his mental equilibrium. At this time of extreme psychological vulnerability, a sudden bout of the Hong Kong flu struck him down. He ended up in hospital.

Unaware of what was taking place at Oxford, Nella and I went down in Trinidad with our own severe bouts of the same notorious influenza. I recall that Vidia, who had arrived in Trinidad at the time of Siri's birth, was not helpful. He suggested that I have a glass of champagne. The Queen, he let us know, had sent the renowned broadcaster Richard Dimbleby a bottle of champagne when he was feeling 'very low'. With my brain aching in my skull, I brushed aside his foolish suggestion and sought the help of my neighbour's daughter, Nilsa, to help with bathing and feeding our still very small baby. Vidia did what he could to help: he recorded our pale, sick faces with his camera!

Switching from his original course in Philosophy and Psychology, Shiva left Oxford with a degree in Classical Chinese. He was also lucky in love, at just the right time. I have no idea how and when Shiva was fortunate to meet a very classy, clever and level-headed young woman named Virginia Stuart. Her father, Douglas Stuart, presented a nightly current affairs programme on the BBC. Jenny, as she has always been known, was one of three children who pursued their degrees at Oxford. She guided Shiva back

Shiva and Jenny's wedding, 1967

to better health and supported his vocation to be a writer.

Early in their marriage, Mel and I visited Shiva and Jenny in their studio apartment in Notting Hill. I found Shiva no longer the lanky and lean young man we had seen off at the docks in Port of Spain. For one thing, he had become – and would remain – a more than competent fudge-maker.

The image of Jenny I took away from that first meeting was of a very tall, thin and pale young lady sitting erect at the typewriter (she was preparing Shiva's first novel, *Fireflies*, for the publishers). Over the years, Mel and I would get to know Jenny's parents, Douglas and Margaret, and her elder brother, Nicky. Douglas and Margaret lived in a cottage in the country with a beautiful hedge of pink roses that remains unforgettable in its profusion.

Our visit to Notting Hill was short, because we were on our way to Europe with our friends Naz and Zahida Ahamad. But we felt reassured about Shiva, who had put his Oxford crisis and near-breakdown behind him, though surely not forgotten. In the end, however, his relationship with his brother became a source mainly of pain, when it could easily have been otherwise if Vidia had been a different, more loving and generous person.

In Shiva's essay, 'My Brother and I', published in his posthumous volume *An Unfinished Journey*, he set down, in language both poised and obviously painful for him to compose, what Vidia had meant to him as a newcomer at Oxford and in the years that followed. According to Shiva, his brother Vidia, away in England during his youth, had been mainly a shadowy if glamorous abstraction to him:

> Abstraction only began to lessen when I myself went to England (even unto Oxford!) at the age of eighteen. Yet, the gap of twelve or thirteen years that separates us remained important. We did not, overnight, cease to be strangers to one another. He perplexed me; and I, no doubt, perplexed him. We had, after all, come out of different worlds. The Hindu Trinidad of his youth was not the Hindu Trinidad of my youth. We did not have a shared past; we did not have a shared pool of memory, ancestral or otherwise. I had vulnerabilities he did not always find easy to understand. Our natural ties of affection would have to discover new modes of expression – and for a long time, neither of us knew what those might be; for a long time there was mutual distress. No grand solutions have ever occurred. But there have been a series of small resolutions along that difficult, treacherous road. We have come to recognise each other's autonomy, to acknowledge the existence of areas of privacy and inaccessibility. Writing has helped, not hindered, that process of slow accommodation. It has offered a means of communication.

Far less equivocal, and distressingly contemptuous, Vidia would tell his own biographer many years after Shiva's death that 'my brother was a gatherer of injustice... When he drew breath, he whined.' And, later: 'I was really hoping when my brother came along – before I was told about his alcoholic idleness – that he would, as it were, show me a new way. But he was just using me as a template. He was patterning himself on me.'

Like Mira and Amar, Shiva and Jenny, when they stayed in Trinidad from 1969 to 1970, lived with Ma in Nepaul Street as Shiva sought facts and inspiration for his second novel, *The Chip-Chip Gatherers*. During their stay, Jenny took a job in the Library at the University of the West Indies in St. Augustine, where her boss was Dr. Alma Jordan, who had been ahead of Kamla at St. Joseph's Convent. From Trinidad, Shiva and Jenny travelled back to England via Jamaica, where they visited Kamla and Hari and their three children, Ved, Shalini and Surya Roshni.

*Fireflies*, Shiva's first novel, was published in 1970 by André Deutsch. It is now a Penguin Modern Classic. Previously, three of his short stories had been brought out in a Penguin publication. The reviewer Mary Borg wrote of Shiva in the *New Statesman*: 'It is not necessary to compare him with his brother: he is obviously going to stand alone in his own right.' That opinion mirrored what I had always felt. Shiva was born to write: his genial humour was a special gift.

With Shiva's marriage, six of Ma's seven children now had spouses. We led independent and separate lives. No demands were made on one another. Now only Sati, Nella and I still lived in Trinidad. We got along beautifully. Our children were growing up together without any sign of competitiveness among them. Neil, Sati's eldest, was born in 1954. My youngest, Siri, was born in 1965. The range of ages made them tolerant and not combative in dealing with one another. Nella, born in 1952 and thus only two years older than Neil, was more of a sister than an aunt to them all. Despite the scattering of the family, we tried our best to remain close to one another. Although Mira, who also had three children, had moved to the USA when her children were still under six, we managed to maintain – and still maintain – close contact and meet each other as often as we can.

However, this closeness was not true for all of Ma's children.

From 1964, when Mel and I built our home and moved into Valsayn, until the mid-seventies, Vidia stayed with us whenever he made his intermittent visits to Trinidad. With age and marriage, for a while our relationship became a lot more wholesome than in the past, and we seemed to understand each other better as the years rolled by. Vidia was writing a number of long pieces for the *New York Review of Books* and the *Observer* in the UK, and even for individuals such as a certain Mr. Epstein, who apparently had commissioned from Vidia a story on which he could base a film.

When Vidia came to Trinidad, it was always on a writing assignment. He was never on vacation. Trinidad was, more often than not, a port of call, except for his coverage of the infamous Michael Abdul Malik trial in 1971. Malik, also known as Michael X and, originally, Michael de Freitas, was a Trinidadian grown sensationally famous in the UK as a Black Power advocate. He had returned to Trinidad to live, attracting to him various friends and admirers from the UK. One day he murdered with a cutlass one of the latter, a young Englishwoman named Gail Benson, and buried her body on his estate. Vidia saw a book in the events and the trial, a project that brought him home. On that trip, Pat accompanied him and regularly attended the trial in Arima with him. I believe they stayed with us over Christmas that year, and we celebrated the arrival of the New Year at the Hilton Hotel in Port of Spain, overlooking the Grand Savannah, with Ralph and Rhoda Walker, Sati and Crisen, and Sonny and Norma Johnson.

What few people know is that Vidia found it difficult to write when he was in Trinidad. Now that we were older, we could see and understand the complex person he was and the private ordeal he faced in coming to the island. We tried as best we could to accommodate him and give him as much space as possible. A desk in his bedroom did not help. The empty house during the day, when he could roam anywhere without the annoying background noises of household activities, did not help. Vidia even tried a stay at the guest house at Mount St. Benedict, the monastery in the hills overlooking the northern plain. That, too, did not help.

Trinidad itself distracted him. The light, the colours, the sounds, the people, the events, the racism, the politics, the hopelessness, the stagnation: all distracted him. It was as if Trinidad was a quagmire that stultified, a land of quicksand that swallowed him. Trinidad always made Vidia restless. He liked talking to the rural people of simple lives and background, especially those who did not know him and had no idea of what he did for a living. With other people he seemed chronically unhappy. He also made some people unhappy.

His visits coincided with the formative years of our children. They remember him well from their most impressionable ages. While Vidia was never one to interfere with their routine activities, and he gladly joined them in playing cricket on the beach, they were also aware that he was always checking on their knowledge of their surroundings, of the names of plants and shrubs and trees. Noises, particularly the radio and TV being left on when no one was listening or looking, caused him to rage. Oddly enough, the hum of the vacuum cleaner or the sound of the broom knocking against the furniture was pleasing.

To our children, Uncle Vido (as they called him) was 'strange,' 'odd', 'impossible', or just 'plain nuts'. They were not in awe of him, but they also never disrespected him in our presence, much less to his face. 'Clear the battlefield!' he would declare as they ended breakfast and set off at 6.30 am for school. While Vidia stayed with us, Kiran and Siri often mimicked his words and Oxonian accent when he was not in earshot. 'Orf' and 'orn' were among their favourites. They would extemporise in the back seat of the car until the mocking sound of 'rum' (room) and 'cawfee' (coffee) got the better of my patience.

Vidia and Pat with Kiro and Siri in the garden at Valsayn

Valsayn: botanical lessons for Kiro and Siri with Pat and Vidia

Pat (I think it was in 1971) took on the role of teacher to the children during a sudden shutdown of schools because of an outbreak of polio. When Siri received the higher grade in Pat's report, Kiran was mortified. We still have Pat's bundle of assignments and reports and Mel managed to get a few charming pictures of one of their sessions.

Vidia depended solely on the success of his writing for his income, but his rising literary acclaim was not yet matched by his earnings. Pat was no longer working. Some books did not sell well. I recall his disappointment after the publication of both *The Loss of El Dorado*, about Caribbean history, and later *Guerrillas*, based on the Abdul Malik murders. He was slow in changing both his agent and his publishers. And this hesitancy cost him dearly and kept him constantly looking for the next dollar to keep him secure.

Working with Robert Silvers of the *New York Review of Books* led to special assignments to write about Jorge Luis Borges and the Perons. These assignments naturally took him to their country, Argentina. Vidia was well aware that at that time Argentina was a cauldron of upheaval. His journeys within the country and his work on its people and culture could be dangerous. He soon found out just how perilous it could be. As he left Trinidad he instructed me what to do if he ran into serious trouble. And run into trouble he soon did. Travelling for some reason without any identification on him, he was dragged off a bus with a gun to his head. Forced to lie on a floor, he was body-searched before being thrown into a cell. He was escorted even to the bathroom. His guards seemed trigger-happy. Eventually, through the intervention, I believe, of the British High Commission, he was released from jail. It was a most unpleasant episode.

At our home in Valsayn we developed a kind of routine for Vidia on these trips. He tended to arrive at short notice. We were never sure of his proposed length of stay, but when he went off to Argentina, as he often did, we knew he would be back for his return flight to England. From Pat's first stay in Valsayn we had moved Vidia to the girls' room, where there was a double bed. From then, until October 1984, this is the room in which he stayed.

One morning, right after his return from one of his trips to Argentina, for the first time that I could remember, Vidia knocked on my bedroom door and asked me to delay my departure to Port of Spain. He needed to talk to me. It was dawn and I was making arrangements to take the children to school. (Against my instincts, I had become the driver for the neighbourhood.)

Vidia had always been prudish with me. At times he had even spoken of his deep admiration for the life of an ascetic. I knew that was rubbish. Vidia liked nice things. From a china teacup, a crystal wine glass and fine wine to lily-white linen and gourmet food, little that he cared for was in line with any sort of asceticism. So I was jolted that morning when he spoke in revealing detail about some apparently mesmerising sexual encounters, starting in Argentina, he had enjoyed with a woman named Margaret Gooding (or Margaret Murray – she used both names).

He was animated and more candid with me than I had ever seen him. In disbelief, I listened to his account of a new, intimate and compulsive friendship he had started with Margaret. Many years later, on reading Patrick French's unabashedly frank biography of Vidia, *The World is What It Is*, I learned that the story Vidia gave me that morning in my home in Valsayn was part-truth, part-fabrication. He had not been struck with frantic sexual desire on seeing Margaret for the first time across a room, as he had told me, nor was the feeling mutual that evening. But what happened subsequently had indeed become sexually intoxicating. Vidia was so invigorated by the turn of events that he was compelled to share the news with me.

I did not know what to say, how to react. My eyes must have opened like two saucers. I confess that I was not sufficiently versed in the ways of the world to participate fully in the conversation. All the same, this revelation about unbridled extramarital sexual pleasures, initiated by my self-proclaimed 'ascetic' brother Vidia of all persons, left me stunned.

I needed to leave the house and go out to school. I needed to be distracted and I needed to think. I needed to reassure myself that such an overly erotic episode between my brother and a woman other than his wife would soon self-destruct. That evening, I learned that he had not said a word to Mel about this liaison. While it was an almost welcome change to see Vidia so animated, so liberated, I also found it sad. Sad for him and sad for Pat – and sad for me. In that one morning I had learned a lot more about my brother than I wished to know.

The affair continued and, in fact, grew in intensity. When Vidia was not going to Argentina to meet Margaret, he brought her to Trinidad or met her in Caracas. Whenever Margaret came to Trinidad, Vidia with no fuss went to stay with her at the Queen's Park Hotel, at one time our leading hotel, overlooking the Savannah and not far from QRC. I noticed that while Vidia always complained about lacking money and having to spend it, he seemed to have no problems paying Margaret's and his own air fares and hotel bills.

With time, Vidia become ever bolder in flaunting his relationship with Margaret in public. In Trinidad he took her everywhere. Since Ralph Roopchand was no longer employed by us, he often needed a chauffeur. With the help of Naz Ahamad, who ran a car dealership, we found him one. After breakfast, Vidia would drive to Tranquillity School with us. The chauffeur would collect the car and Vidia at Tranquillity, and then return the car with him to Tranquillity at the end of the day. Often our housekeeper Pinky would have prepared a picnic basket for Vidia.

We were glad on the whole when the time came for Margaret to leave for Argentina, or for Vidia to return to Pat in England.

Shiva and Jenny had long been back in England. They had been in Trinidad for some of the worst days of the tumultuous Black Power uprising in 1970. For her own safety and protection, Jenny used to travel daily from St James to her work at UWI in St. Augustine in the company of another librarian, a Trinidadian.

Life remained bad enough in this regard in the mid-seventies in Trinidad. In Jamaica, where Kamla lived with her family, it was much worse. Trapped in Prime Minister Michael Manley's ultra-socialist policies, Jamaica lapsed into a state of turmoil that made Trinidad's menacing Black Power marches seem almost as harmless as Carnival parades. Looting and burning, and what the police primly termed 'serious crimes against persons', became the order of the day. Punitive property taxes threatened the landed families. Under siege, prosperous residents in the wealthier districts fled in droves to Canada and the United States. Kamla reported how you woke up on mornings to find old neighbours gone, vanished without a goodbye. Looters sacked businesses with impunity. Foreign currency was difficult to get and businessmen faced not only severe cash-flow problems but an epidemic of bankruptcy. Poorer people refused to pay rent to their landlords. Unscrupulous foreigners ran off with other people's cash.

In this atmosphere, Father Arthur Lai-Fook, a Trinidadian priest and for many years a leading teacher at CIC, urgently advised Kamla to get out of Jamaica with the children. Hari, her husband, was defiant: he insisted that he would be the last man left on the island. Heeding Father Lai-Fook, however, Kamla packed five suitcases and landed in Trinidad with her three children. Ved, her eldest, was about fourteen, Shalini was twelve and Surya Roshni just ten.

Away from their father and unsettled, they were at some level traumatised by this uprooting. Getting into schools, especially very good schools, was the easiest part. To that they responded well. But they were not in Trinidad on vacation and they knew it. They were under severe stress. Roshni fell ill almost every day at school. Kamla, who several years before had started the Higher School Certificate classes at St. Augustine's Girls, could get a teaching job but only at base salary. Her sixteen years at the prominent Wolmer's Boys School in Jamaica, as well as her previous years in Trinidad, were not taken into account. Hari visited from Jamaica, but he was accustomed to a particular lifestyle as a well-known and respected businessman in Jamaica and simply did not fit into Trinidad. Nevertheless, he moved back and forth valiantly between the two islands to try to salvage what he could to keep the family going.

Things remained in a state of flux until a house was found for Kamla and her family around the corner from our own home in Valsayn. Sati and Crisen now also lived nearby, in South Valsayn. Eager to maintain family morale, we shared some of our resources. To ensure Kamla's mobility, I was happy to let her use the car in which we travelled to school daily. We also visited constantly as a family among the various houses. Our garage at No. 3 Woodlands no longer housed cars. Instead there was a table-tennis board, two hammocks and a few comfortable wooden chairs. Sati came regularly to do her forty laps in the pool. The garage, on the cooler side of the house, became the place where we gathered informally but regularly for tea and chatting.

Valsayn, garage activities

On his visits to Trinidad, Vidia now stayed with Kamla when Hari was not in the island. (Vidia had never accepted Hari Tewari as Kamla's husband. He was always hostile, inexplicably so, to Hari.) This arrangement, which seemed natural at first, would precipitate probably the most divisive crisis in our family history.

Since her return from India many years before, Kamla had been given to more than occasional tantrums. After Pa's death, we in the household had no choice but to live with them. There was a pattern to these occurrences. She would storm out of the house and visit friends who never knew that she had just 'blown a fuse' at home. She would then return as if nothing had happened, just as Bhuppie had done after his memorable 'stroll' with Vidia. Now, many years later, and under stress after her forced return from Jamaica, she blasted me one day.

Vidia had teasingly invited me to join him on a visit to Argentina. When Kamla heard of the invitation, she was forceful and thorough in her condemnation of Mel and me for what she seemed to think was our encouragement of Vidia in what she called his unscrupulous affair. Yet not long after that, we found out that Kamla was on her way to meet Vidia and, presumably, Margaret in Caracas. Mel and I believed that this would have been her first meeting with Margaret 'Whatever', as we sometimes called her – Margaret, whose only wish, according to Vidia's rather boastful words, was to hang her clothes in his cupboards in Wiltshire.

On one of our garage afternoons, Kamla arrived and announced that Vidia and Margaret were on their way to Trinidad. Her mission was to suggest that Mel and I should house them at No 3 Woodlands. Our refusal, for the most obvious of reasons (our children were all at an impressionable age, and we felt that to have Vidia in the house with an unknown woman was a bad example to set), caused the biggest altercation I have ever known in this family, and a fracture that never quite healed. While Sati and I were both present, I was singled out.

I shall never know or understand why Kamla sought to change the way we had accommodated Vidia and managed to keep ourselves, for the most part, out of his adventure in infidelity. What I did learn on the evening of his arrival, however, was that she had announced to Vidia that no one in the family, apart from her, wished to have him in their home again. This falsehood led to the sad situation that no one, including our mother, would meet or see Vidia until Sati's sudden and untimely death in October 1984. For almost ten years he communicated only with Kamla. He would tell people, both in Trinidad and abroad, that he had only one sister. And when writers or journalists came to Trinidad, Ma, Sati and I were never introduced or indicated as family members. During those years of silence, Sati made efforts more than once to meet him at Kamla's home. She had entered the house and called out to him, knowing he was at home; but he had refused to see her, without even speaking to her. Mel and I simply kept away.

Kamla would repeat these untruths and almost uncanny somersaults of personality when Vidia visited Trinidad with his second wife Nadira, a Pakistani Muslim journalist. (Pat had died of cancer in February 1996.) Kamla's first apparently vigorous disapproval of the couple would turn into cordial reception of them and rejection of us, after which her attitude would again metamorphose into a renewal of pleasant sisterhood.

In 2001, Mel and I met Nadira for the first time. She had already been married to Vidia for five years. We were in Miami visiting our two children, Kiran and Siri, who were living and working there, and Vidia was appearing at the Miami Book Fair. Our meeting, over lunch, though brief was pleasant. Vidia, hitherto always energetic and active, complained about pain in walking. (Mel, being a doctor, seemed to invite such confidences.) Circumstances and commitments did not allow us to meet again on that visit. The following year, however, Nadira travelled to Trinidad without Vidia for our daughter Siri's wedding in April. He chose not to attend; instead, Nadira was accompanied by Gillon Aitken, Vidia's literary agent. No one had bothered to inform us, and when Nadira and Gillon showed up with Kamla on the eve of the wedding it was quite awkward. We hardly knew Nadira, had never met Gillon and we were in the middle of final preparations for the wedding which was being held at our home in Valsayn.

In the following years, Vidia travelled more often to India and Pakistan than to the Caribbean. As luck would have it, we happened to meet him and Nadira twice in Delhi during that period. On these chance occasions, Mel and I were travelling with friends and found that Vidia with his wife and stepdaughter were staying at the same hotels. What a coincidence! What a small world! On the first occasion we surprised Vidia and family by knocking on their door. He was one of the featured speakers at an international conference the theme of which I would describe as 'Whither India?'. Among the many speakers were Hillary Rodham Clinton, Hamid Karzai and Amitabh Bachchan, the Indian superstar. Nadira arranged for Mel and me to attend Vidia's session. All went well until the question-and-answer section. Vidia became typically riled and testy when he deemed the questions thoughtless. On the second occasion, Vidia was in the hotel alone while Nadira was in Pakistan visiting her family. He waited hours for us to arrive at the poolside before giving up. But we did eventually meet, only to find out once more that he was not in good health.

Vidia came back to Trinidad late in 2010 with a BBC crew led by Adam Low, whom we had met previously when he had done a 'Writers and Places' film about Shiva. We hosted the BBC crew to dinner and saw very little of Vidia, who was busy visiting old island sites with his new family. Walking had definitely become a serious problem, and he tended towards a Mahatma pose, using his wife and stepdaughter to support him on either side. Mel arranged for a group of specialist doctors to investigate the cause of his problems. Nadira, anguished, had her own family remedies.

Kamla was then approaching her eightieth birthday. Suffering by then from the onset of dementia, she would barely be able to recall or explain the vanishing of Ma's diary after her death, the destruction of her wedding album and the pillaging of letters, documents and receipts that Ma had secreted in her wardrobe at No. 26, and about which she had formerly told me. Where had they gone? Who had taken them? A mystery. But in Patrick French's biography of Vidia, Ma's diary is quoted.

When Kamla decided not to return to Jamaica but instead to stay on in Trinidad, Ma, seeking to help her, gave her an acre of land in Felicity, near Chaguanas, on which to build a home. This was part of the five acres of low-lying land that Ma's mother, Soogie Capildeo, had given to each of her nine daughters out of her agricultural estates spreading over several villages and hundreds of acres in that area. Ma knew that Kamla would not be alone there. Our cousin Phoola MacIntosh and her husband Dave lived next door. Phoola, a trained nurse, had built and ran a geriatric home. Dave was a teacher at St. Peter's in Pointe-à-Pierre, an oil-refining area in south Trinidad. Kamla found a job at St. Peter's with a higher salary than that offered by St Augustine's, plus insurance and medical cover. That job put an end to a business venture Kamla and I had started as joint owners of a boutique we had called Tikal.

The plot in Felicity on which Kamla built was agricultural land, left fallow for decades. Through all her hardships Ma had never rented out her piece of land, as most of her sisters had done. The plot was below street level and needed landfill and proper drainage. The commercial banks would not accept the title that Ma had received. She had to apply to the government for a proper deed through the Real Property Ordinance. Legal fees, surveying fees, bank fees and so on added to Hari's and Kamla's expenditure before the foundation of the new house was finally laid. Hari was both architect and building supervisor. Eventually the Tewari family were able to move into their Trinidad home at 69 Pierre Road.

Their house remains the only house built on the land so far. Ma had left half-acre parcels for most of her other surviving children, but no one else has been able to benefit from their parcel of land as the government will still not allow subdivision of the land without the necessary infrastructure of roads, drainage, electricity and water. The land lies fallow to this day, a burden to me as Ma's sole executor.

As for Ma herself, she did not allow the raw conflicts among certain of her children, their celebrity, education, professional successes or personal failures, to divert her from the path through the world she had chosen for herself, or which had been chosen for her by fate.

Cloistered by her mother when she was young, aside from the few years of formal schooling allotted to her by Soogie Capildeo, Ma had truly begun to know the world only with her marriage to Pa. His work as a newspaperman, and the resulting emphasis in our household on news both local and foreign, gradually enlightened her beyond the relatively few books she had read as a child and the few poems she had learnt and understood.

Radio, and with it, music – especially popular Western music – had not been part of her everyday experience growing up in the Lion House under her mother's careful watch. When we first moved as a family to Port of Spain, we had no radio in Luis Street in Woodbrook. Only when we went on to St. James in 1947, and Pa had a Rediffusion box installed in his own home on Nepaul Street, did radio and music became not only part of our world but hers as well. Ma then became familiar with the popular music of the day as well as with local news broadcasts and the BBC World News from London.

To hear Ma within a few years singing the praises of Frank Sinatra or her absolute favourite, Johnny Mathis, was an eye-opener. Unlike Pa, however, she never became a cinema-goer. When television finally reached Trinidad in the early sixties, Ma occasionally looked at shows with the grandchildren. But she was never interested in getting a set for herself.

For thirty years Ma devoted herself to her family. Looking back, I see that it must have been a life mainly of drudgery, single-handedly doing all the things that one needed to do for the family. She kept busy and seemed apparently fulfilled in cooking, cleaning, washing, ironing and sewing for her girls and herself. With little or no social life and interests, family weddings or organised family prayers by her mother's family or by others were her major outings. Then she would return hoarse and happy from being part of the choir of her sisters who knew all the songs that accompanied the various rites. Even there, however, her sister Tara, not Ma, was the star performer.

Pinky and Ma making roti at Valsayn

Kamla would always say that our mother was 'vain'. It is hardly an adjective that I would choose to use. Ma had a sense of self, a dignity without being self-centred. She never wore make-up. Pond's vanishing cream was her only beauty product. Coconut oil was her only body oil, and Johnson's baby powder her only talcum powder during her youthful years. She sewed her own clothes and my father forbade her to wear anything red or with red. Ma wore her skirts a little below mid-calf and liked high heels. In dress she was different from her sisters. A pair of gold bracelets, simple earrings and her wedding band comprised her only jewellery. Ma never left the house without her *orhani* or veil, even to go around the corner to the grocery or to buy vegetables.

Going out to work after Pa's death and after my marriage was Ma's deliverance. She was just forty-six. Only Shiva and Nella were left in

Nepaul Street. The job at the quarry allowed her not only to be self-sufficient but, at last, to be able to save some money. In spite of her thrift over the years she had many petty debts to settle as well as what seemed like the eternal mortgaging of the house to erase. Ma was determined that no child would pay off the mortgage. Now that she was employed and had an income, she saw it as her burden and hers alone.

When Shiva left home in 1964 and Nella came to live with Mel and me, Ma found herself truly alone for the first time in her life. A whole new world would open to her. She would travel abroad. Her religious fervour was rekindled, as well as her interest in history, especially her family history. Finally, and most importantly, she would journey to India to visit the village from whence her father had come. Ma treated her visit to India as a pilgrimage. She was also determined to go there alone. Information from the family about the village or *nagar* was conflicting. She remembered her mother's injunction to Kamla in 1948 never to visit her grandfather's village. Ma had also heard from her brother Simbhoo that no such village existed, that there was no one there for her to meet. Four of Ma's sisters had visited India before she did. The tour they took had been centred on the religious sites of Hardwar, Rishikesh, Ayodhya and Varanasi (called Benares in the years Kamla had attended university there). Believing implicitly in their brother Simbhoo, they never ventured to Gorakhpur, in or near which city one could find the so-called 'village of the Dubes'. Then along came Ma's son Vidia. In exploring the land of his ancestors and the area to which his elder sister Kamla had ventured at the age of eighteen in 1948, Vidia had found the village. In addition, he had met with the remnants of the family still there, as well as the relict who in her younger days had accompanied Pundit Capildeo on that ill-fated trip home. Her name was Jassodra; she was married to a man called Phagoo, whom the family had known in Trinidad.

In the Capildeo family there were apparently some things never to be discussed. These things, most of which I was too young to know about, were stored away in the category of family lore. Vidia's exposure of this piece of family business in *An Area of Darkness* brought vilification on Ma by members of the family who had chosen to believe in Simbhoo's, their Dada's, account. Simbhoonath's wife and daughter announced that Ma should hang her head in shame as the mother of Vidia, a treacherous child whom Simbhoo had held lovingly in his arms as a baby! Vidia had sullied the name Capildeo. While *A House for Mr. Biswas*, which satirised and ridiculed life among the Capildeos in the loose disguise of fiction, was bad, *An Area of Darkness*, offered as fact, was much worse. An edict went out: the name Naipaul could not be mentioned in Uncle Simbhoonath's house again.

Ma would have recalled the wrath and ire that Pa received from the Indian community, including members of his own family, on the publication of *Gurudeva and Other Indian Tales* (although the book was financed, in fact, by Simbhoo, with a loan later repaid). She became deaf and defiant in the face of criticism and warnings. She would travel to India and find the village herself. Ma ignored all the poison-pen letters and midnight phone calls from Simbhoonath's only daughter. She was sixty-five years old and the year was 1978. She booked her flights before telling anyone. She would not be dissuaded; she would not postpone; she would not ask anyone to accompany her.

Ma flew to London, where she spent some time with Nella and her husband Nigel and with Shiva and Jenny. She was ready for her first trip to India, but nothing had really prepared her for the emotions and trepidations she felt on her arrival in Delhi. She was glad she had someone to call there. Nirad Chaudhuri, a journalist and essayist working for the *Times of India,* had visited us in Valsayn, where he had met Ma. He had given her his address and telephone contact information, and invited her to stay with his family. From her hotel she contacted Nirad and paid a visit to the family home in an apartment block. An independent woman, Ma stayed at the hotel and refused to impose on the family's generosity. But she welcomed other offers of help, especially with planning her travels within India. Her journey to Gorakhpur, north of Delhi, should be by car and not train, which required too many stops and changes. Nirad arranged for her to have a reliable driver and car. She needed to be reassured about the driver and remained a little uneasy about him.

With money stitched into the pockets in her petticoat and her passport strapped to her body in a paper-thin leather case, Ma set off. She travelled with all her luggage, prepared for the long haul. She was aware that she would have to stay overnight somewhere. Once outside the city, she saw the great plains stretching ahead. Scattered trees lined some of the main roads and the general feeling was one of heat and dust. The car passed many uninviting roadside inns covered with corrugated iron sheeting. Open-sided and exposed, they revealed men sitting on stringed beds sipping cups of tea or *nimbu pani* (lemonade). Trucks lined the area. Occasionally, a bear or a camel lazed by the roadside. The women squatted and swept the roadside in one motion. Some carried bundles of twigs or grasses on their heads. With rings in their noses, fingers and toes and in their brightly coloured garb, the women seemed to be doing the hard work while the men lazed. Low thatched cottages, looking quite similar to the ones in Trinidad, dotted the landscape, which was more brown than green in colour.

Ma had travelled from Trinidad with a supply of our local Crix biscuits, correctly marketed at home as 'vital supplies'. As the first evening closed in, the search began for a reasonable place to spend the night. She confessed to panicking a little because of the communal bathrooms almost everywhere. They had driven for nearly six hours. The car had proved reliable and the driver willing to please. While he did not understand the Bhojpuri she spoke, they were able to get by with the use of English. Tomorrow would be another day, she decided, as she quelled her anxiety and found a rest house that was 'reasonable'. A bath with a bucket of water and a cup as a dipper was welcome. The following day Ma was ready to move on. Because of the state of the roads it took another three hours to get to Gorakhpur. The clustering of houses, the temples, the bustle of the place, the grimy walls and the bleak and rundown buildings dismayed her. After many dead ends and wayward directions, many stops and starts, many twists and turns, it seemed almost a miracle when finally they arrived at the *nagar*, called indeed the village of the Dubes.

If Ma had any doubts about where they were, these were soon dispelled by the reception she received on getting out of the car. With shouts of '*Kapil ke beti, Kapil ke beti*' (Kapil's daughter), residents ran towards the car. Ma recoiled in fear. She was overwhelmed and apprehensive. How, she asked the driver, did they know who she was? Her sisters had not gone to the village. Did someone inform them of her coming? A little stunned, she sought to find out who among them was the head of the family. No one looked like anyone in Trinidad. No one looked vaguely like her father. Still feeling unsure of the people surrounding her, she finally accepted an invitation to go into one of the tapia dwellings.

The low ceiling of the hut meant an even lower door. Ma, just five feet tall, had to bend her head to enter. The pitch-dark interior made her see poorly for a while. Did she sit on a bench as in Trinidad, or on the floor? She did ascertain at some point the nature of her relationship to these people, but memory fails me about the precise details, and there is no one left to ask. The main person she met was a mature man, a grandson or great-nephew of Ma's father, about fifty years old. He assumed that Ma had brought money for the family.

Ma's father had died in 1926, at the age of fifty-three. Ma was thirteen years old when he left for India with plenty of money to buy goods for trading. His sudden death was a shock, and had caused Nanee to request a death certificate as proof of his demise. She must have known about the woman he had travelled with, Jassodra. Was that the reason for asking Kamla not to go to Gorakhpur? Yet Nanee continued to send money to India, and even today members of the family still live at the same address and worship at the same family temple. Did the family in Trinidad, mainly Simbhoonath, continue to send money after Nanee's death in 1952?

Ma was not comfortable being there in the village. For almost seventy years or more these Brahmins, these Dubes, had expected to be kept. Times had changed. India had changed. They should have changed. To her they seemed a parasitic crew. When she was offered a chance to rest and take a meal, she knew it would be unforgivable to refuse. She compromised and agreed to have a cup of tea. The tea arrived. They offered her sugar, which she accepted, but when her host used his index finger to stir in the sugar, she was mortified. Obliged to drink the tea, she felt her stomach heave, and she almost retched.

It was time to leave. Trinidad was home. It was a long way off. She did not fit in here. She did not belong here. She must have given some money in her father's memory.

On her return I asked: 'Well, Ma, how was your trip?' Her reply was: '*Beti*, India is for the Indians!' She could not see the lighter side of her reply. She was simply happy to be home.

Ma's religious fervour was not dampened by her visit to the home of her ancestors. The Hindu temple in Ethel Street in St. James became a kind of refuge outside her home. She and her younger sister Tara would scarcely miss a Sunday worship or any of the many special Hindu observances. Instead of schoolbooks in her house, her *Ramayan* now stood on its carved stand at one end of the dining table. While most of her pujas and prayers were said at the temple, she kept a small shrine on the wall of her bedroom where Pa's desk and typewriter once stood, and an outdoor shrine where she lit her earthen oil lamp before dark.

Ma and Tara in the temple, Tara in foreground

Vidia and Shiva at Ma's outdoor shrine at Nepaul Street

Tara's death in 1988 would leave Ma without her favourite sister and best friend. Ma's years at the quarry had ended in 1985, the year of Shiva's death. The quarry would be closed, leased or sold within two or three years. She had worked for thirty years, or until she was seventy-two. With her gratuity she asked her nephew Suren to buy the land on which the house stood at 26 Nepaul Street. She used her last will and testament to show her appreciation to Kamla and Vidia for what they had given in her time of need and dependency. They were to be left all her bank shares, as well as a share of 26 Nepaul Street. By this time, Kamla had already received land from our mother. Now Vidia received his portion of the five acres our mother had owned.

Ma continued to live in and look after 26 Nepaul Street, trimming the irascible bougainvillea and pruning the ever-faithful roses. She kept a talking parrot which she called Hanuman. Shiva, making a film for the BBC, captured images of Ma in the temple and with Hanuman the parrot at No. 26. To escape the loneliness she undoubtedly felt, she continued to travel. In this way, she kept pace with not only her children but her growing number of grandchildren. Nevertheless, she also continued to recognise the importance of keeping her distance. When Sati's daughter Shayle was getting married, someone asked Ma what she thought of Shayle's choice of husband. Ma's reply summed up her relinquishment of responsibilities. '*Beti*,' she said, 'I looked after my children. Now they must look after theirs.'

Ma with Kamla and Vidia at Valsayn

# CHAPTER 9

## *In and Out of Politics*

'*Beti*, India is for the Indians!' Ma had said shrewdly. But was Trinidad for Trinidadians like us? Many people, including some in our immediate family, continued to emigrate or to flee from Trinidad and Tobago. Mel and I did not run. We stayed. However, I can say that we chose to remain where we were born not out of any noble sense of a need to sacrifice our comfort and help our nation, or be loyal to it through thick and thin. There were many times when we felt like packing up and moving on, just as many other people felt – people like us and also people utterly unlike us, of different backgrounds and perspectives – when they faced the problems of life in Trinidad and Tobago. In the early 1970s, in particular, Mel and I gave serious consideration to leaving. When that idea did not work out, and Mel happened to fall ill and took months to recover, it was at that point that we (as Eric Williams put it in the mid-1950s about himself) decided to let our bucket down in Trinidad. In the end, we stayed because the circumstances of our life made it necessary to stay. That is the simple truth.

Life in Trinidad and Tobago was never easy. It represented a virtually never-ending challenge, of blows to the mind and heart, not least of all in the realm of politics. As ordinary citizens, Mel and I and our children lived through changes that shook the country almost continuously and made many people pessimistic about its future. All the major political parties seemed to be in constant turmoil. In addition, crime rose steadily, especially after the trade in illegal drugs became commonplace. The level of both violent and non-violent crime only grew.

In 1965, three years after Independence, the government declared a State of Emergency. Among those placed under house arrest was C.L.R. James. An acclaimed writer about cricket, culture and politics, and an ex-QRC man, he had founded the PNM's main journal, *The Nation*, and had been Eric Williams's mentor until he dared to criticise his protégé. On one of Vidia's visits to Trinidad, while James was under house arrest, Mel and I drove him to James's home in Barataria so the two men could talk. They had known one another in London. Security was tight around the house.

Mel and I stayed in our car while Vidia tried to get into the house, but the heavy police presence intimidated him and the meeting never took place. Eventually James was released from house arrest and left the country.

The excitement, the turbulence, never stopped. Five years later, in April 1970, two young army officers led an attempted military coup against the government, which was still in the hands of the PNM. The revolt was quickly put down, but in a sense the country was changed forever. An attempted military coup in Trinidad? Very few people had thought such a thing possible. Around this time, too, Black Power became a dominant, disruptive movement that provoked fresh racial and political tensions. Ironically, one of its main targets was the PNM government and Williams himself. He was seen as a leader too closely allied to US and European powers, too unsympathetic to leftist leaders such as Fidel Castro. In 1976, partly in response to Black Power, Trinidad and Tobago became a Republic. (Rebelliousness was part of our landscape. As a tutor at the University of the West Indies, I had witnessed the bizarre day in 1963 when students locked out the Prime Minister of Canada, John Diefenbaker, when he was on campus for the opening of Canada Hall, a residential facility which was a gift from his government and people to the students! Their demonstration was prompted by the destructive actions of West Indian students at Sir George Williams University in Canada, some of whom claimed they were the victims of racism because of poor marks they had received.)

Through all of these changes, Dr. Williams continued as Prime Minister. Then, in 1981, he died suddenly. His party, the PNM, held on to power for another five-year term. In 1986, however, torn by internal dissension, it finally fell. After thirty years in office, it was brought down by the National Alliance for Reconstruction (NAR), a new alliance of opposition political forces that crossed racial lines and included strong support from Indian voters. A.N.R. Robinson, a former pillar of the PNM from Tobago, became the new Prime Minister. Finally, Indians of all persuasions, but Hindus in particular, seemed to have a major stake in helping to run the affairs of the nation.

From the outset, however, the coalition was shaky. Basdeo Panday, the main Indian leader in the new governing alliance, began to challenge Robinson's leadership. Before the alliance, he had been able to win several seats in Parliament for his political party. As a veteran trade unionist he was the kind of street-fighter politician who, with his lively, often ingenious language, had over the years developed a winning way with words and with people. For a while, at least, he seemed to have a clear, strong vision of himself and of the nation moving into the future. But Panday's bid for further power became a critical source of concern in some quarters. In 1987, a national daily newspaper, the *Trinidad Express*, featured an article raising concern about 'the Indianisation of the Government', with an accompanying headline alerting readers that 'Trinidadians Still Fear Take-over of the State by East Indians'. In other words, as some people saw it, an Indian was never to be allowed to become Prime Minister, because such a development would violate the 'natural' order of power in Trinidad and Tobago.

Through all these and other political and racial agitations, Mel and I stood very much on the sidelines. We had our own reservations about trusting Mr. Panday. Our gestures, if we made them, were largely token. Then, in July 1990, two events shook the nation. One was relatively benign. Mr. Panday formally inaugurated the United National Congress (UNC) as a national party, virtually eliminating the NAR as a major force. Led by A.N.R. Robinson, the NAR now controlled only Tobago. The other event was not benign in any way. Some days later, more than a hundred armed members of the Jamaat-al-Muslimeen, or Black Muslims, made up largely of Muslims of African descent, tried to take over the country by force. The plotters seized the Red House, where Parliament was meeting. They took Prime Minister Robinson and others, including journalists, hostage. Robinson was shot, but not killed. They also seized our only television station. The actions of the Muslimeen came as a shock to me and practically everyone else. Parts of the country seemed to go mad. Looters struck at over a hundred businesses, setting fire to many of them. Six days passed before the insurgents were compelled to surrender to the authorities.

A year later, in December 1991, the PNM returned to power. Patrick Manning became Prime Minister, with Panday as Leader of the Opposition. But four years after that, in November 1995, the electoral moment long feared by Afro-centric voters came to pass. When the PNM and Panday's UNC won the identical number of seats in the general elections, Robinson and his NAR, which had won the two Tobago seats, threw their support behind the UNC. Basdeo Panday became the first Indian to hold the post of Prime Minister. He kept the position from that year until 2001. In the 2001 national elections, history repeated itself – almost. The two main parties again won the same number of seats, resulting in a hung Parliament (the NAR won none). This time, however, Mr. Robinson, who had become President of the nation, invited Mr. Manning of the PNM to form the new government. The next year, 2002, Manning called new elections. The PNM then regained unambiguous control of the government.

Following such events closely, but not too closely, Mel and I tried to keep up, as best we could, with the ever-shifting shape of politics in our country. We felt closer to the action whenever we socialised with our good friends Romesh and Indra Mootoo of San Fernando. Making a foursome, we went to political meetings whenever and wherever possible.

We had known Romesh and Indra even before we had left for Scotland. When we returned in 1963, we had picked up as friends where we left off. Our gatherings were always lively and full of laughter and fun, especially with Romesh's irrepressible delivery of his many 'golf jokes'. Our children – they had five – grew up knowing one another well. They shared many holidays together, especially in our tiny holiday home overlooking the beach in Mayaro, on the eastern side of the island. Like us, the Mootoos had decided to forgo emigration. They, too, had cast down their bucket in Trinidad. Like Mel, Romesh was a general practitioner, who had studied in Ireland at the Royal College of Surgeons, but he was also keenly interested in law and politics. In fact, he became mayor, and a highly successful one, of San Fernando, running as a member of the NAR.

Mel and I always tried hard not to let political affiliation determine our friendships. After all, our friends the Mahabir family in Port of Spain had been deeply associated with the leadership of the PNM for some years, including the years when my uncle Rudranath Capildeo had been Leader of the Opposition. That did not lessen our appreciation of their many fine qualities or our mutual admiration and our pleasure in their company. In addition to the Mootoos, in San Fernando we were close to the Kangaloos, and Carlyle Kangaloo had himself become mayor of San Fernando as a member of the PNM. The reality is that Mel and I were never fully satisfied by either major party, or by any of the major parties that emerged over the decades. We were certainly not entranced by what we saw as the divisive politics of Dr. Williams, but we were also never committed to the various incarnations of the political opposition to the PNM.

Nevertheless, we kept up the hope that farsighted leaders of integrity would emerge to command the respect of the electorate as a whole. One day in the early 1990s, as we began to be more and more aware of Mr. Panday's political shortcomings, Mel and Romesh decided to leave Mayaro and pay a visit to a politician named Winston Dookeran. Mr. Dookeran lived in Trincity, at that time a developing suburb east of Valsayn and close to the Piarco Airport. Mel and Romesh would be among the first of many who would urge Winston Dookeran to assume a greater role in the Opposition – to try eventually to supplant Mr. Panday, then still head of the NAR.

To us, Winston Dookeran was and is one of the few genuine statesmen among the many would-be leaders pushing themselves forward in Trinidad and Tobago politics. A tall and imposing man, with slightly stooped shoulders and a mop of grey hair, he embodies courtesy and mild manners. He tends to think things through rather than act rashly and colourfully. As a result, he does not fit the image of the ideal leader for the many Trinidadians of all backgrounds who tend to favour flash and brashness.

Largely because of what he says and does, I have grown to know and admire him over the years. He may seem to some people overly hesitant and cautious, but no one can accuse him of behaving in such a way as to damage his integrity and our sense of him as a competent man. To me, he remains an unsung hero, as is Kenneth Lalla, who spent only five years as a legislator, but then withdrew with grace and of his own volition from the political fracas. Both men were hamstrung by our racially divisive politics, which will, it seems, always shut out the people best qualified to guide our tiny nation.

For a brief moment it seemed as though Mr. Dookeran would get his chance within his party, which was now the United National Congress, led by Mr. Panday. The UNC formed the main opposition to the PNM. In September 2005, after various charges of corruption were levied against him, Mr. Panday was compelled to step down as Leader of the Opposition in Parliament. That month, he publicly turned over the position of political leader of the UNC to Mr. Dookeran. The way seemed clear for a rejuvenated UNC to move forward. Urging the party faithful to try to look at politics in a new way, Mr. Dookeran pledged to make the UNC truly representative of all the people of the nation. He set as an explicit goal the effective ending of racial bigotry in our politics. But it did not take long for the volatile Mr. Panday to change his mind about giving up power. He did so in a way that offended me and made me question his integrity.

One evening, I was at home in a pleasant and expectant mood, watching the television broadcast of a huge UNC rally. Its top leaders, including Mr. Panday and Mr. Dookeran, were present to address the gathering. Then, to my astonishment, I witnessed something bizarre. Acting obviously in collusion with Mr. Panday, most of the other major leaders of the party openly snubbed Mr. Dookeran. They even went so far as to prevent him from speaking. I was incensed. I also felt despondent about the future of the UNC, and the nation.

Respecting Mr. Dookeran's qualities both as a political leader and a human being who deserved much more courteous treatment, I went straight to my desk and wrote him a warm letter of support and encouragement. With this letter I soon became formally involved for the first time, with a political party: the Congress of the People (COP). Formed mainly by Mr. Dookeran, the COP emerged out of this rift in the UNC leadership but aspired to go beyond it to address the needs of the entire nation. In remarkably quick time he rallied around him a talented and representative group of bright, enterprising minds. Several economists, lecturers, bankers, lawyers, doctors, teachers and businessmen joined its ranks. The party captured the imagination of many Trinidadians and grew so quickly that many of its public meetings led to traffic jams.

I became formally involved with the COP, as I have written, but I do not want to overstate my involvement. For example, I ended up speaking one day to a large gathering in Woodford Square, though I was in no way among the leadership of the party, as some people might have surmised. In fact, my participation that day came as a surprise even to me. Along with my good friend Vernon de Lima, I had agreed to speak as someone who had not previously been involved publicly in politics but was prepared bravely – or rashly – to present to the enthusiastic crowd the COP slate of candidates and to urge the people to embrace 'another new beginning' under Winston Dookeran. The fact that I would be speaking in a setting that Dr. Williams had made famous as a political venue never entered my mind. Mainly, I saw myself as a veteran schoolteacher who would not be flustered by a large audience. My job was to recommend our slate and to encourage the populace not to sit on the fence but to support the new party and the new politics. The usual hecklers had their fun, but I delivered the message. The job was done.

I never had a prominent, enduring role in the COP. I have no stories to tell of incidents and actions behind the scenes as the party planned and schemed. Mainly I spoke up in support of the party whenever it came up as a topic in conversation, as it often did, and I usually argued vigorously in its defence.

In the elections, however, reality asserted itself. Whilst the COP attracted almost 150,00 votes, or almost a quarter of the electorate, that decent showing translated into not a single seat. Winston Dookeran eventually relinquished leadership of the COP. With his withdrawal, Romesh Mootoo's interest and ours waned. A widower now, Romesh leads a quieter and more subdued life with his son, Kavir. His daughter, Shani, a writer with several books published, lives in Toronto.

Politics can seem to be the most pressing issue in the world. In the end, however, certain institutions and values such as family, and especially children, are more important. For the grandchildren of Seepersad Naipaul and Droapatie Capildeo Naipaul, Pa and Ma, the years rolled by almost seamlessly. On reaching the eleven-plus scholastic hurdle, the BissoonDaths, Akals and Tewaris accelerated into the best secondary schools, where they invariably did well. (The Inalsingh family having moved to the United States, all three of their children attended school there.) The teenage-menace years were either largely innocuous or else ignored. All our children loved Ma. My children treated her as Santa Claus whenever she arrived at our home. They often accused me of being a lot less liberal and forward-thinking than Ma.

One of the decisions that Mel and I had made when we started our family was that travel had to be an essential part of our children's upbringing. Every other year we saved so we could take the children abroad. We waited for Siri to be four years old before we began our trips. Our first journey was to Florida, where Kiran complained every day when Siri became tired. Travel revealed certain character traits. Next to our hotel was a grander hotel called the Everglades. While Rai was content, Kiran often let us know that he thought we had made the wrong choice. There were rules to these vacations. There would be no snacking, but a light lunch and good dinner. Each child could choose one gift for himself or herself. And, thankfully, there were no shopping malls in those days to torture them – and us. Siri's regular afternoon exhaustion gave Mel and me a much-appreciated siesta.

In 1971, the youngest of the Naipaul children, Nella, left for Bristol University. Ma and I supported her through her university career there. (Vidia had promised to help by paying her fees, but ended up paying nothing. The fees, if I remember correctly, were modest, with the monthly upkeep costing more – about thirty pounds.) When Nella reached London, Shiva and Jenny were there to meet her, and comfort her in any bout of homesickness she might have felt. Unfortunately, Vidia had other ideas. On her first day in England, he showed up at Shiva and Jenny's home in Earl's Court. He wasn't there long before he launched into a harsh attack on Nella. He ridiculed her Trinidadian accent and her dim prospects as a prospective graduate at what he called a 'third-rate' university. She was likely, he predicted, to end up marrying a bus driver. Shiva asked him to leave. Nella was dismayed but not devastated by Vidia's assault on her. Her above-average exam results had enabled her to attend the university of her choice, and she had chosen Bristol. Eager to start her new life, she travelled on to the university, where she eventually gained an excellent degree in Spanish and Portuguese.

Nella's departure for Britain left a gap in our household that no one could fill. Our daughter Siri, her long-time roommate at our home, was allowed on Friday afternoons to tug the vacuum cleaner up the stairs to continue their practice of cleaning their bedroom on the weekends. All the children, including Sati's, missed their pal and protector. Nella had never allowed any bullying. She usually shook off offenders with a stern warning.

Nella's course at Bristol demanded that she visit both Portugal and Spain during the summer. That year, Mel and I travelled to England and then to Madrid, where we met Nella, who had just completed her stay in Portugal. In my suitcase was the usual dress or dresses I made for her. To celebrate our meeting we overindulged in sangria and missed the midnight liveliness of Madrid. Mel and I made many tours, including a visit to the *corrida*, where thieves picked my purse and where the bull jumped over the ringside, much to Mel's delight and my embarrassment. I had doubted him about the bull!

After graduating, Nella worked for a short while before returning home to marry her fiancé, Nigel Chapman. Despite Vidia's predictions, Nigel was not a bus driver, although in later years Nella and their children loved to tease him by calling him 'the bus driver'. The son of a judge who had been a prominent barrister and appointed a QC, Nigel had attended Rugby school before studying law at Bristol. He and Nella had met there in 1971. The wedding ceremony took place in 1974 at our home in Valsayn. Ma, Kamla, Sati and I were in attendance, as well as a few friends or parents of friends. Hari, Crisen and Mel were in charge of the drinks. By some strange misstep, no one offered the bridegroom a glass of champagne. Nigel therefore stayed sober, perhaps unwillingly, throughout the happy event. He and Nella then returned to London, where they settled down as he began his own successful legal career. Today he is a senior partner in a prestigious international law firm in London.

Nigel's and Nella's wedding, 1974

From tender ages all our children were exposed to sport, but especially to lawn tennis and table tennis. Siri, our daughter, proved to be the only true champion among them. Every year, for five successive years, her class was treated to tubs of ice cream as she won a competition sponsored by Canning's, for a long time the top ice cream-making firm in Trinidad. At thirteen, she won the Silver Medal in the Latin American Table Tennis Tournament in the seventeen-and-under category. Mel and I, along with our friends 'Cap' and Meena Ali, had followed the team to Mexico City. We experienced some panic when it took more than two days for us to locate the venue where the tournament was to be held. We were not careless parents. We had simply accepted that the Table Tennis Association of Trinidad and Tobago would notify us about the site as promised. Mexico City is a sprawling city but it seemed to increase in size with the passage of time. That was not a happy learning experience! The following year, at the age of fourteen, Siri became the Junior Lawn Tennis Champion. Her small size militated against her playing competitively, but she continued with table tennis, where size mattered much less, if at all, and went on to win the 'Trinity Pink' when she was in Ireland at university studying medicine.

After Nella left for Bristol, the exodus of grandchildren to university began. It started with Sati's first-born, Neil Bissoondath (adapted from BissoonDath). Neil, living in Quebec, is an author in his own right, starting with the well-received novel *A Casual Brutality*. His brother Ved and sister Shayle also live in Canada. Kamla's Ved, her only son, now lives in California, and his sister Surya Roshni in Seattle. Their elder sister, Shalini, works with a pharmaceutical company in Trinidad. Mira's three children, Aruna, Nisha and Anil, all attended universities in the USA and now live and work there. Shiva's son Tarun lives and works in London, and Nella's three children, Renuka, Sonali and Rohan, also all make their homes in London, not far from her and from each other.

Except for two grandchildren, all the Tewaris, the BissoonDaths, the Inalsinghs, the Akals, the Naipauls and the Chapmans live abroad. While we do not meet regularly, our meetings are always warm and full of laughter. Strong ties, even the unbearably painful ones, can never be erased or denied. As a family we are fortunate to have had many more pleasant experiences than sad ones. Perhaps because she came to live with us at such a young age, Mel and I take great pleasure in seeing Nella, Nigel and their children as a natural extension of our Akal group.

Of our three children, only our eldest lives in Trinidad. Ashvin Rai, our first-born, studied in Canada and England. He works in insurance and finance and he and his wife Nadira are parents of two girls, Ishana and Arya. Kiran, our second son, is a graduate of the Royal College of Surgeons in Ireland, but after four years of medical practice he gave up the physician's life for the world of creative entertainment. He makes his home mainly in Florida, where he has designed and executed several art installations that have won him acclaim. Siri, our youngest child and only daughter, attended Trinity College in Dublin, and, following in her father's footsteps, chose family medicine as her specialty. Today she owns and runs what many people consider the foremost family clinic in St. Thomas in the US Virgin Islands. She is married to Christopher Mitchell, and they are the happy parents of Kira and Zachary Rai. Even-tempered and pragmatic, and with the quickest of wits, Siri is a joy to be around and gives to others in myriad ways. She was the last person Ma spoke of and blessed before she slipped into eternity. '*Beti*,' she said to me, 'With so many children and so many nephews and nieces, I never thought there was anything like a perfect child. But you have a perfect child. Siri is a perfect child.'

The Akal family, 1983: Rai, Savi, Siri, Mel and Kiro

# CHAPTER 10

## *When Sorrows Come*

'When sorrows come, they come not single spies/But in battalions.' I have never forgotten these lines from Shakespeare's *Hamlet*, one of the plays I studied for my Higher School Certificate. The Naipaul family, like all other families, would have to endure pain and loss. When Pat, Vidia's wife, was gravely ill, Vidia had asked me: 'Why do people not die decently?' By decently I think he meant quickly. The year was 1996. Many of us in the family misinterpreted his reason for haste. We would learn the truth sooner rather than later.

Pa died in 1953. For twenty years our luck held.

In 1972, Mel had fallen ill in San Fernando while at work. He was hospitalised for heart problems. He was forty-three. Remembering Pa and noting our children's ages, I was ridden by anxiety. I had joined the Diploma in Education in-service course introduced at UWI and was determined to complete the course in spite of the difficulties posed. I had never failed an exam and did not intend to fail this one. But with the constant threat of Mel's illness, I knew I would not excel. It took several months for him to improve, but within the year, life had improved still further when he moved his medical practice from San Fernando in the south to St. Augustine in central Trinidad: the daily drives to and from San Fernando had become more and more intolerable. (A new highway, long promised by the government to ease the hideous congestion on the road, had not at that point materialised.)

In 1980, I gave up my job as Vice-Principal of Tranquillity school, perhaps the largest co-ed school in the country. Managing over seventeen hundred students and a staff, as I recall, of about seventy-two teachers had sapped my energy and seriously threatened my health. For the first time in more than twenty years I had no classes to prepare for the Cambridge School Certificate Exams and no responsibility for supervising those who did. No longer did I have the daunting task of creating timetables which required 'setting' and 'streaming' for the fifty forms in the days of very limited technology. So used had I been to 'going to school', I felt liberated, if a little lost.

Tikal, the boutique on the busy Eastern Main Road in St. Augustine that Kamla and I had started together a few years before my retirement, from early on had showed a measure of success, but we shared the view that the boutique would fare better in Valpark Plaza, the new and only shopping mall in Trinidad. It took many months before we were offered a space in the mall, by which time Kamla had accepted a well-paid teaching job in Point-à-Pierre and the boutique had closed. When the offer came, I was encouraged to start a new undertaking of my own. I regarded the change in my work life as a fun venture and a chance, if successful, to earn some money and avoid boredom. Without a name for the shop and no idea of what I was going to sell, I relied on friends to help and guide. I began by selling the furniture of a friend who was venturing outside his profession. With the furniture on consignment, I started by selling plants and flowers. With the help of the children we settled on the name 'Smaks'. It is the acronym for the members of my own family: Savi, Mel, Ashvin, Kiran and Siri. The flowers attracted a competent florist seeking a job and she became my trainer and the store a flower/furniture shop.

Having travelled abroad and been a buyer for Tikal proved to be valuable experience. Joining a friend on a trip to New York changed the direction of the shop. Flowers remained the bread-and-butter line but the shop morphed into a provider of high-end goods, catering to an enriched economy which the oil boom presented in the late seventies in Trinidad and Tobago.

The business proved to be exciting and interesting, and whilst the learning curve was steep, worry and risks were short-term. At Christmas-time the shop became a wonderland of trees and lights and decorations. The long hours of work hardly seemed to matter. Work was a place of chatter, creativity and business. The children, in their free time, enjoyed meeting new and interesting people and the thrill and novelty relieved the pressured days at school. Our clientele became our friends and visited the shop even

Savi, Sati and Crisen in Smaks

when not buying. One particular loyal customer, a busy consultant with a larger-than-life personality, would visit the shop after her business trips to do her 'in bond' shopping. Our little shop strove to cater to the needs of our community and beyond. As the children grew up and went abroad to study, the excitement of the shop waned. But a business which had started on a whim and a fancy became one of the main attractions of the mall.

Sati and I would have tea together in the shop very frequently, not ever thinking that our shared life was to end abruptly and prematurely. In October 1984, shortly after her fiftieth birthday, Sati complained of 'blacking out' while ironing. Off she went to be checked, including for signs of a possible aneurysm. Trinidad as yet had no MRI machines. The specialist she saw assured her that all was well. He told Mel he had checked specifically for the presence of subarachnoid haemorrhaging. The next morning Sati fell into a coma. At the hospital, she was kept her on life support until her two sons could come from Canada. We all knew there was no hope.

The shock of Sati's death was like a thunderbolt. Her husband, Crisen, seemed to crack and lose direction. Both Neil and Shayle were married, but Ved, her youngest, seemed lost and in constant, desperate need of comfort. We did all we could to ease the pain but I felt helpless and hapless. Sati, who had not wanted to go to university; Sati, whose life brought so much joy to others; Sati, who wanted mainly to read and enjoy her books, who thought the ideal kitchen should have wheels like the ones on aeroplanes, who fretted about the KitchenAid I forced her to buy, who never quarrelled with anyone, and in whom my children sought refuge when we scolded them: she would not be with us any more. We had lost a light, a flame in our lives.

Shiva had just returned to London from India when he heard the bad news. He had been covering Indira Gandhi's funeral after her assassination. He flew to Trinidad, arriving on the day of Sati's funeral, but too late for the cremation. He went directly to the site of the pyre. It had been a long and tiring journey for him to get back home, but Mel and I welcomed the sight of him. We needed one another as almost never before. Ma needed the support and comfort of her children, and they gathered for her. Mira travelled alone from Florida to Trinidad for the first time. Kamla, whom we had not seen for many years, arrived with Vidia at our house at 3 Woodlands Road. And Vidia had brought his suitcases. Shiva had to move out. Mel and I should have had the courage to tell Vidia there was no room at the inn. But then Shiva stayed a few days with Kamla, which he had never before done as a visitor to Trinidad.

Kamla was indeed lucky to have had him stay with her. Nine months later, Shiva fell dead of a heart attack in his and Jenny's flat in London. Like Sati, he had been to a doctor and like Sati he had been misdiagnosed. Our hearts broke again. Our dreams shattered. Everyone else travelled

Ma and children after Sati's death: standing, Mira, Shiva, Savi; seated, Kamla, Ma, Nella

After Vidia's arrival

to London for his funeral. I remained in Trinidad, grieving all alone. Jenny, stoic and unimaginably brave, had to look after their young son, Tarun, and also plan Shiva's funeral.

We bore our grief, mourned our loss of one so young, so loving and so beautiful as a son and brother. Vidia erupted in eczema, caused perhaps by remorse for not being compassionate to his much younger brother, who had grown up without a father and had once idolised Vidia and sought his approval and love. Nella, blasted by Shiva's death, lost clumps of her hair. Born seven years apart, living in the shadow cast by Pa's untimely death, she and Shiva had shared a special bond. As children together they had conspired together and not infrequently fought one another, but above all they had loved and comforted one another living together in the house on Nepaul Street.

Once more, Ma was made to suffer by death. Shiva had been truly special to her. She believed she had lost the son who always respected and always loved her, who was not ashamed of her but had proudly showed her to the world, the son who had made her laugh and never ever brought frowns to her face or tears to her eyes. The rest of us had lost our little brother who, as Mira reminded me, once used to call a coconut a 'conkatonut'.

Shiva was cremated in August 1985. He was forty years old.

Mel and I were in New York in 1987 when we heard that Kamla had suffered a near-fatal heart attack. She had survived cardiac arrest and was in a nursing home in Port of Spain. We hastened home and headed almost immediately to her bedside from Piarco airport. On seeing us, Kamla sat bolt upright, tubes and all clinging to her. Urging her to lie back, we made every effort to comfort and encourage her. Only two years had passed since Shiva's death. We feared the worst about her condition, although we tried not to show it. By this time, Kamla wore her burdens for all to see on her face and in her mien. Now we tried to set the old conflicts aside. On her discharge from the hospital, Mel and I brought her to our home to tend to her until she was better. It was one of the few times that I had no help in the house. Hari, who was now back in Jamaica, was himself ailing. While Kamla continued to be attended by specialist doctors, Mel and I and our cousin Phoola, with whom Kamla had also fallen out, watched over her. Her heart muscle, severely damaged, could not be repaired. But evidently her will to live was strong. She survived two more heart attacks as she limped into her eightieth year. But she was never the same in spirit and in health after her first attack. Eventually her daughter Shalini and her husband, Philip Aleong, gave up their home to live with her in the house in Felicity. Many years before, Vidia had relieved her of the financial burden of her mortgage.

Shiva at Valsayn, 1984

Tarun, Shiva and Jenny in London, 1985

As for Vidia, following almost immediately upon Pat's death he married a new wife from a distant land. The twenty-year-old saga of Margaret of Argentina appeared to be over, or dormant. The new wife from a distant land was now hanging her clothes in his cupboards in Wiltshire.

As Kamla approached her last years, dementia overtook her. She died in 2010 at the Mount Hope hospital, almost twenty-six years to the day after Sati's early death. Kamla's funeral was small. Many people did not know of her passing. But her past students, both at St. Augustine's and St. Peter's, still speak in praise and admiration of their beautiful and accomplished teacher. In our time of greatest need, immediately after Pa's death, Kamla had given up her dream of love and marriage and a new life in Fiji in order to help her family in Trinidad. The eldest child, she had set the tone and standard for our education, our ambitions and our social confidence. She was also responsible for our close and lasting relationship with the Sisters of Cluny at St. Joseph's Convent, who remained our friends for life.

In spite of her bad heart, Kamla managed to outlive Ma.

For many years, Ma had awoken in Valsayn every Christmas morning along with her restless grandchildren at the crack of dawn. Presents, which had been placed in piles for days beforehand, which had been counted and rattled and patted or poked, were finally torn open before breakfast. Paper and ribbons littered the floor and carpet. Cleaning up would come later. Meanwhile, presided over by Ma, excitement and anticipation raged.

Ma's last Christmas with the Inalsinghs in Florida, 1990

Christmas 1990 was different. Ma had gone to Mira and Amar in Bradenton, Florida. I believe it was the first Christmas she had spent with Mira in Florida. In Valsayn, she was truly missed, as her arrival with a 'common fowl' in hand and bundles of chives and other seasonings or herbs usually marked for us the true start of Christmas. The children always waited for Ma to come before wrapping their family gifts. On Christmas morning, or late on Christmas Eve, Ma would prepare her special spicy pot-roast chicken for the household. Some among us ate ham, and ham or chicken with hot home-made bread was the standard breakfast fare. That year, as best I could, I did Ma's job of presiding and cooking. Rai and Nadi and their year-old daughter, Ishana, were down from Canada. Ishana, our first grandchild, proved to be the ultimate Christmas toy that year. Rai and Ma had always claimed a special attachment to one another. Rai was determined to stay on an extra week to see Ma before going back to Canada.

Swaddled in her blue-green sari, Ma returned on 12th January. Evidently she had been for a medical check-up. As she entered the house she announced: 'Well, I am back, and I have been given a clean bill of health.' We had no shortage of medical practitioners on hand. Both Kiran and Siri were now in medical practice (after a recurrence of his heart problems in 1990, Mel was taking a break from his work). Ma said she planned to collect herself for one or two days before going back to what she liked to call her 'little box house' on Nepaul Street in St. James.

The Iraqi invasion of Kuwait had initiated the Middle East War. CNN, the cable network, was providing live coverage all day, every day. We were looking at a war as if it were a sci-fi movie. Without sound, as I recall, the recurring images of the missiles on the screen conveyed the terror more than any commentary.

Two days later, in the middle of the evening, Siri reported that Ma was not feeling well. She advised Ma to sit with her eyes averted from the television. We two sat alone, with Ma resting her feet on one of the chairs. Suddenly she began to speak, seemingly at random, about her children. She began with sorrowful words expressing her sense of hurt over Kamla's bizarre wrath over the years, but especially about Vidia's repeated bad behaviour to her and others. 'I had one son,' she said (meaning Shiva), 'and he died many years ago.' In truth, our inner family circle was broken. While we tried to ensure that all ties were not completely severed, and continued to exchange Christmas cards and an occasional telephone call, Vidia was largely gone from our lives. Ma had long grown used to saying little or nothing about him. He had been especially harsh on her when, on a second visit to India, she had spoken to the press there after being tricked into doing so by the local tour operator, who was seeking free publicity for himself and his business. Ma's pleas of innocence had failed to sway Vidia.

That evening in Valsayn, Ma said nothing about Sati, Mira or me, but reminded me of the key to her bank box. She said she would give it to me the next day. As we walked towards the library where recently she had chosen to sleep, I asked: 'Ma, are you feeling better?'

'Yes,' she said with a bit of a sigh, 'I am feeling better.'

Ma went to sleep but never woke up. In medicine, it is said that one has to earn the right to die in that way. It was 15th January 1991. She had died 'decently'. At her funeral she was without the usual number of Brahmins to bear her casket to the crematorium. She had no son to light her pyre or perform the rites. But she had short-circuited these obligations by performing her *shraad* or funeral rites on her second trip to India. She had foreseen this eventuality.

Indeed, sorrows had not come as single spies in the lives of the Seepersad Naipaul family. From the early eighties into the nineties we had lost not only Sati and Shiva but before them Pinky, our old and faithful family housekeeper. And then Ma also left us.

The years that Kamla and Vidia had chosen to stay apart from the rest of us in Trinidad could not be retrieved. For both Kamla and Vidia, their lives were in turmoil. Hari, wracked by illness and a dispirited shadow of his former self, returned to Jamaica, his marriage to Kamla virtually asunder through ill health. The burden of paying off the mortgage on their home in Pierre Road and educating their children fell on Kamla – Ma's history repeating itself. Pat and Vidia were estranged. Pat left the Wiltshire house and moved into their tiny apartment in Queensgate Terrace in London. In these difficult years, Pat, as she was wont to do, retreated into herself and perhaps brooded in her diary. The Christmas cards from her kept coming, always indicating in which continent Vidia was but revealing no more. Meanwhile Vidia's liaison with Margaret Gooding was in its heyday. He would show her off on many continents and continue with his work as if everything was fine. Eventually he would miss the comfort and security he had shared with Pat and they would reconcile and return to their home in Wiltshire. Pat died within five years.

The Bissoondaths sold off the family house in Valsayn, going their separate ways to find new moorings. Jenny, as young a widow as Ma had been, was faced with a life of work and bringing up Tarun, her son and only child. She was fortunate to have compassionate and supportive parents. But loneliness is a difficult load to bear.

When Ma died, she had left nothing undone. Using a favourite phrase of Pa, each child was already in midstream, paddling his or her canoe.

Asvin Rai, Ma, Ishana, Savi: the last photograph.

Ma at 78, taken the day before she died

# CHAPTER 11

## *Never Strangers in a Strange Land*

At about 6.30 in the morning in October 2001, I was on the treadmill at a gym when someone interrupted me to say that our family friend and neighbour Anna Mahase had called on the telephone for me. My heart jumped. My immediate thought was that Mel had fallen ill – perhaps suffered a heart attack, or a stroke. The previous year he had been laid up for quite a while. I needed to know at once what was going on. Mobile phones were not commonplace then, but I was able to get to a telephone and return Anna's call. No, Mel was not ill. In fact, Anna had wonderful news that she knew she had to pass on to me at once. Vidia had won the Nobel Prize for Literature.

As I heard her message, my tears began to flow. Despite all the unpleasantness that had passed and continued to pass between us, I was genuinely happy for my brother. But my deepest reaction came when I thought about our parents. The tears then flowed in earnest. After a while, I decided to drive down to visit Kamla and share a cup of tea with her in celebration. Once again, I had misjudged her. Instead of joining me, she began to upbraid me. Why in heaven's name was I crying? It was almost as if my eldest sister saw little or no connection between Vidia's great victory and the years of effort and struggle and sacrifice and hope that Pa and Ma had put into making Vidia's victory a possibility. She saw no point in mourning the fact that neither of them was still alive to share in the historic moment.

With as little fuss as possible, but eager to be out of her company, I left Kamla's home for my own. I cannot remember if I ever got my cup of tea. However, in a day or two I would learn that she had held a news conference that very afternoon at her home on Pierre Road. A couple of days later we both appeared on television. A burning question in Trinidad was why Vidia had failed to mention Trinidad in his formal announcement on learning of his Nobel victory, which he called 'a great tribute to both England, my home, and India, the home of my ancestors'. (To have mentioned Trinidad, he explained later, might 'encumber the tribute'.) Asked about it, I was about to try to provide an answer when Kamla suggested that I should not. It was a dispiriting moment. Our host was someone who knew the name

V.S. Naipaul, but very little about Vidia's work and even less about the magnitude of the award. In fact, the coverage in general was subdued, notably muted when compared to the triumphant reporting of Derek Walcott's win a few years before.

By 1972, sixteen years after his first book, *The Mystic Masseur*, Vidia had compiled a body of work that merited at least a nomination for the Nobel Prize. From that year, when Patrick White of Australia won it, until 1992, when the Nobel in Literature went to Derek Walcott of St. Lucia (and Trinidad), we had lived on quiet alert every October, when the prize is usually announced. Every day we hoped to hear that the committee had chosen Vidia. Walcott's triumph, however, suggested to most of us that our hopes were permanently dashed. What chance was there that the Swedish committee would select two West Indian-born writers within a few years of one another? Besides, the committee was said to have a liberal bias, and Vidia had long ago forfeited the right to that description. Meanwhile, he continued to earn other top awards and honours of which we had never heard previously. Universities offered him honorary doctorates. Major newspapers and other journals featured him and his work. *Newsweek* placed him on its cover twice, and in 1993 the German magazine *Du* devoted an entire number to 'our' Vidia. There was the often repeated accolade that Vidia was the greatest living writer in the English language. We knew the heights to which he had risen, higher than any one of us had dared to dream for him. And now he had gained the highest honour of all.

Back to my parents went my thoughts, and down came the tears again. Theirs had been such a rugged life. They had pinned their hopes on their children. Ma had lived long enough to see all her children become successful adults and to know her grandchildren and also know that many of them had proven to be above average in ability. No one had married a bus driver, become a cashier or a hairdresser (which, for some reason, had been among Pa's greatest fears for us). Ma had lived long enough to learn about her son Vidia being knighted in 1990 by the Queen. Vidia had told us years before that he had not accepted the offer of an OBE (Order of the British Empire), a highly prized royal award. He never told us, however, about his coming knighthood. Ma and the rest of us had to read about it in the newspapers. He had become Sir Vidia! But Ma also knew that Vidia had deliberately shut her out of that glorious and privileged part of his life. She knew that, unlike Shiva, Vidia was ashamed of her and she no longer had a place in his world. The knowledge must have wounded her terribly, although she never complained to anyone about it. (The only time that Ma, Mel and I were invited to witness Vidia receiving a major honour was when the Government of Trinidad and Tobago awarded him the Trinity Cross, as our highest national award was called then, before non-Christians protested at the name. Despite the other snubs, we attended the ceremony.)

And what about Pa? What would he have felt? Pa would have been ecstatic and would have wept with joy. He would, if he could, have had a shot or two of rum to celebrate. Pa probably would have been both relieved and delighted to learn that his son Vidia was not as mentally and physically fragile as he had feared over the years. He would not have been shocked that Vidia had produced such a staggering body of work, staggering both in quantity as well as quality. For days and weeks Pa would have smiled with pride and pleasure to remember that the little boy to whom he had read from books as a child had gone on to publish many books himself and earn the plaudits of the world.

All the same, Pa would not have liked everything about the man Vidia. His beloved elder son had often been rude and embarrassingly precocious in dealing with his father. Pa had endured these qualities in young Vidia's treatment of him, but he would have been appalled and angry over Vidia's treatment of Shiva. He would have been distressed that Vidia had developed an hauteur and a callousness that upset and wounded so many good people. He would have been horrified by Vidia's treatment of Ma. He would have been more than displeased that Vidia had not invited her or, indeed, a single other member of his family to attend his knighting by Queen Elizabeth or his grand Nobel award from the King of Sweden. And, finally, Pa would have been mortified that Vidia had married a divorced Muslim woman within days of the death from cancer of his long-suffering and loyal wife Pat.

In the beginning, the name Melvin Mervin Marvin Akal had not been music to my ears. But then my own name, Savitri Naipaul, may have been a bit strange to him in turn. The first time we met, Mel asked me to dance. After a moment on the floor he asked: 'What's your name again?' I spelt it out for him. Here, I thought, was another Presbyterian Indian not knowing a good Hindu name! Lost, lost soul. So young and not bad-looking either. But lost.

August 2016 marked fifty-eight years since we got married. At five feet six inches Mel was not of the height I had imagined my husband would be. But he has kept trim and agile and his bodyweight has altered little since 1959. His wedding suit still fits perfectly. Placid in nature, avoiding and hating altercations and happy in his profession, in fulfilling his many and varied roles his aim has always been to please and assist, to make things better not worse. A very gentle man, he has become a great-grandfather in his practice and still works hard at it as he has no other hobby. His major failure in life has been as a toast-maker at weddings. He regrets that his failure rate in keeping those marriages intact is one hundred per cent. He no longer accepts invitations for this role. He also deeply regrets that on the one and only day he tried to take his children to school he had to turn back:

he did not know where their schools were. A handyman he has never been, but he merits serious recognition as a mixer of cocktails, especially gin martinis. While our personalities are quite different we have shared many 'likes' and always attempted to plan our future as a team and in five-year spells. The fact that we did not always succeed never daunted us. We feel contented and comforted at our age, and if one's legacy is one's children we are justifiably proud.

Unlike many of our friends and most of my family, Mel and I chose to stay in Trinidad. Our experience in Scotland, when we had only one child, had taught us that we should live where we could earn a decent salary, where there were good schools to educate our children, where we could, within our means, enjoy a good standard of living and yet travel abroad regularly.

We would also live where we were not strangers in a strange land. We would live out our lives at home.

Valsayn, Trinidad
6th August 2016

## POSTSCRIPT

The house at 26 Nepaul Street was acquired by the government of Trinidad and Tobago by an Act of Parliament in the year 2000. In 2006, a group taking the name of Friends of Mr. Biswas was incorporated, given a lease for ninety-nine years and mandated and entrusted to maintain the property as a living museum and study centre. The group was made up of a chairperson and committee members, including two members of the Naipaul family. They were expected to formulate a constitution and map out an agenda to accomplish the mandate sanctioned by the government. In 2016 a constitution was finally presented by the chairperson to the most recent committee. This was the first known written constitution of the Friends of Mr. Biswas.

In the years before the framing of the constitution, major renovations were undertaken using monies received. These renovations were centred on building two apartments which were attached to the main structure of the small two-storey house. This construction eliminated the garage and the attached bathroom as well as the outdoor shrine where my mother lit her earthen oil lamp before dark. The structure also effectively blocked the light and the free flow of the air currents throughout the house. The various committees, working in fits and starts, never put the apartments to their intended use. Today, one apartment has been reconfigured into an audio-visual room and the other is stacked with unusable furniture. 26 Nepaul Street is no longer a freestanding house with a garage and a garden. While the interior layout of the house remains intact, broken bedroom walls and the removal of doors in the upstairs area make it seem that the occupants had enjoyed no privacy.

In 2014, the government, in an effort to reawaken interest in heritage buildings, installed a plaque calling it 'The Naipaul House', the home of Seepersad and Droapatie Capildeo Naipaul and of V.S. and Shiva Naipaul.

As yet there are no books, magazines or other paraphernalia in the house. Family pictures donated by myself and framed and installed by the government remain the only reminders of the family. The government's generosity in granting the lease is still to be vindicated.

## ACKNOWLEDGEMENTS

The epigraph to my memoir comes from William Wordsworth's well-known 'Michael: A Pastoral Poem'. I have cherished these words since I was fifteen. They comforted me on the death of my father and I have used them as a favourite quotation many times.

I started this memoir at the request of Arnold Rampersad. A Trinidadian by birth and a noted biographer, he is now a retired professor at Stanford University in California. His brief but earnest encouragement at a luncheon in Port of Spain in honour of a mutual friend, coupled with a similar suggestion urged independently by my sister-in-law, Jenny Naipaul, spurred me on.

In fact, I had begun a biography of my mother in 2006. For various reasons I had to set it aside, unsure of when or if ever I would get back to it. My mother has remained a woman largely hidden in the shadows cast by the lives of my father and my two brothers, who were the published writers in the family. I believed strongly that she deserved some public recognition for her intelligence, pragmatism, stoicism and strength. She had stood by my father through difficult and dark days. She had nursed Vidia through his bouts of asthma as a child. She had also believed in and encouraged Shiva, who lost his father while still very young. Certainly, she was always confident about the worth and the promise of her five daughters – from Kamla, the eldest, to Nella, who was a baby when Pa died. I believed that they, too, deserve a greater measure of illumination than they have received.

So I thought of writing a memoir about our family, which includes, of course, my father. In terms of honours, awards and even basic recognition, he was the least successful of the three published writers in our family. But he was an outstanding father to all his children, including his five beloved girls. In addition, he was a pioneering writer of under-appreciated importance in West Indian literature.

Professor Rampersad, who also admires my father's writing, has been a reliable aide. Although he and I have different views about a few areas of Trinidad culture and politics, he served me reliably as an editorial guide, quickly reading my many handwritten pages and various clarifying emails. He asked many fruitful questions. He also dealt cheerfully with my inadequacies in the area of computer literacy.

Finally, let me say that I have tried to be frank here without intruding unduly into the lives of my surviving brother and sisters, my children or my nephews and nieces.

Above all, I thank my husband Melvin and my three children, Ashvin Rai, Kiran and Siri. They provide the wind for my sail.